MARK TWAIN'S
AUTOBIOGRAPHY

I am writing
from the grave.
On these terms
only can a man
be approximately
frank. He cannot
be straitly & un-
qualifiedly frank
either in the grave
or out of it.

MARK TWAIN AT HIS HOME, 21 FIFTH AVENUE,
NEW YORK. THERE, DURING THE MORNING HOURS
IN THE WINTER OF 1906, HE DICTATED MUCH OF HIS
AUTOBIOGRAPHY

MARK TWAIN'S AUTOBIOGRAPHY

WITH AN INTRODUCTION BY
ALBERT BIGELOW PAINE

IN TWO VOLUMES
VOLUME I

HARPER & BROTHERS PUBLISHERS
NEW YORK AND LONDON
MCMXXIV

INTRODUCTION

MARK TWAIN had been a celebrity for a good
many years before he could be persuaded to regard
himself as anything more than an accident, a news-
writer to whom distinction had come as a matter
of good fortune rather than as a tribute to genius.
Sooner or later his "vein" would be worked out,
when he would of necessity embark in other pur-
suits.

He had already owned a newspaper, and ex-
perimented more or less casually—and unfortunately
—with a variety of other enterprises, when in 1884
he capitalized a publishing concern, primarily to
produce his own works, but not without a view to the
establishment of something more dependable than
authorship. It probably never occurred to him during those years that he had achieved anything like
a permanent place in literary history; if the idea of
an autobiography had intruded itself now and then,
it had not seriously troubled him.[1]

But a year later, when the publication by his
firm of the *Memoirs* of Gen. U. S. Grant brought

---

[1] Most of Mark Twain's work up to this time, *Roughing It,
Tom Sawyer, Life on the Mississippi*, etc., had been of an autobiographical nature. Also, as early as 1870 he had jotted down
an occasional reminiscent chapter, for possible publication, though
apparently with no idea of a continuous narrative. Such of these
chapters as have survived are included in Vol. I of the present
work.—A. B. P.

him into daily association with the dying conqueror, the thought came that the story of this episode might be worthy of preservation. It was not, for the present, at least, to be an autobiography, but no more than a few chapters, built around a great historic figure. General Grant's own difficulties in setting down his memories suggested prompt action. Mark Twain's former lecture agent, James Redpath, was visiting him at this time, and with a knowledge of shorthand became his amanuensis. The work they did together was considerable, covering in detail the story of the Grant publishing venture. Clemens may have planned other chapters of a personal sort, but, unaccustomed to dictation, he found the work tedious, with a result, as it seemed to him, unsatisfactory.

A number of important things happened to Mark Twain during the next dozen years, among them his business failure, which left him with a load of debt, dependent entirely upon authorship and the lecture platform for rehabilitation and support. The story of his splendid victory, the payment to the last dollar of his indebtedness, has been widely told. He was in Vienna when he completed this triumph, and, whatever he had been before, he was now unquestionably a world figure with a recognized place in history. Realization of this may have prompted him to begin, during those busy Vienna winters (1897 to 1899), something in the nature of an autobiography, recollections of his Missouri childhood, a picture as primitive and far removed from to-day as anything of the Colonial period.

These chapters were handwritten, his memory was fresh and eager, and in none of his work is there greater charm.

As he proceeded he did not confine himself to his earlier years, but traveled back and forth, setting down whatever was in his mind at the moment. He worked incidentally at this record for two or three years, eventually laying it aside for more immediate things. Five years later, in Florence, where he had taken Mrs. Clemens for her health, he again applied himself to what he now definitely termed his "Autobiography." As in that earlier day, he dictated, and this time found it quite to his liking. He completed some random memories of more or less importance, and might have carried the work further but for his wife's rapidly failing health. Her death and his return to America followed, and there was an interval of another two years before the autobiographical chapters were again resumed.

It was in January, 1906, that the present writer became associated with Mark Twain as his biographer. Elsewhere I have told of that arrangement and may omit most of the story here. It had been agreed that I should bring a stenographer, to whom he would dictate notes for my use, but a subsequent inspiration prompted him to suggest that he might in this way continue his autobiography, from which I would be at liberty to draw material for my own undertaking. We began with this understanding, and during two hours of the forenoon, on several days of each week, he talked pretty steadily to a select audience of two, wandering up and down the years as inclination led him, relating in his inimitable way incidents, episodes, conclusions, whatever the moment presented to his fancy.

It was his custom to stay in bed until noon, and he remained there during most of the earlier dictations, clad in a handsome dressing-gown, propped against great snowy pillows. He loved this loose luxury and ease and found it conducive to thought. On a little table beside him, where lay his cigars, papers, pipes, and various knickknacks, shone a reading lamp, making more brilliant his rich coloring and the gleam of his shining hair. There was daylight, too, but it was north light and the winter days were dull, the walls of the room a deep, unreflecting red. His bed was a vast carved antique affair, its outlines blending into the luxuriant background. The whole, focusing to the striking central figure, made a picture of classic value.

His talk was absorbingly interesting—it never failed to be that, even when it left something to be desired as history. Mark Twain's memory had become capricious and his vivid imagination did not always supply his story with details of crystal accuracy. But always it was a delightful story, amusing, tragic, or instructive, and it was likely to be one of these things at one instant and another at the next. Often he did not know until the moment of beginning what was to be his subject for the day; then he was likely to go drifting among his memories in a quite irresponsible fashion, the fashion of table conversation, as he said, the methodless method of the human mind. He had concluded that this was the proper way to write autobiography, or, as he best conveys it in his own introductory note:

Start at no particular time of your life; wander at your free will all over your life; talk only about the things which interest you for the moment; drop it the moment its interest threatens to pale, and turn your talk upon the new and more interesting thing that has intruded itself into your mind meantime.

Certainly there is something to be said in favor of his plan, and I often thought it the best plan for his kind of autobiography, which was really not auto-biography at all, in the meaning generally conveyed by that term, but a series of entertaining stories and opinions—dinner-table talks, in fact, such as he had always delivered in his own home and elsewhere, and with about the same latitude and elaboration.

I do not wish to convey that his narrative is in any sense a mere fairy tale. Many of the chapters, especially the earlier ones, are vividly true in their presentation; the things he told of Mrs. Clemens and Susy are marvelously and beautifully true in spirit and aspect, and the story as a whole is amaz-ingly faithful in the character picture it presents of the man himself. It was only when he relied upon his memory for details of general history, or when his imagination responded to old prejudice, or when life-long habit prompted a "good story" that he went wandering into fields of elaboration and gathered there such flowers and thorns as his fancy or feelings seemed to require. Mark Twain's soul was built of the very fabric of truth, so far as moral intent was concerned, but memory often betrayed him, even when he tried most to be accurate. He realized this himself, and once said, plaintively:

"When I was younger I could remember anything, whether it happened or not; but I am getting old and soon I shall remember only the latter."

And at another time, paraphrasing Josh Billings:

"It isn't so astonishing the things that I can remember, as the number of things I can remember that aren't so."

Perhaps it is proper to assure the reader that positive mistakes of date and occurrence have been corrected, while, for the rest, the matter of mere detail is of less importance than that the charm of the telling should remain undisturbed.

Our work, begun in the New York house at 21 Fifth Avenue, continued with considerable regularity during a period of about two years, and intermittently during another two. When the first spring came it was transferred to the Upton House, on the slopes of Monadnock, near Dublin, New Hampshire, a perfect setting for the dictations. He no longer remained in bed, but, clad in creamy-white flannels and loose morocco slippers, bareheaded, he paced up and down the long veranda against a background of far-lying forest and distant hill. As I think of that time, now, I can still hear the ceaseless slippered, shuffling walk, and see the white figure, with its rocking, rolling movement, that preternaturally beautiful landscape behind it, and hear his deliberate speech—always deliberate except at rare intervals; always impressive, whatever the subject might be. In September we returned to the New

York house and the work was continued there, that winter and the next. It reached its conclusion at Stormfield, the new home which he had built at Redding, Connecticut, and it was here that he died, April 21, 1910.

In the beginning it was Mark Twain's frequently expressed command that the "Autobiography" was not to be published until he had been dead at least a hundred years. But as the months passed he modified this idea, and himself selected a number of chapters for use in the *North American Review*. Discussing the matter later, he expressed a willingness that any portions of the work not dealing too savagely with living persons or their immediate descendants should be published sooner, either serially or in book form.

The manuscript in time became very large and very inclusive. He even incorporated in it articles and stories which he had written and laid aside, among them "Captain Stormfield's Visit to Heaven." "Is Shakespeare Dead?" was originally a part of the "Autobiography," but he published it separately in a small volume. "The Death of Jean," written (not dictated) immediately following that tragic event, was to be the closing chapter, and such in time it will become. He wished, however, that it should have separate publication and it is for the present included in another volume. It was his last complete writing of any sort, and in all his work from beginning to end there is nothing more perfect —nothing more beautiful.

ALBERT BIGELOW PAINE

PREFACE

AS FROM THE GRAVE

In this Autobiography I shall keep in mind the fact that I am speaking from the grave. I am literally speaking from the grave, because I shall be dead when the book issues from the press.

I speak from the grave rather than with my living tongue, for a good reason: I can speak thence freely. When a man is writing a book dealing with the privacies of his life—a book which is to be read while he is still alive—he shrinks from speaking his whole frank mind; all his attempts to do it fail, he recognizes that he is trying to do a thing which is wholly impossible to a human being. The frankest and freest and privatest product of the human mind and heart is a love letter; the writer gets his limitless freedom of statement and expression from his sense that no stranger is going to see what he is writing. Sometimes there is a breach-of-promise case by and by; and when he sees his letter in print it makes him cruelly uncomfortable and he perceives that he never would have unbosomed himself to that large and honest degree if he had known that he was writing for the public. He cannot find anything in the letter that was not true, honest, and respect-worthy; but no matter, he would have been very much more reserved if he had known he was writing for print.

It has seemed to me that I could be as frank and free and unembarrassed as a love letter if I knew that what I was writing would be exposed to no eye until I was dead, and unaware, and indifferent.

MARK TWAIN

EARLY FRAGMENTS

1870 — 1877

NOTE.—*The various divisions and chapters of this work, in accordance with the author's wish, are arranged in the order in which they were written, regardless of the chronology of events.*

I will construct a text:

What a wee little part of a person's life are his acts and his words! His real life is led in his head, and is known to none but himself. All day long, and every day, the mill of his brain is grinding, and his *thoughts,* not those other things, are his history. His acts and his words are merely the visible, thin crust of his world, with its scattered snow summits and its vacant wastes of water—and they are so trifling a part of his bulk! a mere skin enveloping it. The mass of him is hidden—it and its volcanic fires that toss and boil, and never rest, night nor day. These are his life, and they are not written, and cannot be written. Every day would make a whole book of eighty thousand words—three hundred and sixty-five books a year. Biographies are but the clothes and buttons of the man—the biography of the man himself cannot be written.

M. T.

MARK TWAIN'S AUTOBIOGRAPHY

[*Written about 1870*

THE TENNESSEE LAND [1]

THE monster tract of land which our family own in Tennessee was purchased by my father a little over forty years ago. He bought the enormous area of seventy-five thousand acres at one purchase. The entire lot must have cost him somewhere in the neighborhood of four hundred dollars. That was a good deal of money to pass over at one payment in those days—at least it was considered so away up there in the pineries and the "Knobs" of the Cumberland Mountains of Fentress County, East Tennessee. When my father paid down that great sum, and turned and stood in the courthouse door of Jamestown, and looked abroad over his vast possessions, he said, "Whatever befalls me, my heirs are secure; I shall not live to see these acres' turn to silver and gold, but my children will." Thus with the very kindest intentions in the world toward us, he laid the heavy curse of prospective wealth upon

---

[1] The Tennessee Land is an important feature in a novel by Mark Twain and Charles Dudley Warner, *The Gilded Age.*

3

our shoulders. He went to his grave in the full belief that he had done us a kindness. It was a woeful
mistake, but, fortunately, he never knew it.

He further said: "Iron ore is abundant in this
tract, and there are other minerals; there are thousands of acres of the finest yellow-pine timber in
America, and it can be rafted down Obeds River to
the Cumberland, down the Cumberland to the Ohio,
down the Ohio to the Mississippi, and down the
Mississippi to any community that wants it. There
is no end to the tar, pitch, and turpentine which
these vast pineries will yeld. This is a natural wine
district, too; there are no vines elsewhere in
America, cultivated or otherwise, that yield such
grapes as grow wild here. There are grazing lands,
corn lands, wheat lands, potato lands, there are all
species of timber—there is everything in and on this
great tract of land that can make land valuable. The
United States contain fourteen millions of inhabitants; the population has increased eleven millions
in forty years, and will henceforth increase faster
than ever; my children will see the day that immi-
gration will push its way to Fentress County, Tennessee, and then, with 75,000 acres of excellent land
in their hands, they will become fabulously wealthy."

Everything my father said about the capabilities
of the land was perfectly true—and he could have
added, with like truth, that there were inexhaustible
mines of coal on the land, but the chances are that
he knew very little about the article, for the innocent
Tennesseeans were not accustomed to digging in the
earth for their fuel. And my father might have

added to the list of eligibilities, that the land was only a hundred miles from Knoxville, and right where some future line of railway leading south from Cincinnati could not help but pass through it. But he never had seen a railway, and it is barely possible that he had not even heard of such a thing. Curious as it may seem, as late as eight years ago there were people living close to Jamestown who never had heard of a railroad and could not be brought to believe in steamboats. They do not vote for Jackson in Fentress County; they vote for Washington.

My eldest brother was four or five years old when the great purchase was made, and my eldest sister was an infant in arms. The rest of us—and we formed the great bulk of the family—came afterward, and were born along from time to time during the next ten years. Four years after the purchase came the great financial crash of '34, and in that storm my father's fortunes were wrecked. From being honored and envied as the most opulent citizen of Fentress County—for outside of his great landed possessions he was considered to be worth not less than three thousand five hundred dollars—he suddenly woke up and found himself reduced to less than one-fourth of that amount. He was a proud man, a silent, austere man, and not a person likely to abide among the scenes of his vanished grandeur and be the target for public commiseration. He gathered together his household and journeyed many tedious days through wilderness solitudes, toward what was then the "Far West," and at last pitched his tent in the little town of Florida, Monroe County, Missouri. He "kept store" there several years, but had no luck, except that I was born to him. He presently removed to Hannibal, and prospered somewhat; rose to the dignity of justice of the peace and had been elected to the clerkship of the Surrogate Court, when the summons came which no man may disregard. He had been doing tolerably well, for that age of the world, during the first years of his residence in Hannibal, but ill fortune tripped him once more. He did the friendly office of "going security" for Ira ——, and Ira walked off and deliberately took the benefit of the new bankrupt law—a deed which enabled him to live easily and comfortably along till death called for him, but a deed which ruined my father, sent him poor to his grave, and condemned his heirs to a long and discouraging struggle with the world for a livelihood. But my father would brighten up and gather heart, even upon his death-bed, when he thought of the Tennessee land. He said that it would soon make us all rich and happy. And so believing, he died.

We straightway turned our waiting eyes upon Tennessee. Through all our wanderings and all our ups and downs for thirty years they have still gazed thitherward, over intervening continents and seas, and at this very day they are yet looking toward the same fixed point, with the hope of old habit and a faith that rises and falls, but never dies.

After my father's death we reorganized the domestic establishment, but on a temporary basis, intending to arrange it permanently after the land was sold. My brother borrowed five hundred dollars and bought a worthless weekly newspaper, believing, as we all did, that it was not worth while to go at anything in serious earnest until the land was disposed of and we could embark intelligently in something. We rented a large house to live in, at first, but we were disappointed in a sale we had expected to make (the man wanted only a part of the land and we talked it over and decided to sell all or none) and we were obliged to move to a less expensive one.

[*Written in 1877*

EARLY YEARS IN FLORIDA, MISSOURI

I WAS born the 30th of November, 1835, in the almost invisible village of Florida, Monroe County, Missouri. I suppose Florida had less than three hundred inhabitants. It had two streets, each a couple of hundred yards long; the rest of the avenues mere lanes, with rail fences and cornfields on either side. Both the streets and the lanes were paved with the same material—tough black mud in wet times, deep dust in dry.

Most of the houses were of logs—all of them, indeed, except three or four; these latter were frame ones. There were none of brick, and none of stone. There was a log church, with a puncheon floor and slab benches. A puncheon floor is made of logs whose upper surfaces have been chipped flat with the adz. The cracks between the logs were not filled; there was no carpet; consequently, if you dropped anything smaller than a peach, it was likely to go through. The church was perched upon short sections of logs, which elevated it two or three feet from the ground. Hogs slept under there, and whenever the dogs got after them during services, the minister had to wait till the disturbance was over. In winter there was always a refreshing breeze up through the puncheon floor; in summer there were fleas enough for all.

A slab bench is made of the outside cut of a saw-log, with the bark side down; it is supported on four sticks driven into auger holes at the ends; it has no back and no cushions. The church was twi-lighted with yellow tallow candles in tin sconces hung against the walls. Week days, the church was a schoolhouse.

There were two stores in the village. My uncle, John A. Quarles, was proprietor of one of them. It was a very small establishment, with a few rolls of "bit" calicoes on half a dozen shelves; a few barrels of salt mackerel, coffee, and New Orleans sugar behind the counter; stacks of brooms, shovels, axes, hoes, rakes, and such things here and there; a lot of cheap hats, bonnets, and tinware strung on strings and suspended from the walls; and at the other end of the room was another counter with bags of shot on it, a cheese or two, and a keg of powder; in front of it a row of nail kegs and a few pigs of lead, and behind it a barrel or two of New Orleans molasses and native corn whisky on tap. If a boy bought five or ten cents' worth of anything, he was entitled to half a handful of sugar from the barrel; if a woman bought a few yards of calico she was entitled to a spool of thread in addition to the usual gratis "trimmin's"; if a man bought a trifle, he was at liberty to draw and swallow as big a drink of whisky as he wanted.

Everything was cheap: apples, peaches, sweet potatoes, Irish potatoes, and corn, ten cents a bushel; chickens, ten cents apiece; butter, six cents a pound; eggs, three cents a dozen; coffee and sugar, five cents a pound; whisky, ten cents a gallon. I do not know how prices are out there in interior Missouri now, but I know what they are here in Hartford, Connecticut. To wit: apples, three dollars a bushel; peaches, five dollars; Irish potatoes (choice Bermudas), five dollars; chickens, a dollar to a dollar and a half apiece, according to weight; butter, forty-five to sixty cents a pound; eggs, fifty to sixty cents a dozen; coffee, forty-five cents a pound; native whisky, four or five dollars a gallon, I believe, but I can only be certain concerning the sort which I use myself, which is Scotch and costs ten dollars a gallon when you take two gallons—more when you take less.

Thirty to forty years ago, out yonder in Missouri, the ordinary cigar cost thirty cents a hundred, but most people did not try to afford them, since smoking a pipe cost nothing in that tobacco-growing country. Connecticut is also given up to tobacco raising, today, yet we pay ten dollars a hundred for Connecticut cigars and fifteen to twenty-five dollars a hundred for the imported article.

At first my father owned slaves, but by and by he sold them and hired others by the year from the farmers. For a girl of fifteen he paid twelve dollars a year and gave her two linsey-wolsey frocks and a pair of "stogy" shoes—cost, a modification of nothing; for a negro woman of twenty-five, as general house servant, he paid twenty-five dollars a year and gave her shoes and the aforementioned linsey-wolsey frocks; for a strong negro woman of forty, as cook, washer, etc., he paid forty dollars a year and the customary two suits of clothes; and for an able-bodied man he paid from seventy-five to a hundred dollars a year and gave him two suits of jeans and two pairs of "stogy" shoes—an outfit that cost about three dollars. But times have changed. We pay our German nursemaid $155 a year; Irish housemaid, $150; Irish laundress, $150; negro woman, a cook, $240; young negro man, to wait on door and table, $360; Irish coachman, $600 a year, with gas, hot and cold water, and dwelling consisting of parlor, kitchen, and two bedrooms, connected with the stable, free.[1]

---

[1] These prices of 1877 are as interesting to-day as those of forty years earlier.

THE GRANT DICTATIONS

— 1885 —

THE CHICAGO G. A. R. FESTIVAL

THE first time I ever saw General Grant was in the fall or winter of 1866 at one of the receptions at Washington, when he was general of the army. I merely saw and shook hands with him along with the crowd, but had no conversation. It was there, also, that I first saw General Sheridan.

I next saw General Grant during his first term as President. Senator Bill Stewart, of Nevada, proposed to take me in and see the President. We found him in his working costume, with an old, short, linen duster on, and it was well spattered with ink. I had acquired some trifle of notoriety through some letters which I had written, in the New York *Tribune,* during my trip round about the world in the *Quaker City* expedition. I shook hands, and then there was a pause and silence. I couldn't think of anything to say. So I merely looked into the general's grim, immovable countenance a moment or two, in silence, and then I said: "Mr. President, I am embarrassed. Are you?" He smiled a smile which would have done no discredit to a cast-iron image, and I got away under the smoke of my volley.

I did not see him again for some ten years. In the meantime I had become very thoroughly notorious.

Then, in 1879, the general had just returned from
his journey through the European and Asiatic world,
and his progress from San Francisco eastward had
been one continuous ovation; and now he was to be
feasted in Chicago by the veterans of the Army of
the Tennessee—the first army over which he had
had command. The preparations for this occasion
were in keeping with the importance of it. The
toast committee telegraphed me and asked me if I
would be present and respond at the grand banquet
to the toast to the ladies. I telegraphed back that
the toast was worn out. Everything had been said
about the ladies that could be said at a banquet,
but there was one class of the community that had
always been overlooked upon such occasions and if
they would allow me I would take that class for a
toast—*The Babies*. They were willing, so I prepared my toast and went out to Chicago.

There was to be a prodigious procession. General
Grant was to review it from a rostrum which had
been built out for the purpose from the second-story
window of the Palmer House. The rostrum was
carpeted and otherwise glorified with flags and so on.

The best place of all to see the procession was,
of course, from this rostrum, so I sauntered upon
that rostrum while as yet it was empty, in the hope
that I might be permitted to sit there. It was rather
a conspicuous place, since upon it the public gaze
was fixed and there was a countless multitude below.
Presently two gentlemen came upon that platform
from the window of the hotel and stepped forward
to the front. A prodigious shout went up from

the vast multitude below, and I recognized in one of these two gentlemen General Grant; the other was Carter Harrison, the Mayor of Chicago, with whom I was acquainted. He saw me, stepped over to me, and said wouldn't I like to be introduced to the general? I said I should. So he walked over with me and said, "General, let me introduce Mr. Clemens." We shook hands. There was the usual momentary pause, and then the general said: "I am not embarrassed. Are you?"

It showed that he had a good memory for trifles as well as for serious things.

That banquet was by all odds the most notable one I was ever present at. There were six hundred persons present, mainly veterans of the Army of the Tennessee, and that in itself would have made it a most notable occasion of the kind in my experience, but there were other things which contributed. General Sherman, and in fact nearly all of the surviving great generals of the war, sat in a body on a dais round about General Grant.

The speakers were of a rare celebrity and ability.

That night I heard for the first time a slang expression which had already come into considerable vogue, but I had not myself heard it before.

When the speaking began about ten o'clock, I left my place at the table and went away over to the front side of the great dining room, where I could take in the whole spectacle at one glance. Among others, Colonel Vilas was to respond to a toast, and also Colonel Ingersoll, the silver-tongued infidel, who had begun life in Illinois and was exceedingly popular there. Vilas was from Wisconsin and was very famous as an orator. He had prepared himself superbly for this occasion.

He was about the first speaker on the list of fifteen toasts, and Bob Ingersoll was the ninth.

I had taken a position upon the steps in front of the brass band, which lifted me up and gave me a good general view. Presently I noticed, leaning against the wall near me, a simple-looking young man wearing the uniform of a private and the badge of the Army of the Tennessee. He seemed to be nervous and ill at ease about something; presently, while the second speaker was talking, this young man said, "Do you know Colonel Vilas?" I said I had been introduced to him. He sat silent awhile and then said, "They say he is hell when he gets started!"

I said: "In what way? What do you mean?"

"Speaking! Speaking! They say he is lightning!"

"Yes," I said, "I have heard that he is a great speaker."

The young man shifted about uneasily for a while, and then he said, "Do you reckon he can get away with Bob Ingersoll?"

I said, "I don't know."

Another pause. Occasionally he and I would join in the applause when a speaker was on his legs, but this young man seemed to applaud unconsciously.

Presently he said, "Here, in Illinois, we think there can't nobody get away with Bob Ingersoll."

I said, "Is that so?"

He said, "Yes; we don't think anybody can lay

over Bob Ingersoll." Then he added sadly, "But they do say that Vilas is pretty nearly hell."

At last Vilas rose to speak, and this young man pulled himself together and put on all his anxiety. Vilas began to warm up and the people began to applaud. He delivered himself of one especially fine passage and there was a general shout: "Get up on the table! Get up on the table! Stand up on the table! We can't see you!" So a lot of men standing there picked Vilas up and stood him on the table in full view of the whole great audience, and he went on with his speech. The young man applauded with the rest, and I could hear the young fellow mutter without being able to make out what he said. But presently, when Vilas thundered out something especially fine, there was a tremendous outburst from the whole house, and then this young man said, in a sort of despairing way:

"It ain't no use. Bob can't climb up to that!"

During the next hour he held his position against the wall in a sort of dazed abstraction, apparently unconscious of place or anything else, and at last, when Ingersoll mounted the supper table, his worshiper merely straightened up to an attitude of attention, but without manifesting any hope.

Ingersoll, with his fair and fresh complexion, handsome figure, and graceful carriage, was beautiful to look at.

He was to respond to the toast of "The Volunteers," and his first sentence or two showed his quality. As his third sentence fell from his lips the house let go with a crash and my private looked pleased and for the first time hopeful, but he had been too much frightened to join in the applause. Presently, when Ingersoll came to the passage in which he said that these volunteers had shed their blood and periled their lives in order that a mother might own her own child, the language was so fine, whatever it was (for I have forgotten), and the delivery was so superb that the vast multitude rose as one man and stood on their feet, shouting, stamping, and filling all the place with such a waving of napkins that it was like a snowstorm. This prodigious outburst continued for a minute or two, Ingersoll standing and waiting. And now I happened to notice my private. He was stamping, clapping, shouting, gesticulating like a man who had gone truly mad. At last, when quiet was restored once more, he glanced up at me with the tears in his eyes and said:

"Egod! *He didn't* get left!"

My own speech was granted the perilous distinction of the place of honor. It was the last speech on the list, an honor which no person, probably, has ever sought. It was not reached until two o'clock in the morning. But when I got on my feet I knew that there was at any rate one point in my favor: the text was bound to have the sympathy of nine-tenths of the men present, and of every woman, married or single, of the crowds of the sex who stood huddled in the various doorways.

I expected the speech to go off well—and it did. In it I had a drive at General Sheridan's comparatively new twins and various other things calculated to make it go. There was only one thing in it that I had fears about, and that one thing stood where it could not be removed in case of disaster.

It was the last sentence in the speech.

I had been picturing the America of fifty years hence, with a population of two hundred million souls, and was saying that the future President, admiral, and so forth, of that great coming time were now lying in their various cradles, scattered abroad over the vast expanse of this country, and then said "and now in his cradle somewhere under the flag the future illustrious commander-in-chief of the American armies is so little burdened with his approaching grandeur and responsibilities as to be giving his whole strategic mind at this moment to trying to find some way to get his big toe into his mouth—something, meaning no disrespect to the illustrious guest of this evening, which he turned his entire attention to some fifty-six years ago——"

And here, as I had expected, the laughter ceased and a sort of shuddering silence took its place—for this was apparently carrying the matter too far.

I waited a moment or two to let this silence sink well home, then, turning toward the general, I added:

"And if the child is but the father of the man there are mighty few who will doubt that he succeeded."

Which relieved the house, for when they saw the general break up in good-sized pieces they followed suit with great enthusiasm.

[*Dictated in 1885*

GRANT AND THE CHINESE

EARLY in 1884, or late in 1883, if my memory
serves me, I called on General Grant with Yung
Wing, late Chinese minister at Washington, to introduce Wing and let him lay before General Grant
a propostion. Li Hung-Chang, one of the greatest
and most progressive men in China since the death
of Prince Kung, had been trying to persuade the
imperial government to build a system of military
railroads in China, and had so far succeeded in his
persuasions that a majority of the government were
willing to consider the matter—provided that
money could be obtained for that purpose outside
of China, this money to be raised upon the customs
of the country and by bonding the railway, or in
some such manner. Yung Wing believed that if General Grant would take charge of the matter here
and create the syndicate, the money would be easily
forthcoming. He also knew that General Grant
was better and more favorably known in China than
any other foreigner in the world, and was aware
that if his name were associated with the enterprise
—the syndicate—it would inspire the Chinese government and people and give them the greatest possible sense of security. We found the general
cooped up in his room with a severe rheumatism,
resulting from a fall on the ice which he had got
some months before. He would not undertake a
syndicate, because times were so hard here that

people would be loath to invest money so far away; of course Yung Wing's proposal included a liberal compensation for General Grant for his trouble, but that was a thing that the general would not listen to for a moment. He said that easier times would come by and by, and that the money could then be raised, no doubt, and that he would enter into it cheerfully and with zeal and carry it through to the very best of his ability, but he must do it without compensation. In no case would he consent to take any money for it. Here, again, he manifested the very strongest interest in China, an interest which I had seen him evince on previous occasions. He said he had urged a system of railways on Li Hung-Chang when he was in China, and he now felt so sure that such a system would be a great salvation for the country, and also the beginning of the country's liberation from the Tartar rule and thralldom, that he would be quite willing at a favorable time to do everything he could toward carrying out that project, without other compensation than the pleasure he would derive from being useful to China.

This reminds me of one other circumstance.

About 1879 or 1880 the Chinese pupils in Hartford and other New England towns had been ordered home by the Chinese government. There were two parties in the Chinese government—one headed by Li Hung-Chang, the progressive party, which was striving to introduce Western arts and education into China; the other was opposed to all progressive measures. Li Hung-Chang and the progressive party kept the upper hand for some

time, and during this period the government had
sent one hundred or more of the country's choicest
youth over here to be educated. But now the other
party had got the upper hand and had ordered
these young people home. At this time an old Chinaman named Quong, non-progressionist, was the
chief China minister at Washington, and Yung
Wing was his assistant. The order disbanding the
schools was a great blow to Yung Wing, who had
spent many years in working for their establishment. This order came upon him with the suddenness of a thunderclap. He did not know which way
to turn.

First, he got a petition signed by the presidents
of various American colleges, setting forth the great
progress that the Chinese pupils had made and
offering arguments to show why the pupils should
be allowed to remain to finish their education. This
paper was to be conveyed to the Chinese government through the minister at Peking. But Yung
Wing felt the need of a more powerful voice in the
matter, and General Grant occurred to him. He
thought that if he could get General Grant's great
name added to that petition, that alone would out-
weigh the signatures of a thousand college professors. So the Rev. Mr. Twichell and I went down
to New York to see the general. I introduced Mr.
Twichell, who had come with a careful speech for
the occasion, in which he intended to load the general with information concerning the Chinese pupils
and the Chinese question generally. But he never
got the chance to deliver it. The general took the

word out of his mouth and talked straight ahead, and easily revealed to Twichell the fact that the general was master of the whole matter and needed no information from anybody, and also the fact that he was brimful of interest in the matter. Now, as always, the general was not only ready to do what we asked of him, but a hundred times more. He said, yes, he would sign that paper, if desired, but he would do better than that: he would write a personal letter to Li Hung-Chang, and do it immediately. So Twichell and I went downstairs into the lobby of the Fifth Avenue Hotel, a crowd of waiting and anxious visitors sitting in the anteroom, and in the course of half an hour he sent for us again and put into our hands his letter to Li Hung-Chang, to be sent directly and without the intervention of the American minister, or anyone else. It was a clear, compact, and admirably written statement of the case of the Chinese pupils, with some equally clear arguments to show that the breaking up of the schools would be a mistake. We shipped the letter and prepared to wait a couple of months to see what the result would be.

But we had not to wait so long. The moment the general's letter reached China a telegram came back from the Chinese government, which was almost a copy, in detail, of General Grant's letter, and the cablegram ended with the peremptory command to old Minister Wong to continue the Chinese schools.

It was a marvelous exhibition of the influence of a private citizen of one country over the counsels of an Empire situated on the other side of the globe.

Such an influence could have been wielded by no
other citizen in the world outside of that Empire;
in fact, the policy of the imperial government had
been reversed from Room 45, Fifth Avenue Hotel,
New York, by a private citizen of the United States.

[Dictated in 1885

A CALL WITH W. D. HOWELLS ON GENERAL GRANT

HOWELLS wrote me that his old father, who was
well along in the seventies, was in great distress
about his poor little consulate up in Quebec. Somebody, not being satisfied with the degree of poverty
already conferred upon him by a thoughtful and
beneficent Providence, was anxious to add to it by
acquiring the Quebec consulate. So Howells thought
if we could get General Grant to say a word to
President Arthur it might have the effect of stopping this effort to oust old Mr. Howells from his
position. Therefore, at my suggestion Howells came
down, and we went to New York to lay the matter
before the general. We found him at No. 2 Wall
Street, in the principal office of Grant & Ward,
brokers.

I stated the case and asked him if he wouldn't
write a word on a card which Howells could carry
to Washington and hand to the President.

But, as usual, General Grant was his natural self
—that is to say, ready and also determined to do a
great deal more for you than you could possibly

have the effrontery to ask him to do. Apparently he never meets anybody halfway; he comes nine-tenths of the way himself voluntarily. "No," he said, he would do better than that, and cheerfully; he was going to Washington in a couple of days to dine with the President and he would speak to him and make it a personal matter. Now, as General Grant not only never forgets a promise, but never even the shadow of a promise, he did as he said he would do, and within a week came a letter from the Secretary of State, Mr. Frelinghuysen, to say that in no case would old Mr. Howells be disturbed. And he wasn't. He resigned a couple of years later.

But to go back to the interview with General Grant, he was in a humor to talk—in fact, he was always in a humor to talk when no strangers were present—and he resisted all our efforts to leave him.

He forced us to stay and take luncheon in a private room and continued to talk all the time. (It was bacon and beans. Nevertheless, "How he sits and towers"—Howells, quoting from Dante.)

He remembered "Squibob" Derby at West Point very well. He said that Derby was forever drawing caricatures of the professors and playing jokes of all kinds on everybody. He also told of one thing, which I had heard before but which I have never seen in print. At West Point, the professor was instructing and questioning a class concerning certain particulars of a possible siege, and he said this, as nearly as I can remember. I cannot quote General Grant's words:

Given: that a thousand men are besieging a fortress whose equipment of men, provisions, etc., are so and so—it is a military axiom that at the end of forty-five days the fort will surrender. Now, young men, if any of you were in command of such a fortress, how would you proceed?

Derby held up his hand in token that he had an answer for that question. He said, "I would march out, let the enemy in, and at the end of forty-five days I would change places with him."

I tried very hard to get General Grant to write his personal memoirs for publication, but he would not listen to the suggestion. His inborn diffidence made him shrink from voluntarily coming forward before the public and placing himself under criticism as an author. He had no confidence in his ability to write well, whereas everybody else in the world, excepting himself, is aware that he possesses an admirable literary gift and style. He was also sure that the book would have no sale, and of course that would be a humiliation, too. He instanced the fact that General Badeau's military history of General Grant had had but a trifling sale, and that John Russell Young's account of General Grant's trip around the globe had hardly any sale at all. But I said that these were not instances in point; that what another man might tell about General Grant was nothing, while what General Grant should tell about himself, with his own pen, was a totally different thing. I said that the book would have an enormous sale; that it should be in two volumes, sold, in cash, at $3.50 apiece, and that the sale in two volumes would certainly reach half a million sets. I said that, from my experience, I could save him from making unwise contracts with publishers, and could also suggest the best plan of publication—the subscription plan—and find for him the best men in that line of business.

I had in my mind at that time the American Publishing Comany, of Hartford, and, while I suspected that they had been swindling me for ten years, I was well aware that I could arrange the contract in such a way that they could not swindle General Grant. But the general said that he had no necessity for any addition to his income. I knew that he meant by that that his investments, through the firm in which his sons were partners, were paying him all the money he needed. So I was not able to persuade him to write a book. He said that some day he would make very full notes and leave them behind him; and then, if his children chose to make them into a book, that would answer.

[Dictated in 1885

ABOUT GENERAL GRANT'S "MEMOIRS"

I WANT to set down somewhat of a history of General Grant's *Memoirs*.

By way of preface I will make a remark or two indirectly connected therewith.

During the Garfield campaign Grant threw the whole weight of his influence and endeavor toward the triumph of the Republican party. He made a

progress through many of the states, chiefly the
doubtful ones, and this progress was a daily and
nightly ovation as long as it lasted. He was received
everywhere by prodigious multitudes of enthusiastic
people, and, to strain the facts a little, one might
almost tell what part of the country the general
was in, for the moment, by the red reflections on
the sky caused by the torch processions and fire-
works.

He was to visit Hartford, from Boston, and I
was one of the committee sent to Boston to bring
him down here. I was also appointed to introduce
him to the Hartford people when the population
and the soldiers should pass in review before him.
On our way from Boston in the palace car I fell to
talking with Grant's eldest son, Col. Fred Grant,
whom I knew very well, and it gradually came out
that the general, so far from being a rich man,
as was commonly supposed, had not even income
enough to enable him to live as respectably as a
third-rate physician.

Colonel Grant told me that the general left the
White House, at the end of his second term, a
poor man, and I think he said he was in debt, but
I am not positively sure (I know he was in debt
$45,000, at the end of *one* of his terms). Friends
had given the general a couple of dwelling houses,
but he was not able to keep them or live in either
of them. This was all so shameful and such a reproach to Congress that I proposed to take the
general's straitened circumstances as my text in
introducing him to the people of Hartford.

I knew that if this nation, which was rising up daily to do its chief citizen unparalleled honor, had it in its power, by its vote, to decide the matter, it would turn his poverty into immeasurable wealth in an instant. Therefore the reproach lay not with the people, but with their political representatives in Congress, and my speech could be no insult to the people.

I clove to my plan, and in introducing the general I referred to the dignities and emoluments lavished upon the Duke of Wellington by England and contrasted with that conduct our far finer and higher method toward the savior of our country—to wit, the simple carrying him in our hearts without burdening him with anything to live on.

In his reply the general, of course, said that this country had more than sufficiently rewarded him and that he was well satisfied.

He could not have said anything else, necessarily.

A few months later I could not have made such a speech, for by that time certain wealthy citizens had privately made up a purse of a quarter of a million dollars for the general, and had invested it in such a way that he could not be deprived of it either by his own want of wisdom or the rascality of other people.

Later still, the firm of Grant & Ward, brokers and stock dealers, was established at No. 2 Wall Street, New York City.

This firm consisted of General Grant's sons and a brisk young man by the name of Ferdinand Ward. The general was also, in some way, a partner, but did not take any active part in the business of the house.

In a little time the business had grown to such proportions that it was apparently not only profitable, but it was prodigiously so.

The truth was, however, that Ward was robbing all the Grants and everybody else that he could get his hands on, and the firm was not making a penny.

The general was unsuspicious and supposed that he was making a vast deal of money, whereas, indeed, he was simply losing such as he had, for Ward was getting it.

About the 5th of May, I think it was, 1884, the crash came and the several Grant families found themselves absolutely penniless.

Ward had even captured the interest due on the quarter of a million dollars of the Grant fund, which interest had fallen due only a day or two before the failure.

General Grant told me that that month, *for the first time in his life,* he had paid his domestic bills with *checks.* They came back upon his hands dishonored. He told me that Ward had spared no one connected with the Grant name, however remote— that he had taken all that the general could scrape together and $45,000 that the general had borrowed on his wife's dwelling house in New York; that he had taken $65,000, the sum for which Mrs. Grant had sold, recently, one of the houses which had been presented to the general; that he had taken $7,000, which some poverty-stricken nieces of his in the West had recently received by bequest, and which was all the money they had in the world—that, in a word, Ward had utterly stripped everybody connected with the Grant family.

It was necessary that something be immediately done toward getting bread.

The bill to restore to General Grant the title and emoluments of a full general in the army, on the retired list, had been lagging for a long time in Congress—in the characteristic, contemptible, and stingy congressional fashion. No relief was to be looked for from that source, mainly because Congress chose to avenge on General Grant the veto of the Fitz-John Porter bill by President Arthur.

The editors of the *Century Magazine,* some months before, conceived the excellent idea of getting the surviving heroes of the late Civil War, on both sides, to write out their personal reminiscences of the war and publish them, now, in the magazine. But the happy project had come to grief, for the reason that some of these heroes were quite willing to write out these things only under one condition, that they insisted was essential: they refused to write a line unless the leading actor of the war should also write.[1] All persuasions and arguments failed on General Grant; he would *not* write. So the scheme fell through.

Now, however, the complexion of things had changed and General Grant was without bread, not figuratively, but actually.

The *Century* people went to him once more, and

---

[1] August, 1885. They deny this now, but I go bail I got that statement from Gilder himself.—S. L. C.

now he assented eagerly. A great series of war articles was immediately advertised by the *Century* publishers.

I knew nothing of all this, although I had been a number of times to the general's house, to pass half an hour, talking and smoking a cigar.

However, I was reading one night, in Chickering Hall, early in November, 1884, and as my wife and I were leaving the building we stumbled over Mr. Gilder, the editor of the *Century,* and went home with him to a late supper at his house. We were there an hour or two, and in the course of the conversation Gilder said that General Grant had written three war articles for the *Century* and was going to write a fourth. I pricked up my ears.[1] Gilder went on to describe how eagerly General Grant had entertained the proposition to write when it had last been put to him, and how poor he evidently was, and how eager to make some trifle of bread-and-butter money, and how the handing him a check for five hundred dollars for the first article had manifestly gladdened his heart and lifted from it a mighty burden.

The thing which astounded me was that, admirable man as Gilder certainly is, and with a heart which is in the right place, it had never seemed to occur to him that to offer General Grant five hundred dollars for a magazine article was not only the monumental injustice of the nineteenth century, but of all centuries. He ought to have known that if he

---

[1] In a statement made somewhat later, Mr. Clemens said that he had first heard Gilder mention this fact as they were leaving Chickering Hall.

had given General Grant a check for ten thousand dollars, the sum would still have been trivial; that if he had paid him twenty thousand dollars for a single article, the sum would still have been inadequate; that if he had paid him thirty thousand dollars for a single magazine war article, it still could not be called paid for; that if he had given him forty thousand dollars for a single magazine article, he would still be in General Grant's debt. Gilder went on to say that it had been impossible, months before, to get General Grant to write a single line, but that, now that he had once got started, it was going to be as impossible to stop him again; that, in fact, General Grant had set out deliberately to write his memoirs in full, and to publish them in book form.

I went straight to General Grant's house next morning and told him what I had heard. He said it was all true.

I said I had foreseen a fortune in such a book when I had tried, as early as 1881, to get him to write it; that the fortune was just as sure to fall now. I asked him who was to publish the book, and he said doubtless the Century Company.

I asked him if the contract had been drawn and signed.

He said it had been drawn in the rough, but not signed yet.

I said I had had a long and painful experience in book making and publishing, and that if there would be no impropriety in his showing me the rough contract, I believed I might be useful to him.

He said there was no objection whatever to my seeing the contract, since it had proceeded no further than a mere consideration of its details, without promises given or received on either side. He added that he supposed that the *Century* offer was fair and right and that he had been expecting to accept it and conclude the bargain or contract. He read the rough draft aloud, and I didn't know whether to cry or laugh.

Whenever a publisher in the "trade" thinks enough of the chances of an unknown author's book to print it and put it on the market, he is willing to risk paying the man 10-per-cent royalty, and that is what he does pay him. He can well venture that much of a royalty, but he cannot well venture any more. If that book shall sell 3,000 or 4,000 copies there is no loss on any ordinary book, and both parties have made something; but whenever the sale shall reach 10,000 copies the publisher is getting the lion's share of the profits and would continue to get the lion's share as long thereafter as the book should continue to sell.

When such a book is sure to sell 35,000 copies an author ought to get 15 per cent—that is to say, one-half of the net profit; when a book is sure to sell 80,000 or more, he ought to get 20-per-cent royalty —that is, two-thirds of the total profits.

Now, here was a book that was morally bound to sell several hundred thousand copies in the first year of its publication, and yet the *Century* people had had the hardihood to offer General Grant the very same 10-per-cent royalty which they would have offered to any unknown Comanche Indian whose book they had reason to believe might sell 3,000 or 4,000 or 5,000 copies.

If I had not been acquainted with the *Century* people I should have said that this was a deliberate attempt to take advantage of a man's ignorance and trusting nature to rob him; but I do know the *Century* people, and therefore I know that they had no such base intentions as these, but were simply making their offer out of their boundless resources of ignorance. They were anxious to do book publishing as well as magazine publishing, and had tried one book already, but, owing to their inexperience, had made a failure of it. So I suppose they were anxious, and had made an offer which in the general's instance commended itself as reasonable and safe, showing that they were lamentably ignorant and that they utterly failed to rise to the size of the occasion. This was sufficiently shown in the remark of the head of that firm to me a few months later, a remark which I shall refer to and quote in its proper place.

I told General Grant that the *Century* offer was simply absurd and should not be considered for an instant.

I forgot to mention that the rough draft made two propositions—one at 10-per-cent royalty, and the other the offer of *half the profits on the book,* after subtracting *every sort of expense connected with it,* including *office rent, clerk hire, advertising,* and *everything else,* a most complicated arrangement and one which no business-like author would accept in preference to a 10-per-cent royalty. They manifestly regarded 10-per-cent and half profits as the same thing—which shows that these innocent geese expected the book to sell only 12,000 or 15,000 copies.

I told the general that I could tell him exactly what he ought to receive; that, if he accepted a royalty, it ought to be 20 per cent on the retail price of the book, or, if he preferred the partnership policy, then he ought to have 70 per cent of the profits on each volume, over and above *the mere cost of making* that volume. I said that if he would place these terms before the *Century* people they would accept them, but if they were afraid to accept them he would simply need to offer them to any great publishing house in the country, and not one would decline them. If any should decline them, let *me* have the book. I was publishing my own book, under the business name of Charles L. Webster & Co., I being the company, and Webster being my business man, on a salary, with a one-tenth interest, and I had what I believed to be much the best equipped subscription establishment in the country.

I wanted the general's book, and I wanted it very much, but I had very little expectation of getting it. I supposed that he would lay these new propositions before the *Century* people, that they would accept immediately, and that there the matter would end; for the general evidently felt under great obligations to the *Century* people for saving him from the grip of poverty by paying him $1,500 for three magazine articles which were well worth $100,000, and he seemed wholly unable to free himself from this sense of obligation; whereas, to my mind, he ought rather to have considered the *Century* people under very high obligations to him, not only for making them a present of $100,000, but for procuring for them a great and desirable series of war articles from the other heroes of the war, which, according to Gilder, they could never have got their hands on if he had declined to write.

I now went away on a long Western tour on the platform, but Webster continued to call at the general's house and watch the progress of events.

Col. Fred Grant was strongly opposed to letting the *Century* people have the book, and was, at the same time, as strongly in favor of my having it.

The general's first magazine article had immediately added 50,000 names to their list of subscribers and thereby established the fact that the *Century* people would still have been the gainers if they had paid General Grant $50,000 for the articles—for the reason that they could expect to keep the most of these subscribers for several years, and, consequently, get a profit out of them in the end of $100,000 at least.

Besides this increased circulation, the number of the *Century's* advertising pages at once doubled, a huge addition to the magazine's cash income in itself —(an addition of $25,000 a *month*, as I estimate it from what I have paid them for one-fifth of a page for six months—$1,800).

The *Century* people had eventually added to the original check of $1,500 a check for a thousand dollars, after perceiving that they were going to make a fortune out of the first of the three articles

This seemed a fine liberality to General Grant, who was the most simple-hearted of all men; but, to me, it seemed merely another exhibition of incomparable nonsense, as the added check ought to have been for $30,000 instead of $1,000. Col. Fred Grant looked upon the matter just as I did, and had determined to keep the book out of the *Century* people's hands if possible. This action merely confirmed and hardened him in his purpose.

While I was in the West, propositions from publishers came to General Grant daily, and these propositions had a common form—to wit: "only tell us what your best offer is and we stand ready to make a better one."

These things had their effect. The general began to perceive, from these various views, that he had narrowly escaped making a very bad bargain for his book; and now he began to incline toward me, for the reason, no doubt, that I had been the accidental cause of stopping that bad bargain.

He called in George W. Childs of Philadelphia and laid the whole matter before him and asked his advice. Mr. Childs said to me afterward that it was plain to be seen that the general, on the score of friendship, was so distinctly inclined toward me that the advice which would please him best would be advice to turn the book over to me.

He counseled the general to send competent people

to examine into my capacity to properly publish the book and into the capacity of the other competitors for the book, and (this was done at my own suggestion—Fred Grant being present) if they found that my house was as well equipped in all ways as the others, that he give the book to me.

The general sent persons selected by a couple of great law firms (Clarence Seward's was one) to make examinations, and Col. Fred Grant made similar examinations for himself personally.

The verdict in these several cases was that my establishment was as competent to make a success of the book as was that of any of the firms competing.

The result was that the contract was drawn and the book was placed in my hands.

In the course of one of my business talks with General Grant he asked me if I felt sure I could sell 25,000 copies of his book, and he asked the question in such a way that I suspected that the *Century* people had intimated that that was about the number of the books that they thought ought to sell.[1]

I replied that the best way for a man to express an opinion in such a case was to put it in money— therefore, I would make this offer: if he would give me the book I would advance him the sum of $25,000 on each volume the moment the manuscript was placed in my hands, adding that I would draw the first check immediately. If I never got the $50,000 back again, out of the future copyrights due, I would

---

[1] This had occurred during their first interview.

never ask him to return any part of the money to
me.

The suggestion seemed to *distress* him. He said
he could not think of taking in advance any sum
of money large or small which the publisher would
not be absolutely sure of getting back again. Some
time afterward, when the contract was being drawn
and the question was whether it should be 20-per-
cent royalty or 70 per cent of the profits, he inquired which of the two propositions would be the
best all round. I sent Webster to tell him that the
20-per-cent royalty would be the best for him, for the
reason that it was the surest, the simplest, the easiest to keep track of, and, better still, would pay him
a trifle more, no doubt, than with the other plan.

He thought the matter over and then said in substance that by the 20-per-cent plan he would be sure
to make, while the publisher might possibly lose;
therefore, he would not have the royalty plan, but
the 70-per-cent-profit plan, since, if there were
profits, he could not then get them all, but the publisher would be sure to get 30 per cent of it.

This was just like General Grant. It was absolutely impossible for him to entertain for a moment
any proposition which might prosper him at the risk
of any other man.

After the contract had been drawn and signed, I
remembered I had offered to advance the general
some money and that he had said he might possibly need $10,000 before the book issued. The
circumstance had been forgotten and was not in the
contract, but I had the luck to remember it before

leaving town; so I went back and told Col. Fred Grant to draw upon Webster for the $10,000 whenever it should be wanted.

That was the only thing forgotten in the contract, and it was now rectified and everything was smooth.

And now I come to a circumstance which I have never spoken of and which cannot be known for many years to come, for this paragraph must not be published until the mention of so private a matter cannot offend any living person.

The contract was drawn by the great law firm of Alexander & Green, on my part, and Clarence Seward, son of Mr. Lincoln's Secretary of State, on the part of General Grant.

Appended to the contract was a transfer of the book to General Grant's wife, and the transfer from her to my firm for the consideration of $1,000 in hand paid.

This was to prevent the general's creditors from seizing the proceeds of the book.

Webster had said, "Yes," when the sum named was a thousand dollars, and, after he had signed the contract and was leaving the law office, he mentioned, incidentally, that the thousand dollars was of course a mere formality in such a paper, and meant nothing. But Mr. Seward took him privately aside and said, "No, it means just what it says— *for the general's family have not a penny in the house and they are waiting at this moment with lively anxiety for that small sum of money.*"

Webster was astonished. He drew a check at once and Mr. Seward gave it to a messenger boy and told him to take it swiftly—by the speediest route—to General Grant's house, and not let the grass grow under his feet.

It was a shameful thing that the man who had saved this country and its government from destruction should still be in a position where so small a sum—so trivial an amount—as $1,000 could be looked upon as a godsend. Everybody knew that the general was in reduced circumstances, but what a storm would have gone up all over the land if the people could have known that his poverty had reached such a point as this.

The newspapers all over the land had been lauding the princely generosity of the *Century* people in paying General Grant the goodly sum of $1,500 for three magazine articles, whereas, if they had paid him the amount which was his just due for them, he would still have been able to keep his carriage and not have been worrying about $1,000. Neither the newspapers nor the public were probably aware that fifty-five years earlier the publishers of an annual in London had offered little Tom Moore twice $1,500 for two articles and had told him to make them long or short and to write about whatever he pleased. The difference between the financial value of any article written by Tom Moore in his best day and a war article written by General Grant in these days was about as one to fifty.

To go back awhile. After being a month or two in the West, during the winter of 1884-85, I returned to the East, reaching New York about the 20th of February.

No agreement had at that time been reached as to the contract, but I called at General Grant's house simply to inquire after his health, for I had seen reports in the newspapers that he had been sick and confined to his house for some time.

The last time I had been at his house he told me that he had stopped smoking because of the trouble in his throat, which the physicians had said would be quickest cured in that way. But while I was in the West the newspapers had reported that this throat affection was believed to be in the nature of a cancer. However, on the morning of my arrival in New York the newspapers had reported that the physicians had said that the general was a great deal better than he had been and was getting along very comfortably. So, when I called at the house, I went up to the general's room and shook hands and said I was very glad he was so much better and so well along on the road to perfect health again.

He smiled and said, "If it were only true."

Of course I was both surprised and discomfited, and asked his physician, Doctor Douglas, if the general were in truth not progressing as well as I had supposed. He intimated that the reports were rather rose colored and that this affection was no doubt a cancer.

I am an excessive smoker, and I said to the general that some of the rest of us must take warning by his case, but Doctor Douglas spoke up and said that this result must not be attributed altogether to smoking. He said it was probable that it had its *origin* in excessive smoking; but that was not the certain reason of its manifesting itself at this time; that more than likely the real reason was the general's distress of mind and year-long depression of spirit, arising from the failure of the Grant & Ward firm.

This remark started the general at once to talking; and I found then and afterward that, when he did not care to talk about any other subject, he was always ready and willing to talk about that one.

He told what I have before related about the robberies perpetrated upon him and upon all the Grant connection, by this man Ward whom he had so thoroughly trusted, *but he never uttered a phrase concerning Ward which an outraged adult might not have uttered concerning an offending child.* He spoke as a man speaks who has been deeply wronged and humiliated and betrayed; but he never used a venomous expression or one of a vengeful nature.

As for myself, I was inwardly boiling all the time; I was scalping Ward, flaying him alive, breaking him on the wheel, pounding him to jelly, and cursing him with all the profanity known to the one language that I am acquainted with, and helping it out, in times of difficulty and distress, with odds and ends of profanity drawn from the two other languages of which I have a limited knowledge.

He told his story with deep feeling in his voice, but with no betrayal upon his countenance of what was going on in his heart. He could depend upon that countenance of his in all emergencies. It always stood by him. It never betrayed him.

[July 1st or 2d, at Mount McGregor, 1885, about

three weeks before the general's death, Buck Grant and I sat talking an hour to each other across the general's lap, just to keep him company—he had only to listen. The news had just come that that Marine Bank man (Ward's pal—what *was* that scoundrel's name?) had been sent up for ten years. Buck Grant said the bitterest things about him he could frame his tongue to; I was about as bitter myself. The general listened for some time, then reached for his pad and pencil and wrote, "He was not as bad as the other"—meaning Ward. It was his only comment. Even his *writing* looked gentle.]

While he was talking, Colonel Grant said, "Father is letting you see that the Grant family are a pack of fools, Mr. Clemens!"

The general combated that statement. He said, in substance, that facts could be produced which would show that when Ward laid siege to a man, that man would turn out to be a fool, too—as much of a fool as any Grant; that all men were fools if the being successfully beguiled by Ward was proof, by itself, that the man was a fool. He began to present instances. He said (in effect) that nobody would call the president of the Erie Railroad a fool, yet Ward beguiled him to the extent of $800,000, robbed him of every cent of it. He mentioned another man who could not be called a fool; yet Ward had beguiled that man out of more than half a million dollars and had given him nothing in return for it. He instanced a man with a name something like Fisher, though that was not the name, whom he said nobody could call a fool; on the contrary a man who had made himself very rich by being sharper and smarter than other people and who always prided himself upon his smartness and upon the fact that he could not be fooled, he could not be deceived by anybody; but what did Ward do in his case? He fooled him into buying a portion of a mine belonging to ex-Senator Chaffee—a property which was not for sale, which Ward could produce no authority for selling—yet he got out of *that* man $300,000 in cash, without the passage of a single piece of paper or a line of writing to show that the sale had been made. This man came to the office of Grant & Ward every day for a good while, and talked with Ward about the prospects of that rich mine (and it *was* very rich), and these two would pass directly by Mr. Chaffee and go into the next room and talk. You would think that a man of his reputation for shrewdness would at some time or other have concluded to ask Mr. Chaffee a question or two; but, no, Ward had told this man that Chaffee did not want to be known in the transaction at all, that he must seem to be at Grant & Ward's office on other business, and that he must not venture to speak to Chaffee or the whole business would be spoiled.

There was a man who prided himself on being a smart business man, and yet Ward robbed him of $300,000 without giving him a scrap of anything to show that the transaction had taken place, and to-day that man is not among the prosecutors of Ward at all, for the reason, perhaps, that he would rather lose all of that money than to have the fact get out that he was deceived in so childish a way.

General Grant mentioned another man who was very wealthy, whom no one would venture to call a fool, either businesswise or otherwise, yet this man came into the office one day and said: "Ward, here is my check for $50,000. I have no use for it at present; I am going to make a flying trip to Europe. Turn it over for me; see what you can do with it." Some time afterward I was in the office when this gentleman returned from his trip and presented himself. He asked Ward if he had accomplished anything with that money? Ward said, "Just wait a moment," went to his books, turned over a page, mumbled to himself a few moments, drew a check for $250,000, handed it to this man with the air of a person who had really accomplished nothing worth talking of! The man stared at the check a moment, handed it back to Ward, and said, "That is plenty good enough for me; set that hen again," and he went out of the place. It was the last he ever saw of any of that money.

I had been discovering fools all along when the general was talking, but this instance brought me to my senses. I put myself in this fellow's place and confessed that if I had been in that fellow's clothes it was a hundred to one that I would have done the very thing that he had done, and I was thoroughly well aware that, at any rate, there was not a preacher or a widow in Christendom who would not have done it; for these people are always seeking investments that pay illegitimately large sums; and they never, or seldom, stop to inquire into the nature of the business.

When I was ready to go, Col. Fred Grant went downstairs with me, and stunned me by telling me, confidentially, that the physicians were trying to keep his father's real condition from him, but that in fact they considered him to be under sentence of death and that he would not be likely to live more than a fortnight or three weeks longer.

This was about the 21st of February, 1885.

After the 21st of February, General Grant busied himself, daily, as much as his strength would allow, in revising the manuscript of his book. It was read to him by Colonel Grant, very carefully, and he made the corrections as he went along. He was losing valuable time because only one-half or two-thirds of the second and last volume was as yet written. However, he was more anxious that what was written should be *absolutely correct* than that he should finish the book in an incorrect form, and then find himself unable to correct it. His memory was superb, and nearly any other man with such a memory would have been satisfied to trust it. Not so the general. No matter how sure he was of the fact or the date, he would never let it go until he had verified it with the official records. This constant and painstaking searching of the records cost a great deal of time, but it was not wasted. Everything stated as a fact in General Grant's book may be accepted with entire confidence as being thoroughly trustworthy.

Speaking of his memory, what a wonderful machine it was! He told me one day that he never made a report of the battles of the Wilderness until they were all over and he was back in Washington. Then he sat down and made a full report from memory, and, when it was finished, examined the reports of his subordinates, and found that he had made hardly an error. To be exact, he said he had made two errors.

The general lost some more time in one other way. Three *Century* articles had been written and paid for, but he had during the summer before promised to write a fourth one. He had written it in a rough draft, but it had remained unfinished.

The *Century* people had advertised these articles and were now fearful that the general would never be able to complete them. By this time news of the general's failing health had got abroad and the newspapers were full of reports about his perilous condition. The *Century* people called several times to get the fourth article, and this hurt and offended Col. Fred Grant, because he knew that they were aware, as was all the world, that his father was considered to be in a dying condition. Colonel Grant thought that they ought to show more consideration—more humanity. By fits and starts, the general worked at that article whenever his failing strength would permit him, and was determined to finish it, if possible, *because his promise had been given and he would in no way depart from it while any slight possibility remained of fulfilling it.* I asked if there was no contract or no understanding as to what was to be paid by the *Century* people

for the article. He said there was not. "Then,"
I said, "charge them $20,000 for it. It is well
worth it—worth double the money. Charge them
this sum for it in its unfinished condition and let
them have it, and tell them that it will be worth
still more in case the general shall be able to complete it. This may modify their ardor somewhat
and bring you a rest." He was not willing to put
so large a price upon it, but thought that if he gave
it to them he might require them to pay $5,000.
It was plain that the modesty of the family in money
matters was indestructible.

Just about this time I was talking to General
Badeau there one day, when I saw a pile of type-
writer manuscript on the table and picked up the
first page and began to read it. I saw that it was
an account of the siege of Vicksburg. I counted
a page and there were about three hundred words
on the page; 18,000 or 20,000 words altogether.

General Badeau said it was one of the three articles written by General Grant for the *Century*.

I said, "Then they have no sort of right to require the fourth article, for there is matter enough
in this one to make two or three ordinary magazine
articles." The copy of this and the other two articles were at this moment in the *Century's* safe;
the fourth-article agreement was therefore most
amply fulfilled already, without an additional article; yet the *Century* people considered that the
contract would not be fulfilled without the fourth
article, and so insisted upon having it. At the ordinary price paid me for *Century* articles, this Vicks-

bury article, if I had written it, would have been worth about $700. Therefore, the *Century* people had paid General Grant no more than they would have paid me; and this *including* the $1,000 gratuity which they had given him.

If the *Century* people knew anything at all, they knew that a single page of General Grant's manuscript was worth more than a hundred of mine. They were honest, honorable, and good-hearted people according to their lights, and if anybody could have made them see differently they would have rectified the wrong. But all the eloquence that I was able to pour out upon them went for nothing, utterly nothing. They still thought that they had been quite generous to the general and were not able to see the matter in any other light.

Afterward, at Mount McGregor, they consented to give up half of the Vicksburg article; and they did; they gave up *more* than half of it—cut it from twenty-two galleys down to nine, and only the nine will appear in the magazine, and they added $2,500 to the $2,500 already paid. Those people could learn to be as fair and liberal as anybody if they had the right schooling.

Some time after the contract for General Grant's book was completed, I found that nothing but a verbal understanding existed between General Grant and the Century Company giving General Grant permission to use his *Century* articles in his book. There is a law of custom which gives an author the privilege of using his magazine articles in any way he pleases, after it shall have appeared in the magazine; and this law of custom is so well established that an author never expects to have any difficulty about getting a magazine copyright transferred to him, whenever he shall ask for it, with the purpose in view of putting the article in a book. But in the present case I was afraid that the Century Company might fall back upon their legal rights and ignore the law of custom, in which case we should be debarred from using General Grant's *Century* articles in his book—an awkward state of things, because he was now too sick a man to rewrite them. It was necessary that something should be done in this matter, and done at once.

Mr. Seward, General Grant's lawyer, was a good deal disturbed when he found that there was no writing. But I was not. I believed that the *Century* people could be relied upon to carry out any verbal agreement which they had made. The only thing I feared was that their idea of the verbal agreement, and General Grant's idea of it, might not coincide. So I went back to the general's house and got Col. Fred Grant to write down what he understood the verbal agreement to be, and this piece of writing he read to General Grant, who said it was correct, and then signed it with his own hand, a feeble and trembling signature, but recognizable as his.

Then I sent for Webster and our lawyer, and we three went to the *Century* office, where we found Roswell Smith (the head man of the company) and several of the editors. I stated my case plainly and simply and found that their understanding and General Grant's were identical; so the difficulty was at an end at once and we proceeded to draw a writing to cover the thing.

When the business was finished, or perhaps in the course of it, I made another interesting discovery.

I was already aware that the *Century* people were going to bring out all their war articles in book form, eventually, General Grant's among the number; but, as I knew what a small price had been paid to the general for his articles, I had a vague notion that he would receive a further payment for the use of them in their book—a remuneration which an author customarily receives, in our day, by another unwritten law of custom. But when I spoke of this, to my astonishment they told me that they had bought and paid for every one of these war articles with the distinct understanding that that first payment was the last. In confirmation of this amazing circumstance, they brought out a receipt which General Grant had signed, and therein it distinctly appeared that each $500 not only paid for the use of the article printed in the magazine, *but also in the subsequent book!*

One thing was quite clear to me: if we consider the value of those articles to that book, we must grant that the general was paid very much less than nothing at all for their issue in the magazine.

The *Century* people didn't blush, and, therefore, it is plain that they considered the transaction fair and legitimate; and I believe myself that they had no idea that they were doing an unfair thing. It was easily demonstrable that they were buying ten-dollar gold pieces from General Grant at twenty-five cents apiece, and I think it was as easily demonstrable that they did not know that there was anything unfair about it.

Roswell Smith said to me, with the glad air of a man who has stuck a nail in his foot, "I'm glad you've got the general's book, Mr. Clemens, and glad there was somebody with courage enough to take it, under the circumstances. What do you think the general wanted to require of me?"

"What?"

"He wanted me to insure a sale of twenty-five thousand sets of his book! I wouldn't risk such a guaranty on any book that ever was published." [1]

I did not say anything, but I thought a good deal. This was one more evidence that the *Century* people had no more just idea of the value of the book than as many children might be expected to have. At this present writing (May 25, 1885) we have not advertised General Grant's book in any way; we have not spent a dollar in advertising of any kind; we have not even given notice by circular or otherwise that we are ready to receive applications from book agents; and yet, to-day, we have *bona fide* orders for 100,000 sets of the book—that is to say, 200,000 single volumes; and these orders are from men who

---

[1] This is the remark I have already several times referred to. I've got Smith's exact language (from my notebook); it proves that they thought 10-per-cent royalty would actually represent half profits on General Grant's book!

Note added Sept. 10, 1885, 250,000 sets—500,000 single copies—have been sold to date—and only half the ground canvassed.

have bonded themselves to take and pay for them, and who have also laid before us the most trustworthy evidence that they are financially able to carry out their contracts. The territory which these men have taken is only about one-fourth of the area of the Northern states. We have also under consideration applications for 50,000 sets more; and although we have confidence in the energy and ability of the men who have made these applications, we have not closed with them because, as yet, we are not sufficiently satisfied as to their financial strength.

When it became known that the general's book had fallen into my hands, the New York *World* and a Boston paper (I think the *Herald*) came out at once with the news; and in both instances the position was taken that, by some sort of superior underhanded smartness, I had taken an unfair advantage of the confiding simplicity of the *Century* people and got the book away from them—a book which they had the right to consider their property, inasmuch as the terms of its publication had been mutually agreed upon and the contract covering it was on the point of being signed by General Grant when I put in my meddling appearance.

None of the statements of these two papers was correct, but the Boston paper's account was considered to be necessarily correct, for the reason that it was furnished by the sister of Mr. Gilder, editor of the *Century,* so there was considerable newspaper talk about my improper methods; but nobody seemed to have wit enough to discover that if one gouger *had* captured the general's book, here was evidence that he had only prevented another gouger from getting it, since the *Century's* terms were distinctly mentioned in the Boston paper's account as being *10-per-cent royalty*. No party observed that, and nobody commented upon it. It was taken for granted all round that General Grant would have signed that 10-per-cent contract without being grossly cheated.

It is my settled policy to allow newspapers to make as many misstatements about me or my affairs as they like; therefore I had no mind to contradict either of these newspapers or explain my side of the case in any way. But a reporter came to our house at Hartford (from one of the editors of the *Courant*) to ask me for my side of the matter for use in the Associated Press dispatches. I dictated a short paragraph in which I said that the statement made in the *World*, that there was a coolness between the Century Company and General Grant, and that, in consequence of it, the *Century* would not publish any more articles by General Grant, notwithstanding the fact that they had advertised them far and wide, was not true. I said there was no coolness and no ground for coolness; that the contract for the book had been open for all competitors; that I had put in my application and had asked the general to state its terms to the other applicants in order that he might thereby be enabled to get the best terms possible; that I had got the book, eventually, but by no underhand or unfair method. The statement I made was concise and brief and contained nothing offensive. It was sent over the wires to the Associated Press headquarters

in New York, but it was not *issued* by that concern.
It did not appear in print. I inquired why, and
was told that, although it was a piece of news of
quite universal interest, it was also more or less
of an advertisement for the book—a thing I had
not thought of before. I was also told that if I
had had a friend round about the Associated Press
office, I could have had that thing published all
over the country for a reasonable bribe. I wondered if that were true. I wondered if so great
and important a concern dealt in that sort of thing.

[*Dictated in 1885.*

GERHARDT[1] AND THE GRANT BUST

I WILL make a diversion here, and get back upon
my track again later.

While I was away with G. W. Cable, giving public readings in the theaters, lecture halls, skating
rinks, jails, and churches of the country, the travel
was necessarily fatiguing, and, therefore, I ceased
from writing letters excepting to my wife and children. This foretaste of heaven, this relief from the
fret of letter-answering, was delightful; but it finally
left me in the dark concerning things which I ought
to have been acquainted with at the moment.

Among these the affairs of Karl Gerhardt, the
young artist, should be mentioned.

I had started out on this reading pilgrimage the

---

[1] Karl Gerhardt, a young sculptor sent by Mr. and Mrs.
Clemens to Paris to perfect himself in his art.

day after the presidential election; that is to say, I
had started on the 5th of November, and had visited
my home only once between that time and the 2d
of March following.

During all these four months, Gerhardt had been
waiting for a verdict of a dilatory committee, concerning a Nathan Hale statue, and had taken it out
in waiting; that is to say, he had sat still and done
nothing to earn his bread. He had been tirelessly
diligent in asking for work in the line of his art,
and had used all possible means in that direction;
he had written letters to every man he could hear
of who was likely to need a mortuary monument for
himself, or his friends, or acquaintances, and had
also applied for the chance of a competition for a
soldiers' monument—for all things of this sort—
but always without success; the natural result, as his
name was not known. He had no reputation.

Once, J. Q. A. Ward, in speaking of his early
struggles to get a status as a sculptor, had told me
that he had made his beginning by hanging around
the studios of sculptors of repute and picking up odd
jobs of journey work in them, for the sake of the
bread he could gain in that way.

I may as well say here, and be done with it, that
my connection with Gerhardt had very little sentiment in it, from my side of the house; and no ro-
mance. I took hold of his case, in the first place,
solely because I had become convinced that he had
it in him to become a very capable sculptor. I was
not adopting a child, I was not adding a member
to the family, I was merely taking upon myself a

common duty—the duty of helping a man who was not able to help himself. I never expected him to be grateful, I never expected him to be thankful— my experience of men had long ago taught me that one of the surest ways of begetting an enemy was to do some stranger an act of kindness which should lay upon him the irritating sense of an obligation. Therefore my connection with Gerhardt had nothing sentimental or romantic about it. I told him in the first place that if the time should ever come when he could pay back to me the money expended upon him, and pay it without inconvenience to himself, I should expect it at his hands, and that, when it *was* paid, I should consider the account entirely requited—sentiment and all; that that act would leave him free from any obligation to me. It was well, all round, that things had taken that shape in the beginning, and had kept it, for if the foundation had been sentiment that sentiment might have grown sour.

One evening Gerhardt appeared in the library and I hoped he had come to say he was getting along very well and was contented; so I was disappointed when he said he had come to show me a small bust he had been making, in clay, of General Grant, from a photograph. I was the more irritated for the reason that I had never seen a portrait of General Grant—in oil, water-colors, crayon, steel, wood, photograph, plaster, marble, or any other material—that was to me at all satisfactory; and, therefore, I could not expect that a person who had never even seen the general could accomplish anything worth considering in the way of a likeness of him.

However, when he uncovered the bust my prejudices vanished at once.

The thing was not correct in its details, yet it seemed to me to be a closer approach to a good likeness of General Grant than any one which I had ever seen before. Before uncovering it, Gerhardt had said he had brought it in the hope that I would show it to some member of the general's family and get that member to point out its chief defects, for correction; but I had replied that I could not venture to do that, for there was a plenty of people to pester these folks without me adding myself to the number. But a glance at the bust had changed all that in an instant. I said I would go to New York in the morning and ask the family to look at the bust, and that he must come along to be within call in case they took enough interest in the matter to point out the defects.

We reached the general's house at one o'clock the next afternoon, and I left Gerhardt and the bust below and went upstairs to see the family.

And now, for the first time, the thought came into my mind that perhaps I was doing a foolish thing; that the family must of necessity have been pestered with such matters as this so many times that the very mention of such a thing must be nauseating to them. However, I had started, and so I might as well finish. Therefore, I said I had a young artist downstairs who had been making a small bust of the general from a photograph, and

I wished they would look at it, if they were willing
to do me that kindness.

Jesse Grant's wife spoke up with eagerness and
said, "Is it the artist who made the bust of you
that is in *Huckleberry Finn?*" I said, "Yes." She
said, with great animation, "How good it was of
you, Mr. Clemens, to think of that!" She expressed
this lively gratitude to me in various ways until I
began to feel somehow a great sense of merit in having originated this noble idea of having a bust of
General Grant made by so excellent an artist. I
will not do my sagacity the discredit of saying that
I did anything to remove or modify this impression
that I had originated the idea and carried it out
to its present state through my own ingenuity and
diligence.

Mrs. Jesse Grant added, "How strange it is; only
two nights ago I dreamed that I was looking at
your bust in *Huckleberry Finn* and thinking how
nearly perfect it was, and then I thought that I conceived the idea of going to you and asking you if
you could not hunt up that artist and get him to
make a bust of father!"

Things were going on very handsomely!

The persons present were Col. Fred Grant, Mrs.
Jesse Grant, and Doctor Douglas.

I went down for Gerhardt and he brought up the
bust and uncovered it. All of the family present
exclaimed over the excellence of the likeness, and
Mrs. Jesse Grant expended some more unearned
gratitude upon me.

The family began to discuss the details, and then

checked themselves and begged Gerhardt's pardon
for criticizing. Of course, he said that their criticisms were exactly what he wanted and begged them
to go on. The general's wife said that in that case
they would be glad to point out what seemed to
them inaccuracies, but that he must not take their
speeches as being criticisms upon his art at all. They
found two inaccuracies; in the shape of the nose and
the shape of the forehead. All were agreed that
the forehead was wrong, but there was a lively dispute about the nose. Some of those present contended that the nose was nearly right—the others
contended that it was distinctly wrong. The general's wife knelt on the ottoman to get a clearer
view of the bust, and the others stood about her
—all talking at once. Finally, the general's wife
said, hesitatingly, with the mien of one who is afraid
he is taking a liberty and asking too much, "If Mr.
Gerhardt could see the general's nose and forehead,
himself, that would dispose of this dispute at once.
Finally, "The general is in the next room. Would
Mr. Gerhardt mind going in there and making the
correction himself?"

Things were indeed progressing handsomely!

Of course, Mr. Gerhardt lost no time in expressing his willingness.

While the controversy was going on concerning
the nose and the forehead, Mrs. Fred Grant joined
the group, and then, presently, each of the three
ladies, in turn, disappeared for a few minutes, and
came back with a handful of photographs and hand-
painted miniatures of the general.

These pictures had been made in every quarter of the world. One of them had been painted in Japan. But, good as many of these pictures were, they were worthless as evidence, for the reason that they contradicted one another in every detail.

The photograph apparatus had lied as distinctly and as persistently as had the hands of the miniature-artists. No two noses were alike and no two foreheads were alike.

We stepped into the general's room—all but General Badeau and Doctor Douglas.

The general was stretched out in a reclining chair with his feet supported upon an ordinary chair. He was muffled up in dressing gowns and afghans, with his black woolen skull-cap on his head.

The ladies took the skull-cap off and began to discuss his nose and his forehead, and they made him turn this way and that way and the other way, to get different views and profiles of his features. He took it all patiently and made no complaint. He allowed them to pull and haul him about, in their own affectionate fashion, without a murmur.

Mrs. Fred Grant, who is very beautiful and of the most gentle and loving character, was very active in this service, and very deft, with her graceful hands, in arranging and rearranging the general's head for inspection, and repeatedly called attention to the handsome shape of his head—a thing which reminds me that Gerhardt had picked up an old plug hat of the general's downstairs, and had remarked upon the perfect oval shape of the inside of it, this oval being so uniform that the wearer of the hat could never be able to know, by the feel of it, whether he had it right end in front or wrong end in front; whereas the average man's head is broad at one end and narrow at the other.

The general's wife placed him in various positions, none of which satisfied her, and finally she went to him and said: "Ulyss! Ulyss! Can't you put your feet to the floor?" He did so at once and straightened himself up.

During all this time the general's face wore a pleasant, contented, and I should say benignant, aspect, but he never opened his lips once. As had often been the case before, so now his silence gave ample room to guess at what was passing in his mind—and to take it out in guessing. I will remark, in passing, that the general's hands were very thin, and they showed, far more than did his face, how his long siege of confinement and illness and insufficient food had wasted him. He was at this time suffering great and increasing pain from the cancer at the root of his tongue, but there was nothing ever discoverable in the expression of his face to betray this fact, as long as he was awake. When asleep, his face would take advantage of him and make revelations.

At the end of fifteen minutes, Gerhardt said he believed he could correct the defects now. So we went back to the other room.

Gerhardt went to work on the clay image, everybody standing round, observing and discussing with the greatest interest.

Presently the general astonished us by appearing there, clad in his wraps and supporting himself in a somewhat unsure way upon a cane. He sat down on the sofa and said he could sit there if it would be for the advantage of the artist.

But his wife would not allow that. She said that he might catch cold. She was for hurrying him back at once to his invalid chair. He succumbed and started back, but at the door he turned and said:

"Then can't Mr. Gerhardt bring the clay in here and work?"

This was several hundred times better fortune than Gerhardt could have dreamed of. He removed his work to the general's room at once. The general stretched himself out in his chair, but said that if that position would not do, he would sit up. Gerhardt said it would do very well indeed, especially if it were more comfortable to the sitter than any other would be.

The general watched Gerhardt's swift and noiseless fingers for some time with manifest interest in his face, and no doubt this novelty was a valuable thing to one who had spent so many weeks that were tedious with sameness and unemphasized with change or diversion. By and by, one eyelid began to droop occasionally; then everybody stepped out of the room excepting Gerhardt and myself, and I moved to the rear, where I would be out of sight and not be a disturbing element.

Harrison, the general's old colored body servant, came in presently, and remained awhile, watching

Gerhardt, and then broke out, with great zeal and decision:

"That's the general! Yes, sir, that's the general! Mind! I tell you that's the general!"

Then he went away and the place became absolutely silent.

Within a few minutes afterward the general was sleeping, and for two hours he continued to sleep tranquilly, the serenity of his face disturbed only at intervals by a passing wave of pain. It was the first sleep he had had for several weeks uninduced by narcotics.

To my mind this bust, completed at this sitting, has in it more of General Grant than can be found in any other likeness of him that has ever been made since he was a famous man. I think it may rightly be called the best portrait of General Grant that is in existence. It has also a feature which must always be a remembrancer to this nation of what the general was passing through during the long weeks of that spring. For into the clay image went the pain which he was enduring, but which did not appear in his face when he was awake. Consequently, the bust has about it a suggestion of patient and brave and manly suffering which is infinitely touching.

At the end of two hours General Badeau entered abruptly and spoke to the general, and this woke him up. But for this interruption he might have slept as much longer, possibly.

Gerhardt worked on as long as it was light enough to work, and then he went away. He was to come again, and did come the following day; but at the last moment Col. Fred Grant would not permit another sitting. He said that the face was so nearly perfect that he was afraid to allow it to be touched again, lest some of the excellence might be refined out of it, instead of adding more excellence to it. He called attention to an oil painting on the wall downstairs and asked if we knew that man. We couldn't name him—had never seen his face before. "Well," said Colonel Grant, "that was a perfect portrait of my father once. It was given up by all the family to be the best that had ever been made of him. We were entirely satisfied with it, but the artist, unhappily, was not; he wanted 'to do a stroke or two to make it absolutely perfect' and he insisted on taking it back with him. After he had made those finishing touches it didn't resemble my father or anyone else. We took it, and have always kept it as a curiosity. But with that lesson behind us we will save this bust from a similar fate."

He allowed Gerhardt to work at the hair, however; he said he might expend as much of his talent on that as he pleased, but must stop there.

Gerhardt finished the hair to his satisfaction, but never touched the face again. Colonel Grant required Gerhardt to promise that he would take every pains with the clay bust, and then return it to him, to keep, as soon as he had taken a mold from it. This was done.

Gerhardt prepared the clay as well as he could for permanent preservation and gave it to Colonel Grant.

Up to the present day, May 22, 1885, no later likeness of General Grant, of any kind, has been made from life, and if it shall chance to remain the last ever made of him from life, coming generations can properly be grateful that one so nearly perfect of him was made after the world learned his name.

[*Dictated* 1885

The Reverend Doctor N—— Visits General Grant

July 4, 1885.—General Grant is still living this morning. Many a person between the two oceans lay hours awake last night listening for the booming of the fire bells which should speak to a nation in simultaneous voice and tell it its calamity. The bell strokes are to be thirty seconds apart and there will be sixty-three—the general's age. They will be striking in every town in the United States at the same moment—the first time in the world's history that the bells of a nation have tolled in unison —beginning at the same moment and ending at the same moment.

More than once, during two weeks, the nation stood watching with bated breath, expecting the news of General Grant's death.

The family, in their distress, desired spiritual help, and one Reverend Doctor N—— was sent for to furnish it. N—— had lately gone to California, where he had got a ten-thousand-dollar job to preach a funeral sermon over the son of an ex-governor, a millionaire; and a most remarkable sermon it was —and worth the money. If N—— got the facts right, neither he nor anybody else—any ordinary human being—was worthy to preach that youth's funeral sermon, and it was manifest that one of the disciples ought to have been imported into California for the occasion. N—— came on from California at once and began his ministration at the general's bedside; and, if one might trust his daily reports, the general had conceived a new and perfect interest in spiritual things. It is fair to presume that the most of N——'s daily reports originated in his own imagination.

Col. Fred Grant told me that his father was, in this matter, what he was in all matters and at all times—that is to say, perfectly willing to have family prayers going on, or anything else that could be satisfactory to anybody, or increase anybody's comfort in any way; but he also said that, while his father was a good man, and indeed as good as any man, Christian or otherwise, he was *not* a praying man.

Some of the speeches put into General Grant's mouth were to the last degree incredible to people who knew the general, since they were such gaudy and flowering misrepresentations of that plain-spoken man's utterances.

About the 14th or 15th of April, Reverend Mr. N—— reported that upon visiting the general in his sick chamber, the general pressed his hand and delivered himself of this astounding remark:

"Thrice have I been in the shadow of the Valley of Death and thrice have I come out again."

General Grant never used flowers of speech, and, dead or alive, he never could have uttered anything like that, either as a quotation or otherwise.[1]

[Written in the closing days of 1890

THE MACHINE EPISODE

THIS episode has now spread itself over more than one-fifth of my life—a considerable stretch of time, as I am now fifty-five years old.

Ten or eleven years ago, Dwight Buell, a jeweler, called at our house and was shown up to the billiard room—which was my study; and the game got more study than the other sciences. He wanted me to take some stock in a type-setting machine. He said it was at the Colt arms factory, and was about finished. I took $2,000 of the stock. I was always taking little chances like that—and almost always losing by it, too—a thing which I did not greatly mind, because I was always careful to risk only such amounts as I could easily afford to lose. Some time afterward I was invited to go down to the factory and see the machine. I went, promising myself nothing, for I knew all about type-setting by practical experience, and held the settled and solidified opinion that a successful type-setting machine was an impossibility,

---

[1] The Grant dictations ended here. General Grant died July 23, 1885. More than 300,000 sets, of two vols. each, of his *Memoirs* were sold.

for the reason that a machine cannot be made to *think,* and the thing that sets movable type *must* think or retire defeated. So the performance I witnessed did most thoroughly amaze me. Here was a machine that was really setting type, and doing it with swiftness and accuracy, too. Moreover, it was distributing its case *at the same time.* The distribution was automatic. The machine fed itself from a galley of dead matter, and without human help or suggestion; for it began its work of its own accord when the type channels needed filling, and stopped of its own accord when they were full enough. The machine was almost a complete compositor; it lacked but one feature—it did not "justify" the lines; this was done by the operator's assistant.

I saw the operator set at the rate of 3,000 ems an hour, which, counting distribution, was but little short of four case-men's work.

Mr. H—— was there. I had known him long; I thought I knew him well. I had great respect for him and full confidence in him. He said he was already a considerable owner and was now going to take as much more of the stock as he could afford. Wherefore I set down my name for an additional $3,000. It is here that the music begins.[1]

Before very long H—— called on me and asked me what I would charge to raise a capital of $500,000 for the manufacture of the machine. I said I would undertake it for $100,000. He said,

---

[1] This was the Farnam machine—so called.

"Raise $600,000, then, and take $100,000." I agreed. I sent for my partner, Webster. He came up from New York and went back with the project. There was some correspondence. H—— wrote Webster a letter.

I will remark here that James W. Paige, the little bright-eyed, alert, smartly dressed inventor of the machine is a most extraordinary compound of business thrift and commercial insanity; of cold calculation and jejune sentimentality; of veracity and falsehood; of fidelity and treachery; of nobility and baseness; of pluck and cowardice; of wasteful liberality and pitiful stinginess; of solid sense and weltering moonshine; of towering genius and trivial ambitions; of merciful bowels and a petrified heart; of colossal vanity and—— But there the opposites stop. His vanity stands alone, sky-piercing, as sharp of outline as an Egyptian monolith. It is the only unpleasant feature in him that is not modified, softened, compensated by some converse characteristic. There is another point or two worth mentioning. He can persuade anybody, he can convince nobody. He has a crystal-clear mind as regards the grasping and concreting of an idea which has been lost and smothered under a chaos of baffling legal language; and yet it can always be depended upon to take the simplest half dozen facts and draw from them a conclusion that will astonish the idiots in the asylum. It is because he is a dreamer, a visionary. His imagination runs utterly away with him. He is a poet, a most great and genuine poet, whose sublime creations are written in steel. He is the Shakespeare of mechanical invention. In all the ages he has no peer. Indeed, there is none that even approaches him. Whoever is qualified to fully comprehend his marvelous machine will grant that its place is upon the loftiest summit of human invention, with no kindred between it and the far foothills below.

But I must explain these strange contradictions above listed or the man will be misunderstood and wronged. His business thrift is remarkable, and it is also of a peculiar cut. He has worked at his expensive machine for more than twenty years, but always at somebody else's cost. He spent hundreds and thousands of other folks' money, yet always kept his machine and its possible patents in his own possession, unencumbered by an embarrassing lien of any kind—except once, which will be referred to by and by. He could never be beguiled into putting a penny of his own into his work. Once he had a brilliant idea in the way of a wonderfully valuable application of electricity. To test it, he said, would cost but twenty-five dollars. I was paying him a salary of nearly $600 a month and was spending $1,200 on the machine, besides. Yet he asked me to risk the twenty-five dollars and take half of the result. I declined, and he dropped the matter. Another time he was sure he was on the track of a splendid thing in electricity. It would cost only a trifle—possibly $200—to try some experiments; I was asked to furnish the money and take half of the result. I furnished money until the sum had grown to about a thousand dollars, and everything was pronounced ready for the grand exposition. The

electric current was turned on—the thing declined
to go. Two years later the same thing was successfully worked out and patented by a man in the
State of New York and was at once sold for a huge
sum of money and a royalty reserve besides. The
drawings in the electrical journal showing the stages
by which that inventor had approached the con-
summation of his idea, proving his way step by step
as he went, were almost the twins of Paige's drawings of two years before. It was almost as if the
same hand had drawn both sets. Paige said we had
had it, and we should have *known* it if we had only
tried an alternating current after failing with the
direct current; said he had felt sure, at the time,
that at cost of a hundred dollars he could apply
the alternating test and come out triumphant. Then
he added, in tones absolutely sodden with self-sacri-
fice and just barely touched with reproach:

*"But you had already spent so much money on
the thing that I hadn't the heart to ask you to spend
any more."*

If I had asked him why he didn't draw on his
own pocket, he would not have understood me. He
could not have grasped so strange an idea as that.
He would have thought there was something the
matter with my mind. I am speaking honestly; he
could not have understood it. A cancer of old habit
and long experience could as easily understand the
suggestion that it board itself awhile.

In drawing contracts he is always able to take
care of himself; and in every instance he will work
into the contracts injuries to the other party and

advantages to himself which were never considered or mentioned in the preceding verbal agreement. In one contract he got me to assign to him several hundred thousand dollars' worth of property for a certain valuable consideration—said valuable consideration being the *regiving to me of another piece of property which was not his to give, but already belonged to me!* I quite understand that I am confessing myself a fool; but that is no matter, the reader would find it out anyway as I go along. H—— was our joint lawyer, and I had every confidence in his wisdom and cleanliness.

Once when I was lending money to Paige during a few months, I presently found that he was giving *receipts* to my representative instead of notes! But that man never lived who could catch Paige so nearly asleep as to palm off on him a piece of paper which apparently satisfied a debt when it ought to acknowledge a loan.

I must throw in a parenthesis here or I shall do H—— an injustice. Here and there I have seemed to cast little reflections upon him. Pay no attention to them. I have no feeling about him; I have no harsh words to say about him. He is a great, fat, good-natured, kind-hearted, chicken-livered slave; with no more pride than a tramp, no more sand than a rabbit, no more moral sense than a wax figure, and no more sex than a tapeworm. He sincerely thinks he is honest, he sincerely thinks he is honorable. It is my daily prayer to God that he be permitted to live and die in those superstitions. I gave him a twentieth of my American holding,

at Paige's request; I gave him a twentieth of my
foreign holding, at his own supplication; I advanced
nearly forty thousand dollars in five years to keep
these interests sound and valid for him. In return,
he drafted every contract which I made with Paige
in all that time—clear up to September, 1890—
and pronounced them good and fair; and then I
signed.

Yes, it is as I have said: Paige is an extraordinary
compound of business thrift and commercial insanity. Instances of his commercial insanity are
simply innumerable. Here are some examples.
When I took hold of the machine, February 6, 1886,
its faults had been corrected and a setter and a
justifier could turn out about 3,500 ems an hour
on it, possibly 4,000. There was no machine that
could pretend rivalry to it. Business sanity would
have said, put it on the market as it was, secure
the field, and add improvements later. Paige's business insanity said, add the improvements first and
risk losing the field. And that is what he set out
to do. To add a justifying mechanism to that machine would take a few months and cost $9,000 by
his estimate, or $12,000 by Pratt and Whitney's.
I agreed to add said justifier to *that* machine. There
could be no sense in building a new machine, yet
in total violation of the agreement, Paige went immediately to work to build a new machine, although
aware, by recent experience, that the cost could
not fall below $150,000 and that the time consumed
would be years instead of months. Well, when four
years had been spent and the new machine was able

to exhibit a marvelous capacity, we appointed the 12th of January for Senator Jones of Nevada to come and make an inspection. He was not promised a perfect machine, but a machine which could be perfected. He had agreed to invest one or two hundred thousand dollars in its fortunes, and had also said that if the exhibition was particularly favorable he might take entire charge of the elephant. At the last moment Paige concluded to add an air blast (afterward found to be unnecessary); wherefore, Jones had to be turned back from New York to wait a couple of months and lose his interest in the thing. A year ago Paige made what he regarded as a vast and magnanimous concession, and said I might sell the English patent for $10,000,000! A little later a man came along who thought he could bring some Englishmen who would buy that patent, and he was sent off to fetch them. He was gone so long that Paige's confidence began to diminish, and with it his price. He finally got down to what he said was his very last and bottom price for that patent—$50,000! This was the only time in five years that I ever saw Paige in his right mind. I could furnish other examples of Paige's business insanity—enough of them to fill six or eight volumes, perhaps, but I am not writing his history, I am merely sketching his portrait.

.   .   .   .

I went on footing the bills and got the machine really perfected at last, at a full cost of about $150,000, instead of the original $30,000.

W. tells me that Paige tried his best to cheat

me out of my royalties when making a contract with the Connecticut Company.

Also that he tried to cheat out of all share Mr. North (inventor of the justifying mechanism), but that North frightened him with a lawsuit threat and is to get a royalty until the aggregate is $2,000,000.

Paige and I always meet on effusively affectionate terms, and yet he knows perfectly well that if I had him in a steel trap I would shut out all human succor and watch that trap till he died.[1]

---

[1] The machine in the end proved a complete failure, being too complicated, too difficult to keep in order. It cost Mark Twain a total of about $190,000.—A. B. P.

CHAPTERS BEGUN IN VIENNA

Written 1897-8

Early Days

. . . So much for the earlier days, and the New England branch of the Clemenses.[1] The other brother settled in the South and is remotely responsible for me. He has collected his reward generations ago, whatever it was. He went South with his particular friend Fairfax, and settled in Maryland with him, but afterward went further and made his home in Virginia. This is the Fairfax whose descendants were to enjoy a curious distinction— that of being American-born English earls. The founder of the house was the Lord General Fairfax of the Parliamentary arm, in Cromwell's time. The earldom, which is of recent date, came to the American Fairfaxes through the failure of male heirs in England. Old residents of San Francisco will remember "Charley," the American earl of the mid-'sixties—tenth Lord Fairfax according to Burke's Peerage, and holder of a modest public office of some sort or other in the new mining town of Virginia City, Nevada. He was never out of America. I knew him, but not intimately. He had a golden character, and that was all his fortune. He laid his title aside, and gave it a holiday until

[1] Mr. Clemens evidently intended to precede this paragraph with some data concerning his New England ancestry, but he never did so.—A. B. P.

his circumstances should improve to a degree consonant with its dignity; but that time never came, I think. He was a manly man and had fine generosities in his make-up. A prominent and pestilent creature named Ferguson, who was always picking quarrels with better men than himself, picked one with him one day, and Fairfax knocked him down. Ferguson gathered himself up and went off, mumbling threats. Fairfax carried no arms, and refused to carry any now, though his friends warned him that Ferguson was of a treacherous disposition and would be sure to take revenge by base means, sooner or later. Nothing happened for several days; then Ferguson took the earl by surprise and snapped a revolver at his breast. Fairfax wrenched the pistol from him and was going to shoot him, but the man fell on his knees and begged, and said: *"Don't* kill me. I have a wife and children." Fairfax was in a towering passion, but the appeal reached his heart, and he said, *"They* have done me no harm," and he let the rascal go.

Back of the Virginian Clemenses is a dim procession of ancestors stretching back to Noah's time. According to tradition, some of them were pirates and slavers in Elizabeth's time. But this is no discredit to them, for so were Drake and Hawkins and the others. It was a respectable trade then, and monarchs were partners in it. In my time I have had desires to be a pirate myself. The reader, if he will look deep down in his secret heart, will find —but never mind what he will find there. I am not writing his autobiography, but mine. Later, according to tradition, one of the procession was ambassador to Spain in the time of James I, or of Charles I, and married there and sent down a strain of Spanish blood to warm us up. Also, according to tradition, this one or another—Geoffrey Clement, by name—helped to sentence Charles to death. I have not examined into these traditions myself, partly because I was indolent and partly because I was so busy polishing up this end of the line and trying to make it showy; but the other Clemenses claim that they have made the examination and that it stood the test. Therefore I have always taken for granted that I did help Charles out of his troubles, by ancestral proxy. My instincts have persuaded me, too. Whenever we have a strong and persistent and ineradicable instinct, we may be sure that it is not original with us, but inherited—inherited from away back, and hardened and perfected by the petrifying influence of time. Now I have been always and unchangingly bitter against Charles, and I am quite certain that this feeling trickled down to me through the veins of my forebears from the heart of that judge; for it is not my disposition to be bitter against people on my own personal account. I am not bitter against Jeffreys. I ought to be, but I am not. It indicates that my ancestors of James II's time were indifferent to him; I do not know why; I never could make it out; but that is what it indicates. And I have always felt friendly toward Satan. Of course that is ancestral; it must be in the blood, for I could not have originated it.

. . . And so, by the testimony of instinct, backed
by the assertions of Clemenses, who said they had
examined the records, I have always been obliged
to believe that Geoffrey Clement, the martyr maker,
was an ancestor of mine, and to regard him with
favor, and in fact, pride. This has not had a good
effect upon me, for it has made me vain, and that
is a fault. It has made me set myself above people
who were less fortunate in their ancestry than I, and
has moved me to take them down a peg, upon occasion, and say things to them which hurt them before company.

A case of the kind happened in Berlin several
years ago. William Walter Phelps was our minister at the Emperor's court then, and one evening
he had me to dinner to meet Count S———, a Cabinet Minister. This nobleman was of long and illustrious descent. Of course I wanted to let out the
fact that I had some ancestors, too; but I did not
want to pull them out of their graves by the ears,
and I never could seem to get the chance to work
them in in a way that would look sufficiently casual. I
suppose Phelps was in the same difficulty. In fact,
he looked distraught now and then—just as a person
looks who wants to uncover an ancestor purely by
accident and cannot think of a way that will seem
accidental enough. But at last, after dinner, he
made a try. He took us about his drawing-room,
showing us the pictures, and finally stopped before
a rude and ancient engraving. It was a picture of
the court that tried Charles I. There was a pyra-
mid of judges in Puritan slouch hats, and below

them three bareheaded secretaries seated at a table. Mr. Phelps put his finger upon one of the three and said, with exulting indifference:

"An ancestor of mine."

I put my finger on a judge, and retorted with scathing languidness:

"Ancestor of mine. But it is a small matter. I have others."

It was not noble in me to do it. I have always regretted it since. But it landed him. I wonder how he felt! However, it made no difference in our friendship; which shows that he was fine and high, notwithstanding the humbleness of his origin. And it was also creditable in me, too, that I could over-look it. I made no change in my bearing toward him, but always treated him as an equal.

But it was a hard night for me in one way. Mr. Phelps thought I was the guest of honor, and so did Count S——, but I didn't, for there was nothing in my invitation to indicate it. It was just a friendly offhand note, on a card. By the time dinner was announced Phelps was himself in a state of doubt. Something had to be done, and it was not a handy time for explanations. He tried to get me to go out with him, but I held back; then he tried S——, and he also declined. There was another guest, but there was no trouble about him. We finally went out in a pile. There was a decorous plunge for seats and I got the one at Mr. Phelps's left, the count captured the one facing Phelps, and the other guest had to take the place of honor, since he could not help himself. We returned to the drawing-room in the original disorder. I had new shoes on and they were tight. At eleven I was privately crying; I couldn't help it, the pain was so cruel. Conversation had been dead for an hour. S—— had been due at the bedside of a dying official ever since half past nine. At last we all rose by one blessed impulse and went down to the street door without explanations—in a pile, and no precedence; and so parted.

The evening had its defects; still, I got my ancestor in, and was satisfied.

Among the Virginian Clemenses were Jere and Sherrard. Jere Clemens had a wide reputation as a good pistol-shot, and once it enabled him to get on the friendly side of some drummers when they wouldn't have paid any attention to mere smooth words and arguments. He was out stumping the state at the time. The drummers were grouped in front of the stand and had been hired by the opposition to drum while he made his speech. When he was ready to begin he got out his revolver and laid it before him and said, in his soft, silky way:

"I do not wish to hurt anybody and shall try not to, but I have got just a bullet apiece for those six drums, and if you should want to play on them don't stand behind them."

Sherrard Clemens was a republican Congressman from West Virginia in the war days, and then went out to St. Louis, where the James Clemens branch lived and still lives, and there he became a warm rebel. This was after the war. At the time that he was a Republican I was a rebel; but by the time he had become a rebel I was become (temporarily) a Republican. The Clemenses have always done the best they could to keep the political balances level, no matter how much it might inconvenience them. I did not know what had become of Sherrard Clemens; but once I introduced Senator Hawley to a Republican mass meeting in New England, and then I got a bitter letter from Sherrard from St. Louis. He said that the Republicans of the North—no, the "mudsills of the North"—had swept away the old aristocracy of the South with fire and sword, and it ill became me, an aristocrat by blood, to train with that kind of swine. Did I forget that I was a Lambton?

That was a reference to my mother's side of the house. My mother was a Lambton—Lambton with a p, for some of the American Lamptons could not spell very well in early times, and so the name suffered at their hands. She was a native of Kentucky, and married my father in Lexington in 1823, when she was twenty years old and he twenty-four. Neither of them had an overplus of property. She brought him two or three negroes, but nothing else, I think. They removed to the remote and secluded village of Jamestown, in the mountain solitudes of east Tennessee. There their first crop of children was born, but as I was of a later vintage, I do not remember anything about it. I was postponed—postponed to Missouri. Missouri was an unknown new state and needed attractions.

I think that my eldest brother, Orion, my sisters Pamela and Margaret, and my brother Benjamin

were born in Jamestown. There may have been
others, but as to that I am not sure. It was a great
lift for that little village to have my parents come
there. It was hoped that they would stay, so that
it would become a city. It was supposed that they
would stay. And so there was a boom; but by and
by they went away, and prices went down, and it
was many years before Jamestown got another start.
I have written about Jamestown in the *Gilded Age,*
a book of mine, but it was from hearsay, not from
personal knowledge. My father left a fine estate
behind him in the region roundabout Jamestown—
75,000 acres.[1] When he died in 1847 he had owned
it about twenty years. The taxes were almost nothing (five dollars a year for the whole), and he had
always paid them regularly and kept his title perfect.
He had always said that the land would not become
valuable in his time, but that it would be a com-
modious provision for his children some day. It
contained coal, copper, iron, and timber, and he said
that in the course of time railways would pierce
to that region and then the property would be
property in fact as well as in name. It also produced a wild grape of a promising sort. He had
sent some samples to Nicholas Longworth of Cincinnati to get his judgment upon them, and Mr.
Longworth had said that they would make as good
wine as his Catawbas. The land contained all these
riches; and also oil, but my father did not know
that, and of course in those early days he would
have cared nothing about it if he had known it.

---

[1] Correction (1906)—it was above 100,000, it appears.

The oil was not discovered until about 1895. I wish I owned a couple of acres of the land now, in which case I would not be writing autobiographies for a living. My father's dying charge was, "Cling to the land and wait; let nothing beguile it away from you." My mother's favorite cousin, James Lampton, who figures in the *Gilded Age* as Colonel Sellers, always said of that land—and said it with blazing enthusiasm, too—"There's millions in it—millions!" It is true that he always said that about everything—and was always mistaken, too, but this time he was right; which shows that a man who goes around with a prophecy-gun ought never to get discouraged. If he will keep up his heart and fire at everything he sees, he is bound to hit something by and by.

Many persons regarded Colonel Sellers as a fiction, an invention, an extravagant impossibility, and did me the honor to call him a "creation"; but they were mistaken. I merely put him on paper as he was; he was not a person who could be exaggerated. The incidents which looked most extravagant, both in the book and on the stage, were not inventions of mine, but were facts of his life; and I was present when they were developed. John T. Raymond's audiences used to come near to dying with laughter over the turnip-eating scene; but, extravagant as the scene was, it was faithful to the facts, in all its absurd details. The thing happened in Lampton's own house, and I was present. In fact, I was myself the guest who ate the turnips. In the hands of a great actor that piteous scene would have dimmed any manly spectator's eyes with tears, and racked his ribs apart with laughter at the same time. But Raymond was great in humorous portrayal only. In that he was superb, he was wonderful—in a word, great; in all things else he was a pygmy of pygmies. The real Colonel Sellers, as I knew him in James Lampton, was a pathetic and beautiful spirit, a manly man, a straight and honorable man, a man with a big, foolish, unselfish heart in his bosom, a man born to be loved; and he was loved by all his friends, and by his family worshiped. It is the right word. To them he was but little less than a god. The real Colonel Sellers was never on the stage. Only half of him was there. Raymond could not play the other half of him; it was above his level. There was only one man who could have played the whole of Colonel Sellers, and that was Frank Mayo.[1]

It is a world of surprises. They fall, too, where one is least expecting them. When I introduced Sellers into the book, Charles Dudley Warner, who was writing the story with me, proposed a change of Sellers's Christian name. Ten years before, in a remote corner of the West, he had come across a man named Eschol Sellers, and he thought that Eschol was just the right and fitting name for our Sellers, since it was odd and quaint and all that. I liked the idea, but I said that that man might turn up and object. But Warner said it couldn't

---

[1] Raymond was playing Colonel Sellers in 1876 and along there. About twenty years later Mayo dramatized *Pudd'nhead Wilson* and played the title rôle delightfully.

happen; that he was doubtless dead by this time and, be he dead or alive, we must have the name; it was exactly the right one and we couldn't do without it. So the change was made. Warner's man was a farmer in a cheap and humble way. When the book had been out a week, a college-bred gentleman of courtly manners and ducal upholstery arrived in Hartford in a sultry state of mind and with a libel suit in his eye, and *his* name was Eschol Sellers! He had never heard of the other one and had never been within a thousand miles of him. This damaged aristocrat's program was quite definite and business-like: the American Publishing Company must suppress the edition as far as printed and change the name in the plates, or stand a suit for $10,000. He carried away the company's promise and many apologies, and we changed the name back to Colonel Mulberry Sellers in the plates. Apparently there is nothing that cannot happen. Even the existence of two unrelated men wearing the impossible name of Eschol Sellers is a possible thing.

James Lampton floated, all his days, in a tinted mist of magnificent dreams, and died at last without seeing one of them realized. I saw him last in 1884, when it had been twenty-six years since I ate the basin of raw turnips and washed them down with a bucket of water in his house. He was become old and white-headed, but he entered to me in the same old breezy way of his earlier life, and he was all there yet—not a detail wanting; the happy light in his eye, the abounding hope in his heart, the persuasive tongue, the miracle-breeding imagination

—they were all there; and before I could turn around he was polishing up his Aladdin's lamp and flashing the secret riches of the world before me. I said to myself: "I did not overdraw him by a shade, I set him down as he was; and he is the same man to-day. Cable will recognize him." I asked him to excuse me a moment and ran into the next room, which was Cable's. Cable and I were stumping the Union on a reading tour. I said:

"I am going to leave your door open so that you can listen. There is a man in there who is interesting."

I went back and asked Lampton what he was doing now. He began to tell me of a "small venture" he had begun in New Mexico through his son; "only a little thing—a mere trifle—partly to amuse my leisure, partly to keep my capital from lying idle, but mainly to develop the boy—develop the boy. Fortune's wheel is ever revolving; he may have to work for his living some day—as strange things have happened in this world. But it's only a little thing—a mere trifle, as I said."

And so it was—as he began it. But under his deft hands it grew and blossomed and spread— oh, beyond imagination. At the end of half an hour he finished; finished with the remark, uttered in an adorably languid manner:

"Yes, it is but a trifle, as things go nowadays— a bagatelle—but amusing. It passes the time. The boy thinks great things of it, but he is young, you know, and imaginative; lacks the experience which comes of handling large affairs, and which tempers the fancy and perfects the judgment. I suppose there's a couple of millions in it, possibly three, but not more, I think; still, for a boy, you know, just starting in life, it is not bad. I should not want him to make a fortune—let that come later. It could turn his head, at his time of life, and in many ways be a damage to him."

Then he said something about his having left his pocketbook lying on the table in the main drawing-room at home, and about its being after banking hours, now, and——

I stopped him there and begged him to honor Cable and me by being our guest at the lecture—with as many friends as might be willing to do us the like honor. He accepted. And he thanked me as a prince might who had granted us a grace. The reason I stopped his speech about the tickets was because I saw that he was going to ask me to furnish them to him and let him pay next day; and I knew that if he made the debt he would pay it if he had to pawn his clothes. After a little further chat he shook hands heartily and affectionately and took his leave. Cable put his head in at the door and said:

"That was Colonel Sellers."

.   .   .   .   .   .

As I have said, that vast plot of Tennessee land was held by my father twenty years—intact. When he died in 1847 we began to manage it ourselves. Forty years afterward we had managed it all away except 10,000 acres, and gotten nothing to remember the sales by. About 1887—possibly it was earlier—the 10,000 went. My brother found a chance to

trade it for a house and lot in the town of Corry,
in the oil regions of Pennsylvania. About 1894 he
sold this property for $250. That ended the Ten-
nessee land.

If any penny of cash ever came out of my father's
wise investment but that, I have no recollection of
it. No, I am overlooking a detail. It furnished
me a field for Sellers and a book. Out of my half
of the book I got $20,000, perhaps something more;
out of the play I got $75,000—just about a dollar
an acre. It is curious; I was not alive when my
father made the investment, therefore he was not
intending any partiality; yet I was the only member
of the family that ever profited by it. I shall have
occasion to mention this land again now and then,
as I go along, for it influenced our life in one way
or another during more than a generation. Whenever things grew dark it rose and put out its hopeful
Sellers hand and cheered us up, and said, "Do not
be afraid—trust in me—wait." It kept us hoping
and hoping during forty years, and forsook us at
last. It put our energies to sleep and made vision-
aries of us—dreamers and indolent. We were always going to be rich next year—no occasion to
work. It is good to begin life poor; it is good to
begin life rich—these are wholesome; but to begin
it poor and *prospectively* rich! The man who has
not experienced it cannot imagine the curse of it.

My parents removed to Missouri in the early
'thirties; I do not remember just when, for I was
not born then and cared nothing for such things.
It was a long journey in those days, and must have

been a rough and tiresome one. The home was made in the wee village of Florida, in Monroe County, and I was born there in 1835. The village contained a hundred people and I increased the population by 1 per cent. It is more than many of the best men in history could have done for a town. It may not be modest in me to refer to this, but it is true. There is no record of a person doing as much—not even Shakespeare. But I did it for Florida, and it shows that I could have done it for any place—even London, I suppose.

Recently some one in Missouri has sent me a picture of the house I was born in. Heretofore I have always stated that it was a palace, but I shall be more guarded now.

I used to remember my brother Henry walking into a fire outdoors when he was a week old. It was remarkable in me to remember a thing like that, and it was still more remarkable that I should cling to the delusion, for thirty years, that I *did* remember it—for of course it never happened; he would not have been able to walk at that age. If I had stopped to reflect, I should not have burdened my memory with that impossible rubbish so long. It is believed by many people that an impression deposited in a child's memory within the first two years of its life cannot remain there five years, but that is an error. The incident of Benvenuto Cellini and the salamander must be accepted as authentic and trustworthy; and then that remarkable and indisputable instance in the experience of Helen Keller— However, I will speak of that at another time. For many

years I believed that I remembered helping my
grandfather drink his whisky toddy when I was six
weeks old, but I do not tell about that any more,
now; I am grown old and my memory is not as active
as it used to be. When I was younger I could remember anything, whether it had happened or not;
but my faculties are decaying now, and soon I shall
be so I cannot remember any but the things that
never happened. It is sad to go to pieces like this,
but we all have to do it.

My uncle, John A. Quarles, was a farmer, and
his place was in the country four miles from Florida.
He had eight children and fifteen or twenty negroes,
and was also fortunate in other ways, particularly
in his character. I have not come across a better
man than he was. I was his guest for two or
three months every year, from the fourth year after
we removed to Hannibal till I was eleven or twelve
years old. I have never consciously used him or
his wife in a book, but his farm has come very
handy to me in literature once or twice. In *Huck
Finn* and in *Tom Sawyer, Detective* I moved it
down to Arkansas. It was all of six hundred miles,
but it was no trouble; it was not a very large
farm—five hundred acres, perhaps—but I could
have done it if it had been twice as large. And
as for the morality of it, I cared nothing for that;
I would move a state if the exigencies of literature
required it.

It was a heavenly place for a boy, that farm of
my uncle John's. The house was a double log one,
with a spacious floor (roofed in) connecting it with

the kitchen. In the summer the table was set in the middle of that shady and breezy floor, and the sumptuous meals—well, it makes me cry to think of them. Fried chicken, roast pig; wild and tame turkeys, ducks, and geese; venison just killed; squirrels, rabbits, pheasants, partridges, prairie-chickens; biscuits, hot batter cakes, hot buckwheat cakes, hot "wheat bread," hot rolls, hot corn pone; fresh corn boiled on the ear, succotash, butter-beans, string-beans, tomatoes, peas, Irish potatoes, sweet potatoes; buttermilk, sweet milk, "clabber"; water-melons, muskmelons, cantaloupes—all fresh from the garden; apple pie, peach pie, pumpkin pie, apple dumplings, peach cobbler—I can't remember the rest. The way that the things were cooked was perhaps the main splendor—particularly a certain few of the dishes. For instance, the corn bread, the hot biscuits and wheat bread, and the fried chicken. These things have never been properly cooked in the North—in fact, no one there is able to learn the art, so far as my experience goes. The North thinks it knows how to make corn bread, but this is mere superstition. Perhaps no bread in the world is quite so good as Southern corn bread, and perhaps no bread in the world is quite so bad as the Northern imitation of it. The North seldom tries to fry chicken, and this is well; the art cannot be learned north of the line of Mason and Dixon, nor anywhere in Europe. This is not hearsay; it is experience that is speaking. In Europe it is imagined that the custom of serving various kinds of bread blazing hot is

"American," but that is too broad a spread; it is custom in the South, but is much less than that in the North. In the North and in Europe hot bread is considered unhealthy. This is probably another fussy superstition, like the European superstition that ice-water is unhealthy. Europe does not need ice-water and does not drink it; and yet, notwithstanding this, its word for it is better than ours, because it describes it, whereas ours doesn't. Europe calls it "iced" water. Our word describes water made from melted ice—a drink which has a characterless taste and which we have but little acquaintance with.

It seems a pity that the world should throw away so many good things merely because they are unwholesome. I doubt if God has given us any refreshment which, taken in moderation, is unwholesome, except microbes. Yet there are people who strictly deprive themselves of each and every eatable, drinkable, and smokable which has in any way acquired a shady reputation. They pay this price for health. And health is all they get for it. How strange it is! It is like paying out your whole fortune for a cow that has gone dry.

The farmhouse stood in the middle of a very large yard, and the yard was fenced on three sides with rails and on the rear side with high palings; against these stood the smoke-house; beyond the palings was the orchard; beyond the orchard were the negro quarters and the tobacco fields. The front yard was entered over a stile made of sawed-off logs of graduated heights; I do not remember any gate. In a corner of the front yard were a dozen lofty hickory trees and a dozen black walnuts, and in the nutting season riches were to be gathered there.

Down a piece, abreast the house, stood a little log cabin against the rail fence; and there the woody hill fell sharply away, past the barns, the corn-crib, the stables, and the tobacco-curing house, to a limpid brook which sang along over its gravelly bed and curved and frisked in and out and here and there and yonder in the deep shade of overhanging foliage and vines—a divine place for wading, and it had swimming pools, too, which were forbidden to us and therefore much frequented by us. For we were little Christian children and had early been taught the value of forbidden fruit.

In the little log cabin lived a bedridden white-headed slave woman whom we visited daily and looked upon with awe, for we believed she was upward of a thousand years old and had talked with Moses. The younger negroes credited these statistics and had furnished them to us in good faith. We accommodated all the details which came to us about her; and so we believed that she had lost her health in the long desert trip coming out of Egypt, and had never been able to get it back again. She had a round bald place on the crown of her head, and we used to creep around and gaze at it in reverent silence, and reflect that it was caused by fright through seeing Pharaoh drowned. We called her "Aunt" Hannah, Southern fashion. She was superstitious, like the other negroes; also, like them, she was deeply religious. Like them, she had great faith in prayer and employed it in all ordinary exigencies, but not in cases where a dead certainty of result was urgent. Whenever witches were around she tied up the remnant of her wool in little tufts, with white thread, and this promptly made the witches impotent.

All the negroes were friends of ours, and with those of our own age we were in effect comrades. I say in effect, using the phrase as a modification. We were comrades, and yet not comrades; color and condition interposed a subtle line which both parties were conscious of and which rendered complete fusion impossible. We had a faithful and affectionate good friend, ally, and adviser in "Uncle Dan'l," a middle-aged slave whose head was the best one in the negro quarter, whose sympathies were wide and warm, and whose heart was honest and simple and knew no guile. He has served me well these many, many years. I have not seen him for more than half a century, and yet spiritually I have had his welcome company a good part of that time, and have staged him in books under his own name and as "Jim," and carted him all around —to Hannibal, down the Mississippi on a raft, and even across the Desert of Sahara in a balloon— and he has endured it all with the patience and friendliness and loyalty which were his birthright. It was on the farm that I got my strong liking for his race and my appreciation of certain of its fine qualities. This feeling and this estimate have stood the test of sixty years and more, and have suffered no impairment. The black face is as welcome to me now as it was then.

In my schoolboy days I had no aversion to slavery. I was not aware that there was anything wrong about it. No one arraigned it in my hearing; the local papers said nothing against it; the local pulpit taught us that God approved it, that it was a holy thing, and that the doubter need only look in the Bible if he wished to settle his mind —and then the texts were read aloud to us to make the matter sure; if the slaves themselves had an aversion to slavery, they were wise and said nothing. In Hannibal we seldom saw a slave misused; on the farm, never.

There was, however, one small incident of my boyhood days which touched this matter, and it must have meant a good deal to me or it would not have stayed in my memory, clear and sharp, vivid and shadowless, all these slow-drifting years. We had a little slave boy whom we had hired from some one, there in Hannibal. He was from the eastern shore of Maryland, and had been brought away from his family and his friends, halfway across the American continent, and sold. He was a cheery spirit, innocent and gentle, and the noisiest creature that ever was, perhaps. All day long he was singing, whistling, yelling, whooping, laughing—it was maddening, devastating, unendurable. At last, one day, I lost all my temper, and went raging to my mother and said Sandy had been singing for an hour without a single break, and I couldn't stand it, and *wouldn't* she please shut him up. The tears came into her eyes and her lip trembled, and she said something like this:

"Poor thing, when he sings it shows that he is not remembering, and that comforts me; but when he is still I am afraid he is thinking, and I cannot bear it. He will never see his mother again; if he can sing, I must not hinder it, but be thankful for it. If you were older, you would understand me; then that friendless child's noise would make you glad."

It was a simple speech and made up of small words, but it went home, and Sandy's noise was not a trouble to me any more. She never used large words, but she had a natural gift for making small ones do effective work. She lived to reach the neighborhood of ninety years and was capable with her tongue to the last—especially when a meanness or an injustice roused her spirit. She has come handy to me several times in my books, where she figures as Tom Sawyer's Aunt Polly. I fitted her out with a dialect and tried to think up other improvements for her, but did not find any. I used Sandy once, also; it was in *Tom Sawyer*. I tried to get him to whitewash the fence, but it did not work. I do not remember what name I called him by in the book.

I can see the farm yet, with perfect clearness. I can see all its belongings, all its details; the family room of the house, with a "trundle" bed in one corner and a spinning-wheel in another—a wheel whose rising and falling wail, heard from a distance, was the mournfulest of all sounds to me, and made me homesick and low spirited, and filled my atmosphere with the wandering spirits of the dead; the vast fireplace, piled high, on winter nights, with flaming hickory logs from whose ends a sugary sap bubbled out, but did not go to waste, for we scraped it off and ate it; the lazy cat spread out on the rough hearthstones; the drowsy dogs braced against the jambs and blinking; my aunt in one chimney corner, knitting; my uncle in the other, smoking his corn-cob pipe; the slick and carpetless oak floor faintly mirroring the dancing flame tongues and freckled with black indentations where fire coals had popped out and died a leisurely death; half a dozen children romping in the background twilight; "split"-bottomed chairs here and there, some with rockers; a cradle—out of service, but waiting, with confidence; in the early cold mornings a snuggle of children, in shirts and chemises, occupying the hearthstone and procrastinating—they could not bear to leave that comfortable place and go out on the wind-swept floor space between the house and kitchen where the general tin basin stood, and wash.

Along outside of the front fence ran the country road, dusty in the summertime, and a good place for snakes—they liked to lie in it and sun themselves; when they were rattlesnakes or puff adders, we killed them; when they were black snakes, or racers, or belonged to the fabled "hoop" breed, we fled, without shame; when they were "house snakes," or "garters," we carried them home and

put them in Aunt Patsy's work basket for a surprise; for she was prejudiced against snakes, and
always when she took the basket in her lap and
they began to climb out of it it disordered her
mind. She never could seem to get used to them;
her opportunities went for nothing. And she was
always cold toward bats, too, and could not bear
them; and yet I think a bat is as friendly a bird
as there is. My mother was Aunt Patsy's sister
and had the same wild superstitions. A bat is beautifully soft and silky; I do not know any creature
that is pleasanter to the touch or is more grateful
for caressings, if offered in the right spirit. I know
all about these coleoptera, because our great cave,
three miles below Hannibal, was multitudinously
stocked with them, and often I brought them home
to amuse my mother with. It was easy to manage
if it was a school day, because then I had ostensibly
been to school and hadn't any bats. She was not
a suspicious person, but full of trust and confidence;
and when I said, "There's something in my coat
pocket for you," she would put her hand in. But
she always took it out again, herself; I didn't have
to tell her. It was remarkable, the way she couldn't
learn to like private bats. The more experience
she had, the more she could not change her
views.

I think she was never in the cave in her life;
but everybody else went there. Many excursion
parties came from considerable distances up and
down the river to visit the cave. It was miles in
extent and was a tangled wilderness of narrow and

lofty clefts and passages. It was an easy place to get lost in; anybody could do it—including the bats. I got lost in it myself, along with a lady, and our last candle burned down to almost nothing before we glimpsed the search party's lights winding about in the distance.

"Injun Joe," the half-breed, got lost in there once, and would have starved to death if the bats had run short. But there was no chance of that; there were myriads of them. He told me all his story. In the book called *Tom Sawyer* I starved him entirely to death in the cave, but that was in the interest of art; it never happened. "General" Gaines, who was our first town drunkard before Jimmy Finn got the place, was lost in there for the space of a week, and finally pushed his handkerchief out of a hole in a hilltop near Saverton, several miles down the river from the cave's mouth, and somebody saw it and dug him out. There is nothing the matter with his statistics except the handkerchief. I knew him for years and he hadn't any. But it could have been his nose. That would attract attention.

The cave was an uncanny place, for it contained a corpse—the corpse of a young girl of fourteen. It was in a glass cylinder inclosed in a copper one which was suspended from a rail which bridged a narrow passage. The body was preserved in alcohol, and it was said that loafers and rowdies used to drag it up by the hair and look at the dead face. The girl was the daughter of a St. Louis surgeon of extraordinary ability and wide celebrity. He was

an eccentric man and did many strange things. He
put the poor thing in that forlorn place himself.

.   .   .   .

Beyond the road where the snakes sunned themselves was a dense young thicket, and through it a
dim-lighted path led a quarter of a mile; then out
of the dimness one emerged abruptly upon a level
great prairie which was covered with wild strawberry
plants, vividly starred with prairie pinks, and walled
in on all sides by forests. The strawberries were
fragrant and fine, and in the season we were generally there in the crisp freshness of the early morning, while the dew beads still sparkled upon the grass
and the woods were ringing with the first songs
of the birds.

Down the forest slopes to the left were the
swings. They were made of bark stripped from
hickory saplings. When they became dry they were
dangerous. They usually broke when a child was
forty feet in the air, and this was why so many
bones had to be mended every year. I had no ill
luck myself, but none of my cousins escaped. There
were eight of them, and at one time and another
they broke fourteen arms among them. But it cost
next to nothing, for the doctor worked by the year
—twenty-five dollars for the whole family. I remember two of the Florida doctors, Chowning and
Meredith. They not only tended an entire family
for twenty-five dollars a year, but furnished the
medicines themselves. Good measure, too. Only
the largest persons could hold a whole dose. Castor
oil was the principal beverage. The dose was half

a dipperful, with half a dipperful of New Orleans molasses added to help it down and make it taste good, which it never did. The next standby was calomel; the next, rhubarb; and the next, jalap. Then they bled the patient, and put mustard plasters on him. It was a dreadful system, and yet the death rate was not heavy. The calomel was nearly sure to salivate the patient and cost him some of his teeth. There were no dentists. When teeth became touched with decay or were otherwise ailing, the doctor knew of but one thing to do—he fetched his tongs and dragged them out. If the jaw remained, it was not his fault. Doctors were not called in cases of ordinary illness; the family grandmother attended to those. Every old woman was a doctor, and gathered her own medicines in the woods, and knew how to compound doses that would stir the vitals of a cast-iron dog. And then there was the "Indian doctor"; a grave savage, remnant of his tribe, deeply read in the mysteries of nature and the secret properties of herbs; and most backwoodsmen had high faith in his powers and could tell of wonderful cures achieved by him. In Mauritius, away off yonder in the solitudes of the Indian Ocean, there is a person who answers to our Indian doctor of the old times. He is a negro, and has had no teaching as a doctor, yet there is one disease which he is master of and can cure and the doctors can't. They send for him when they have a case. It is a child's disease of a strange and deadly sort, and the negro cures it with a herb medicine which he makes, himself, from a prescription which has come down to him from his father and grandfather. He will not let anyone see it. He keeps the secret of its components to himself, and it is feared that he will die without divulging it; then there will be consternation in Mauritius. I was told these things by the people there, in 1896.

We had the "faith doctor," too, in those early days—a woman. Her specialty was toothache. She was a farmer's old wife and lived five miles from Hannibal. She would lay her hand on the patient's jaw and say, "Believe!" and the cure was prompt. Mrs. Utterback. I remember her very well. Twice I rode out there behind my mother, horseback, and saw the cure performed. My mother was the patient.

Doctor Meredith removed to Hannibal, by and by, and was our family physician there, and saved my life several times. Still, he was a good man and meant well. Let it go.

I was always told that I was a sickly and precarious and tiresome and uncertain child, and lived mainly on allopathic medicines during the first seven years of my life. I asked my mother about this, in her old age—she was in her eighty-eighth year—and said:

"I suppose that during all that time you were uneasy about me?"

"Yes, the whole time."

"Afraid I wouldn't live?"

After a reflective pause—ostensibly to think out the facts—"No—afraid you would."

The country schoolhouse was three miles from my uncle's farm. It stood in a clearing in the woods and would hold about twenty-five boys and girls. We attended the school with more or less regularity once or twice a week, in summer, walking to it in the cool of the morning by the forest paths, and back in the gloaming at the end of the day. All the pupils brought their dinners in baskets—corn dodger, buttermilk, and other good things—and sat in the shade of the trees at noon and ate them. It is the part of my education which I look back upon with the most satisfaction. My first visit to the school was when I was seven. A strapping girl of fifteen, in the customary sunbonnet and calico dress, asked me if I "used tobacco"—meaning did I chew it. I said no. It roused her scorn. She reported me to all the crowd, and said:

"Here is a boy seven years old who can't chew tobacco."

By the looks and comments which this produced I realized that I was a degraded object, and was cruelly ashamed of myself. I determined to reform. But I only made myself sick; I was not able to learn to chew tobacco. I learned to smoke fairly well, but that did not conciliate anybody and I remained a poor thing, and characterless. I longed to be respected, but I never was able to rise. Children have but little charity for one another's defects.

As I have said, I spent some part of every year at the farm until I was twelve or thirteen years old. The life which I led there with my cousins was

full of charm, and so is the memory of it yet. I
can call back the solemn twilight and mystery of
the deep woods, the earthy smells, the faint odors
of the wild flowers, the sheen of rain-washed foliage,
the rattling clatter of drops when the wind shook
the trees, the far-off hammering of woodpeckers and
the muffled drumming of wood pheasants in the re-
moteness of the forest, the snapshot glimpses of
disturbed wild creatures scurrying through the grass
—I can call it all back and make it as real as it
ever was, and as blessed. I can call back the prairie,
and its loneliness and peace, and a vast hawk hanging motionless in the sky, with his wings spread
wide and the blue of the vault showing through
the fringe of their end feathers. I can see the
woods in their autumn dress, the oaks purple, the
hickories washed with gold, the maples and the
sumachs luminous with crimson fires, and I can hear
the rustle made by the fallen leaves as we plowed
through them. I can see the blue clusters of wild
grapes hanging among the foliage of the saplings,
and I remember the taste of them and the smell.
I know how the wild blackberries looked, and how
they tasted, and the same with the pawpaws, the
hazelnuts, and the persimmons; and I can feel the
thumping rain, upon my head, of hickory nuts and
walnuts when we were out in the frosty dawn to
scramble for them with the pigs, and the gusts
of wind loosed them and sent them down. I know
the stain of blackberries, and how pretty it is, and
I know the stain of walnut hulls, and how little it
minds soap and water, also what grudged experi-

ence it had of either of them. I know the taste
of maple sap, and when to gather it, and how
to arrange the troughs and the delivery tubes, and
how to boil down the juice, and how to hook the
sugar after it is made, also how much better hooked
sugar tastes than any that is honestly come by, let
bigots say what they will. I know how a prize
watermelon looks when it is sunning its fat ro-
tundity among pumpkin vines and "simblins"; I
know how to tell when it is ripe without "plug-
ging" it; I know how inviting it looks when it is
cooling itself in a tub of water under the bed, waiting; I know how it looks when it lies on the table
in the sheltered great floor space between house and
kitchen, and the children gathered for the sacrifice
and their mouths watering; I know the crackling
sound it makes when the carving knife enters its
end, and I can see the split fly along in front of the
blade as the knife cleaves its way to the other
end; I can see its halves fall apart and display the
rich red meat and the black seeds, and the heart
standing up, a luxury fit for the elect; I know how
a boy looks behind a yard-long slice of that melon,
and I know how he feels; for I have been there.
I know the taste of the watermelon which has been
honestly come by, and I know the taste of the watermelon which has been acquired by art. Both taste
good, but the experienced know which tastes best.
I know the look of green apples and peaches and
pears on the trees, and I know how entertaining
they are when they are inside of a person. I know
how ripe ones look when they are piled in pyramids

under the trees, and how pretty they are and how
vivid their colors. I know how a frozen apple
looks, in a barrel down cellar in the wintertime,
and how hard it is to bite, and how the frost makes
the teeth ache, and yet how good it is, notwithstanding. I know the disposition of elderly people
to select the specked apples for the children, and
I once knew ways to beat the game. I know the
look of an apple that is roasting and sizzling on
a hearth on a winter's evening, and I know the
comfort that comes of eating it hot, along with
some sugar and a drench of cream. I know the
delicate art and mystery of so cracking hickory nuts
and walnuts on a flatiron with a hammer that the
kernels will be delivered whole, and I know how
the nuts, taken in conjunction with winter apples,
cider, and doughnuts, make old people's old tales
and old jokes sound fresh and crisp and enchanting,
and juggle an evening away before you know what
went with the time. I know the look of Uncle
Dan'l's kitchen as it was on the privileged nights,
when I was a child, and I can see the white and
black children grouped on the hearth, with the fire-
light playing on their faces and the shadows flick-
ering upon the walls, clear back toward the cavern-
ous gloom of the rear, and I can hear Uncle Dan'l
telling the immortal tales which Uncle Remus
Harris was to gather into his book and charm the
world with, by and by; and I can feel again the
creepy joy which quivered through me when the
time for the ghost story was reached—and the sense
of regret, too, which came over me, for it was al-

ways the last story of the evening and there was nothing between it and the unwelcome bed.

I can remember the bare wooden stairway in my uncle's house, and the turn to the left above the landing, and the rafters and the slanting roof over my bed, and the squares of moonlight on the floor, and the white cold world of snow outside, seen through the curtainless window. I can remember the howling of the wind and the quaking of the house on stormy nights, and how snug and cozy one felt, under the blankets, listening; and how the powdery snow used to sift in, around the sashes, and lie in little ridges on the floor and make the place look chilly in the morning and curb the wild desire to get up—in case there was any. I can remember how very dark that room was, in the dark of the moon, and how packed it was with ghostly stillness when one woke up by accident away in the night, and forgotten sins came flocking out of the secret chambers of the memory and wanted a hearing; and how ill chosen the time seemed for this kind of business; and how dismal was the hoo-hooing of the owl and the wailing of the wolf, sent mourning by on the night wind.

I remember the raging of the rain on that roof, summer nights, and how pleasant it was to lie and listen to it, and enjoy the white splendor of the lightning and the majestic booming and crashing of the thunder. It was a very satisfactory room, and there was a lightning rod which was reachable from the window, an adorable and skittish thing to climb up and down, summer nights, when there were duties on hand of a sort to make privacy desirable.

I remember the 'coon and 'possum hunts, nights, with the negroes, and the long marches through the black gloom of the woods, and the excitement which fired everybody when the distant bay of an experienced dog announced that the game was treed; then the wild scramblings and stumblings through briers and bushes and over roots to get to the spot; then the lighting of a fire and the felling of the tree, the joyful frenzy of the dogs and the negroes, and the weird picture it all made in the red glare —I remember it all well, and the delight that everyone got out of it, except the 'coon.

I remember the pigeon seasons, when the birds would come in millions and cover the trees and by their weight break down the branches. They were clubbed to death with sticks; guns were not necessary and were not used. I remember the squirrel hunts, and prairie-chicken hunts, and wild-turkey hunts, and all that; and how we turned out, mornings, while it was still dark, to go on these expeditions, and how chilly and dismal it was, and how often I regretted that I was well enough to go. A toot on a tin horn brought twice as many dogs as were needed, and in their happiness they raced and scampered about, and knocked small people down, and made no end of unnecessary noise. At the word, they vanished away toward the woods, and we drifted silently after them in the melancholy gloom. But presently the gray dawn stole over the world, the birds piped up, then the sun rose and poured light and comfort all around, everything

was fresh and dewy and fragrant, and life was a
boon again. After three hours of tramping we arrived back wholesomely tired, overladen with game,
very hungry, and just in time for breakfast.

JANE LAMPTON CLEMENS

This was my mother. When she died, in October, 1890, she was well along in her eighty-eighth
year, a mighty age, a well-contested fight for life
for one who at forty was so delicate of body as
to be accounted a confirmed invalid and destined
to pass soon away. I knew her well during the
first twenty-five years of my life; but after that I
saw her only at wide intervals, for we lived many
days' journey apart. I am not proposing to write
about her, but merely to talk about her; not give
her formal history, but merely make illustrative extracts from it, so to speak; furnish flashlight
glimpses of her character, not a processional view
of her career. Technically speaking, she had no
career; but she had a character, and it was of a
fine and striking and lovable sort.

What becomes of the multitudinous photographs
which one's mind takes of people? Out of the million which my mental camera must have taken of
this first and closest friend, only one clear and
strongly defined one of early date remains. It dates
back forty-seven years; she was forty years old then,
and I was eight. She held me by the hand, and
we were kneeling by the bedside of my brother,
two years older than I, who lay dead, and the tears

were flowing down her cheeks unchecked. And she was moaning. That dumb sign of anguish was perhaps new to me, since it made upon me a very strong impression—an impression which holds its place still with the picture which it helped to intensify and make memorable.

She had a slender, small body, but a large heart —a heart so large that everybody's grief and everybody's joys found welcome in it, and hospitable accommodation. The greatest difference which I find between her and the rest of the people whom I have known, is this, and it is a remarkable one: those others felt a strong interest in a few things, whereas to the very day of her death she felt a strong interest in the whole world and everything and everybody in it. In all her life she never knew such a thing as a half-hearted interest in affairs and people, or an interest which drew a line and left out certain affairs and was indifferent to certain people. The invalid who takes a strenuous and indestructible interest in everything and everybody but himself, and to whom a dull moment is an unknown thing and an impossibility, is a formidable adversary for disease and a hard invalid to vanquish. I am certain that it was this feature of my mother's make-up that carried her so far toward ninety.

Her interest in people and other animals was warm, personal, friendly. She always found something to excuse, and as a rule to love, in the toughest of them—even if she had to put it there herself. She was the natural ally and friend of the friendless. It was believed that, Presbyterian as she was, she could be beguiled into saying a soft word for the devil himself, and so the experiment was tried. The abuse of Satan began; one conspirator after another added his bitter word, his malign reproach, his pitiless censure, till at last, sure enough, the unsuspecting subject of the trick walked into the trap. She admitted that the indictment was sound, that Satan was utterly wicked and abandoned, just as these people had said; *but* would any claim that he had been treated fairly? A sinner was but a sinner; Satan was just that, like the rest. What saves the rest?—their own efforts alone? No —or none might ever be saved. To their feeble efforts is added the mighty help of pathetic, appealing, imploring prayers that go up daily out of all the churches in Christendom and out of myriads upon myriads of pitying hearts. But who prays for Satan? Who, in eighteen centuries, has had the common humanity to pray for the one sinner that needed it most, our one fellow and brother who most needed a friend yet had not a single one, the one sinner among us all who had the highest and clearest *right* to every Christian's daily and nightly prayers, for the plain and unassailable reason that his was the first and greatest need, he being among sinners the supremest?

This friend of Satan was a most gentle spirit, and an unstudied and unconscious pathos was her native speech. When her pity or her indignation was stirred by hurt or shame inflicted upon some defenseless person or creature, she was the most eloquent person I have heard speak. It was seldom

eloquence of a fiery or violent sort, but gentle, pitying, persuasive, appealing; and so genuine and so
nobly and simply worded and so touchingly uttered,
that many times I have seen it win the reluctant and
splendid applause of tears. Whenever anybody or
any creature was being oppressed, the fears that
belonged to her sex and her small stature retired
to the rear and her soldierly qualities came promptly
to the front. One day in our village I saw a
vicious devil of a Corsican, a common terror in
the town, chasing his grown daughter past cautious
male citizens with a heavy rope in his hand, and
declaring he would wear it out on her. My mother
spread her door wide to the refugee, and then, instead of closing and locking it after her, stood
in it and stretched her arms across it, barring the
way. The man swore, cursed, threatened her with
his rope; but she did not flinch or show any sign
of fear; she only stood straight and fine, and lashed
him, shamed him, derided him, defied him in tones
not audible to the middle of the street, but audible
to the man's conscience and dormant manhood; and
he asked her pardon and gave her his rope and said
with a most great and blasphemous oath that she
was the bravest woman he ever saw; and so went
his way without other word and troubled her no
more. He and she were always good friends after
that, for in her he had found a long-felt want
—somebody who was not afraid of him.

One day in St. Louis she walked out into the
street and greatly surprised a burly cartman who
was beating his horse over the head with the butt

of his heavy whip; for she took the whip away from him and then made such a persuasive appeal in behalf of the ignorantly offending horse that he was tripped into saying he was to blame; and also into volunteering a promise which of course he couldn't keep, for he was not built in that way— a promise that he wouldn't ever abuse a horse again.

That sort of interference in behalf of abused animals was a common thing with her all her life; and her manner must have been without offense and her good intent transparent, for she always carried her point, and also won the courtesy, and often the friendly applause, of the adversary. All the race of dumb animals had a friend in her. By some subtle sign the homeless, hunted, bedraggled, and disreputable cat recognized her at a glance as the born refuge and champion of his sort—and followed her home. His instinct was right, he was as welcome as the prodigal son. We had nineteen cats at one time, in 1845. And there wasn't one in the lot that had any character, not one that had any merit, except the cheap and tawdry merit of being unfortunate. They were a vast burden to us all—including my mother—but they were out of luck, and that was enough; they had to stay. However, better these than no pets at all; children must have pets, and we were not allowed to have caged ones. An imprisoned creature was out of the question—my mother would not have allowed a rat to be restrained of its liberty.

In the small town of Hannibal, Missouri, when

I was a boy, everybody was poor, but didn't know it; and everybody was comfortable, and did know it. And there were grades of society—people of good family, people of unclassified family, people of no family. Everybody knew everybody, and was affable to everybody, and nobody put on any visible airs; yet the class lines were quite clearly drawn and the familiar social life of each class was restricted to that class. It was a little democracy which was full of liberty, equality, and Fourth of July, and sincerely so, too; yet you perceived that the aristocratic taint was there. It was there, and nobody found fault with the fact, or ever stopped to reflect that its presence was an inconsistency.

I suppose that this state of things was mainly due to the circumstance that the town's population had come from slave states and still had the institution of slavery with them in their new home. My mother, with her large nature and liberal sympathies, was not intended for an aristocrat, yet through her breeding she was one. Few people knew it, perhaps, for it was an instinct, I think, rather than a principle. So its outward manifestation was likely to be accidental, not intentional, and also not frequent. But I knew of that weak spot. I knew that privately she was proud that the Lambtons, now Earls of Durham, had occupied the family lands for nine hundred years; that they were feudal lords of Lambton Castle and holding the high position of ancestors of hers when the Norman Conqueror came over to divert the Englishry. I argued—cautiously, and with mollifying circumlocutions, for one had to be careful when he was on that holy ground, and mustn't cavort—that there was no particular merit in occupying a piece of land for nine hundred years, with the friendly assistance of an entail; anybody could do it, with intellect or without; therefore the entail was the thing to be proud of, just the entail and nothing else; consequently, she was merely descended from an entail, and she might as well be proud of being descended from a mortgage. Whereas my own ancestry was quite a different and superior thing, because it had the addition of an ancestor—one Clemens—who *did* something; something which was very creditable to him and satisfactory to me, in that he was a member of the court that tried Charles I and delivered him over to the executioner. Ostensibly this was chaff, but at the bottom it was not. I had a very real respect for that ancestor, and this respect has increased with the years, not diminished. He did what he could toward reducing the list of crowned shams of his day. However, I can say this for my mother, that I never heard her refer in any way to her gilded ancestry when any person not a member of the family was present, for she had good American sense. But with other Lamptons whom I have known, it was different. "Colonel Sellers" was a Lampton, and a tolerably near relative of my mother's; and when he was alive, poor old airy soul, one of the earliest things a stranger was likely to hear from his lips was some reference to the "head of our line," flung off with a painful casualness that was wholly beneath criticism as a work of art. It compelled inquiry, of course; it was intended to compel it. Then followed the whole disastrous history of how the Lambton heir came to this country a hundred and fifty years or so ago, disgusted with that foolish fraud, hereditary aristocracy, and married, and shut himself away from the world in the remotenesses of the wilderness, and went to breeding ancestors of future American claimants, while at home in England he was given up as dead and his titles and estates turned over to his younger brother, usurper and personally responsible for the perverse and unseatable usurpers of our day. And the colonel always spoke with studied and courtly deference of the claimant of his day—a second cousin of his—and referred to him with entire seriousness as "the earl." "The earl" was a man of parts, and might have accomplished something for himself but for the calamitous accident of his birth. He was a Kentuckian, and a well-meaning man; but he had no money, and no time to earn any; for all his time was taken up in trying to get me, and others of the tribe, to furnish him capital to fight his claim through the House of Lords with. He had all the documents, all the proofs; he knew he could win. And so he dreamed his life away, always in poverty, sometimes in actual want, and died at last, far from home, and was buried from a hospital by strangers who did not know he was an earl, for he did not look it. That poor fellow used to sign his letters "Durham," and in them he would find fault with me for voting the Republican ticket, for the reason that it was unaristocratic, and by consequence un-Lamptonian. And presently along would come a letter from some red-hot Virginian, son of my other branch, and abuse me bitterly for the same vote—on the ground that the Republican was an aristocratic party and it was not becoming in the descendant of a regicide to train with that kind of animals. And so I used to almost wish I hadn't had any ancestors, they were so much trouble to me.

As I have said, we lived in a slaveholding community; indeed, when slavery perished my mother had been in daily touch with it for sixty years. Yet, kind-hearted and compassionate as she was, I think she was not conscious that slavery was a bald, grotesque, and unwarrantable usurpation. She had never heard it assailed in any pulpit, but had heard it defended and sanctified in a thousand; her ears were familiar with Bible texts that approved it, but if there were any that disapproved it they had not been quoted by her pastors; as far as her experience went, the wise and the good and the holy were unanimous in the conviction that slavery was right, righteous, sacred, the peculiar pet of the Deity, and a condition which the slave himself ought to be daily and nightly thankful for. Manifestly, training and association can accomplish strange miracles. As a rule our slaves were convinced and content. So, doubtless, are the far more intelligent slaves of a monarchy; they revere and approve their masters, the monarch and the noble, and recognize no degradation in the fact that they are slaves—slaves with the name blinked, and less respectworthy than were our black ones, if to be a slave by meek consent is baser than to be a slave by compulsion —and doubtless it is.

However, there was nothing about the slavery of the Hannibal region to rouse one's dozing humane instincts to activity. It was the mild domestic slavery, not the brutal plantation article. Cruelties were very rare, and exceedingly and wholesomely unpopular. To separate and sell the members of a slave family to different masters was a thing not well liked by the people, and so it was not often done, except in the settling of estates. I have no recollection of ever seeing a slave auction in that town; but I am suspicious that that is because the thing was a common and commonplace spectacle, not an uncommon and impressive one. I vividly remember seeing a dozen black men and women chained to one another, once, and lying in a group on the pavement, awaiting shipment to the Southern slave market. Those were the saddest faces I have ever seen. Chained slaves could not have been a common sight, or this picture would not have made so strong and lasting an impression upon me.

The "nigger trader" was loathed by everybody. He was regarded as a sort of human devil who bought and conveyed poor helpless creatures to hell —for to our whites and blacks alike the Southern plantation was simply hell; no milder name could describe it. If the threat to sell an incorrigible slave "down the river" would not reform him, nothing would—his case was past cure.

It is commonly believed that an infallible effect of slavery was to make such as lived in its midst hard hearted. I think it had no such effect—speaking in general terms. I think it stupefied everybody's humanity, as regarded the slave, but stopped there. There were no hard-hearted people in our town—I mean there were no more than would be found in any other town of the same size in any other country; and in my experience hard-hearted people are very rare everywhere.

[*Written about 1898*

Playing "Bear"—Herrings—Jim Wolf and the Cats

This was in 1849. I was fourteen years old, then. We were still living in Hannibal, Missouri, on the banks of the Mississippi, in the new "frame" house built by my father five years before. That is, some of us lived in the new part, the rest in the old part back of it and attached to it. In the autumn my sister gave a party and invited all the marriageable young people of the village. I was too young for this society, and was too bashful to mingle with young ladies, anyway, therefore I was not invited— at least not for the whole evening. Ten minutes of it was to be my whole share. I was to do the part of a bear in a small fairy play. I was to be disguised all over in a close-fitting brown hairy stuff proper for a bear. About half past ten I was told to go to my room and put on this disguise, and be ready in half an hour. I started, but changed my mind, for I wanted to practice a little, and that room was very small. I crossed over to the large unoccupied house on the corner of Main Street, unaware that a dozen of the young people were also going there to dress for their parts. I took the little black boy, Sandy, with me, and we selected a roomy and empty chamber on the second floor. We entered it talking, and this gave a couple of half-dressed young ladies an opportunity to take refuge behind a screen undiscovered. Their gowns and things were hanging on hooks behind the door, but I did not see them; it was Sandy that shut the door, but all his heart was in the theatricals, and he was as unlikely to notice them as I was myself.

That was a rickety screen, with many holes in it, but, as I did not know there were girls behind it, I was not disturbed by that detail. If I had known, I could not have undressed in the flood of cruel moonlight that was pouring in at the curtainless windows; I should have died of shame. Untroubled by apprehensions, I stripped to the skin and began my practice. I was full of ambition, I was determined to make a hit, I was burning to establish a reputation as a bear and get further engagements; so I threw myself into my work with an abandon that promised great things. I capered back and forth from one end of the room to the other on all fours, Sandy applauding with enthusiasm; I walked upright and growled and snapped and snarled, I stood on my head, I flung handsprings,

I danced a lubberly dance with my paws bent and my imaginary snout sniffing from side to side, I did everything a bear could do, and many things which no bear could ever do and no bear with any dignity would want to do, anyway; and of course I never suspected that I was making a spectacle of myself to anyone but Sandy. At last, standing on my head, I paused in that attitude to take a minute's rest. There was a moment's silence, then Sandy spoke up with excited interest and said:

"Mars Sam, has you ever seed a dried herring?"

"No. What is that?"

"It's a fish."

"Well, what of it? Anything peculiar about it?"

"Yes, suh, you bet you dey is. *Dey* eats 'em innards and all!"

There was a smothered burst of feminine snickers from behind the screen! All the strength went out of me and I toppled forward like an undermined tower and brought the screen down with my weight, burying the young ladies under it. In their fright they discharged a couple of piercing screams—and possibly others—but I did not wait to count. I snatched my clothes and fled to the dark hall below, Sandy following. I was dressed in half a minute, and out the back way. I swore Sandy to eternal silence, then we went away and hid until the party was over. The ambition was all out of me. I could not have faced that giddy company after my adventure, for there would be two performers there who

knew my secret and would be privately laughing at
me all the time. I was searched for, but not found,
and the bear had to be played by a young gentleman
in his civilized clothes. The house was still and
everybody asleep when I finally ventured home. I
was very heavy hearted and full of a bitter sense
of disgrace. Pinned to my pillow I found a slip of
paper which bore a line which did not lighten my
heart, but only made my face burn. It was written
in a laboriously disguised hand, and these were its
mocking terms:

You probably couldn't have played bear, but you played
bare very well—oh, very *very* well!

We think boys are rude, unsensitive animals, but
it is not so in all cases. Each boy has one or two
sensitive spots, and if you can find out where they
are located you have only to touch them and you
can scorch him as with fire. I suffered miserably
over that episode. I expected that the facts would
be all over the village in the morning, but it was
not so. The secret remained confined to the two
girls and Sandy and me. That was some appease-
ment of my pain, but it was far from sufficient—
the main trouble remained: I was under four mocking eyes, and it might as well have been a thousand,
for I suspected all girls' eyes of being the ones I
so dreaded. During several weeks I could not look
any young lady in the face; I dropped my eyes in
confusion when any one of them smiled upon me
and gave me greeting; I said to myself, "That is

one of them," and got quickly away. Of course I was meeting the right girls everywhere, but if they ever let slip any betraying sign I was not bright enough to catch it. When I left Hannibal, four years later, the secret was still a secret; I had never guessed those girls out, and was no longer hoping or expecting to do it.

One of the dearest and prettiest girls in the village at the time of my mishap was one whom I will call Mary Wilson, because that was not her name. She was twenty years old; she was dainty and sweet, peach-blooming and exquisite, gracious and lovely in character. I stood in awe of her, for she seemed to me to be made out of angel clay and rightfully unapproachable by just any unholy ordinary kind of boy like me. I probably never suspected *her*. But——

The scene changes to Calcutta—forty-seven years later. It was in 1896. I arrived there on a lecturing trip. As I entered the hotel a vision passed out of it, clothed in the glory of the Indian sunshine—the Mary Wilson of my long-vanished boyhood! It was a startling thing. Before I could recover from the pleasant shock and speak to her she was gone. I thought maybe I had seen an apparition, but it was not so, she was flesh. She was the granddaughter of the other Mary. The other Mary, now a widow, was upstairs, and presently sent for me. She was old and gray-haired, but she looked young and was very handsome. We sat down and talked. We steeped our thirsty souls in the reviving wine of the past, the pathetic past, the beautiful past, the dear and lamented past; we uttered the names that had been silent upon our lips for fifty years, and it was as if they were made of music; with reverent hands we unburied our dead, the mates of our youth, and caressed them with our speech; we searched the dusty chambers of our memories and dragged forth incident after incident, episode after episode, folly after folly, and laughed such good laughs over them, with the tears running down; and finally Mary said, suddenly, and without any leading up:

"Tell me! What is the special peculiarity of dried herrings?"

It seemed a strange question at such a hallowed time as this. And so inconsequential, too. I was a little shocked. And yet I was aware of a stir of some kind away back in the deeps of my memory somewhere. It set me to musing—thinking—searching. Dried herrings? Dried herrings? The peculiarity of dri . . . I glanced up. Her face was grave, but there was a dim and shadowy twinkle in her eye which— All of a sudden I knew and far away down in the hoary past I heard a remembered voice murmur, "Dey eats 'em innards and all!"

"At—last! I've found one of you, anyway! Who was the other girl?"

But she drew the line there. She wouldn't tell me.

But a boy's life is not all comedy; much of the tragic enters into it. The drunken tramp—mentioned elsewhere—who was burned up in the village jail lay upon my conscience a hundred nights afterward and filled them with hideous dreams—

dreams in which I saw his appealing face as I had seen it in the pathetic reality, pressed against the window bars, with the red hell glowing behind him— a face which seemed to say to me, "If you had not given me the matches, this would not have happened; you are responsible for my death." I was *not* responsible for it, for I had meant him no harm, but only good, when I let him have the matches; but no matter, mine was a trained Presbyterian conscience and knew but the one duty—to hunt and harry its slave upon all pretexts and on all occasions, particularly when there was no sense nor reason in it. The tramp—who was to blame—suffered ten minutes; I, who was not to blame, suffered three months.

The shooting down of poor old Smarr in the main street at noonday supplied me with some more dreams; and in them I always saw again the grotesque closing picture—the great family Bible spread open on the profane old man's breast by some thoughtful idiot, and rising and sinking to the labored breathings, and adding the torture of its leaden weight to the dying struggles. We are curiously made. In all the throng of gaping and sympathetic onlookers there was not one with common sense enough to perceive that an anvil would have been in better taste there than the Bible, less open to sarcastic criticism, and swifter in its atrocious work. In my nightmares I gasped and struggled for breath under the crush of that vast book for many a night.

All within the space of a couple of years we

had two or three other tragedies, and I had the ill luck to be too near by, on each occasion. There was the slave man who was struck down with a chunk of slag for some small offense; I saw him die. And the young Californian emigrant who was stabbed with a bowie knife by a drunken comrade; I saw the red life gush from his breast. And the case of the rowdy young brothers and their harmless old uncle: one of them held the old man down with his knees on his breast while the other one tried repeatedly to kill him with an Allen revolver which wouldn't go off. I happened along just then, of course.

Then there was the case of the young Californian emigrant who got drunk and proposed to raid the "Welshman's house" all alone one dark and threatening night. This house stood halfway up Holliday's Hill and its sole occupants were a poor but quite respectable widow and her blameless daughter. The invading ruffian woke the whole village with his ribald yells and coarse challenges and obscenities. I went up there with a comrade—John Briggs, I think—to look and listen. The figure of the man was dimly visible; the women were on their porch, not visible in the deep shadow of its roof, but we heard the elder woman's voice. She had loaded an old musket with slugs, and she warned the man that if he stayed where he was while she counted ten it would cost him his life. She began to count, slowly; he began to laugh. He stopped laughing at "six"; then through the deep stillness, in a steady voice, followed the rest of the tale: "Seven . . .

eight . . . nine"—a long pause, we holding our breaths—"ten!" A red spout of flame gushed out into the night, and the man dropped with his breast riddled to rags. Then the rain and the thunder burst loose and the waiting town swarmed up the hill in the glare of the lightning like an invasion of ants. Those people saw the rest; I had had my share and was satisfied. I went home to dream, and was not disappointed.

My teaching and training enabled me to see deeper into these tragedies than an ignorant person could have done. I knew what they were for. I tried to disguise it from myself, but down in the secret deeps of my troubled heart I knew—and I *knew* I knew. They were inventions of Providence to beguile me to a better life. It sounds curiously innocent and conceited, now, but to me there was nothing strange about it; it was quite in accordance with the thoughtful and judicious ways of Providence as I understood them. It would not have surprised me, nor even overflattered me, if Providence had killed off that whole community in trying to save an asset like me. Educated as I had been, it would have seemed just the thing, and well worth the expense. *Why* Providence should take such an anxious interest in such a property, that idea never entered my head, and there was no one in that simple hamlet who would have dreamed of putting it there. For one thing, no one was equipped with it.

It is quite true, I took all the tragedies to myself, and tallied them off in turn as they happened, saying to myself in each case, with a sigh, "Another

one gone—and on my account; this ought to bring
me to repentance; the patience of God will not always endure." And yet privately I believed it would.
That is, I believed it in the daytime; but not in the
night. With the going down of the sun my faith
failed and the clammy fears gathered about my
heart. It was then that I repented. Those were
awful nights, nights of despair, nights charged with
the bitterness of death. After each tragedy I recognized the warning and repented; repented and
begged; begged like a coward, begged like a dog;
and not in the interest of those poor people who
had been extinguished for my sake, but only in my
own interest. It seems selfish, when I look back
on it now.

My repentances were very real, very earnest; and
after each tragedy they happened every night for a
long time. But as a rule they could not stand the
daylight. They faded out and shredded away and
disappeared in the glad splendor of the sun. They
were the creatures of fear and darkness, and they
could not live out of their own place. The day
gave me cheer and peace, and at night I repented
again. In all my boyhood life I am not sure that
I ever tried to lead a better life in the daytime—
or wanted to. In my age I should never think of
wishing to do such a thing. But in my age, as in
my youth, night brings me many a deep remorse.
I realize that from the cradle up I have been like
the rest of the race—never quite sane in the night.
When "Injun Joe" died . . . But never mind.
Somewhere I have already described what a raging

hell of repentance I passed through then. I believe that for months I was as pure as the driven snow. After dark.

Jim Wolf and the Cats

It was back in those far-distant days—1848 or '49—that Jim Wolf came to us. He was from a hamlet thirty or forty miles back in the country, and he brought all his native sweetnesses and gentlenesses and simplicities with him. He was approaching seventeen, a grave and slender lad, trustful, honest, honorable, a creature to love and cling to. And he was incredibly bashful. He was with us a good while, but he could never conquer that peculiarity; he could not be at ease in the presence of any woman, not even in my good and gentle mother's; and as to speaking to any girl, it was wholly impossible. He sat perfectly still, one day—there were ladies chatting in the room—while a wasp up his leg stabbed him cruelly a dozen times; and all the sign he gave was a slight wince for each stab and the tear of torture in his eye. He was too bashful to move.

It is to this kind that untoward things happen. My sister gave a "candy-pull" on a winter's night. I was too young to be of the company, and Jim was too diffident. I was sent up to bed early, and Jim followed of his own motion. His room was in the new part of the house and his window looked out on the roof of the L annex. That roof was six inches deep in snow, and the snow had an ice crust upon it which was as slick as glass. Out of the comb of the roof projected a short chimney, a common resort for sentimental cats on moonlight nights—and this was a moonlight night. Down at the eaves, below the chimney, a canopy of dead vines spread away to some posts, making a cozy shelter, and after an hour or two the rollicking crowd of young ladies and gentlemen grouped themselves in its shade, with their saucers of liquid and piping-hot candy disposed about them on the frozen ground to cool. There was joyous chaffing and joking and laughter—peal upon peal of it.

About this time a couple of old, disreputable tomcats got up on the chimney and started a heated argument about something; also about this time I gave up trying to get to sleep and went visiting to Jim's room. He was awake and fuming about the cats and their intolerable yowling. I asked him, mockingly, why he didn't climb out and drive them away. He was nettled, and said overboldly that for two cents he *would*.

It was a rash remark and was probably repented of before it was fairly out of his mouth. But it was too late—he was committed. I knew him; and I knew he would rather break his neck than back down, if I egged him on judiciously.

"Oh, of course you would! Who's doubting it?"

It galled him, and he burst out, with sharp irritation, "Maybe *you* doubt it!"

"I? Oh no! I shouldn't think of such a thing. You are always doing wonderful things, with your mouth."

He was in a passion now. He snatched on his

yarn socks and began to raise the window, saying in a voice quivering with anger:

"*You* think I dasn't—you do! Think what you blame please. *I* don't care what you think. I'll show you!"

The window made him rage; it wouldn't stay up. I said, "Never mind, I'll hold it."

Indeed, I would have done anything to help. I was only a boy and was already in a radiant heaven of anticipation. He climbed carefully out, clung to the window sill until his feet were safely placed, then began to pick his perilous way on all-fours along the glassy comb, a foot and a hand on each side of it. I believe I enjoy it now as much as I did then; yet it is nearly fifty years ago. The frosty breeze flapped his short shirt about his lean legs; the crystal roof shone like polished marble in the intense glory of the moon; the unconscious cats sat erect upon the chimney, alertly watching each other, lashing their tails and pouring out their hollow grievances; and slowly and cautiously Jim crept on, flapping as he went, the gay and frolicsome young creatures under the vine canopy unaware, and outraging these solemnities with their misplaced laughter. Every time Jim slipped I had a hope; but always on he crept and disappointed it. At last he was within reaching distance. He paused, raised himself carefully up, measured his distance deliberately, then made a frantic grab at the nearest cat—and missed it. Of course he lost his balance. His heels flew up, he struck on his back, and like a rocket he darted down the roof feet first, crashed

through the dead vines, and landed in a sitting position in fourteen saucers of red-hot candy, in the
midst of all that party—and dressed as *he* was—
this lad who could not look a girl in the face with
his clothes on. There was a wild scramble and a
storm of shrieks, and Jim fled up the stairs, dripping
broken crockery all the way.

The incident was ended. But I was not done with
it yet, though I supposed I was. Eighteen or twenty
years later I arrived in New York from California,
and by that time I had failed in all my other under-
takings and had stumbled into literature without
intending it. This was early in 1867. I was offered
a large sum to write something for the *Sunday Mer-
cury,* and I answered with the tale of "Jim Wolf
and the Cats." I also collected the money for it—
twenty-five dollars. It seemed over-pay, but I did
not say anything about that, for I was not so
scrupulous then as I am now.

A year or two later "Jim Wolf and the Cats"
appeared in a Tennessee paper in a new dress—as
to spelling; it was masquerading in a Southern dialect. The appropriator of the tale had a wide reputation in the West and was exceedingly popular.
Deservedly so, I think. He wrote some of the breez-
iest and funniest things I have ever read, and did
his work with distinguished ease and fluency. His
name has passed out of my memory.

A couple of years went by; then the original story
cropped up again and went floating around in the
original spelling, and with my name to it. Soon,
first one paper and then another fell upon me vig-

orously for "stealing" "Jim Wolf and the Cats"
from the Tennessee man. I got a merciless basting,
but I did not mind it. It's all in the game. Besides,
I had learned, a good while before that, that it is
not wise to keep the fires going under a slander
unless you can get some large advantage out of
keeping it alive. Few slanders can stand the wear
of silence.

But I was not done with "Jim and the Cats"
yet. In 1873 I was lecturing in London in the
Queen's Concert Rooms, Hanover Square, and living at the Langham Hotel, Portland Place. I had
no domestic household on that side of the water, and
no official household except George Dolby, lecture
agent, and Charles Warren Stoddard, the Californian poet, now professor of English literature
in the Roman Catholic University, Washington.
Ostensibly Stoddard was my private secretary; in
reality he was merely my comrade—I hired him in
order to have his company. As secretary there was
nothing for him to do except to scrap-book the daily
reports of the great trial of the Tichborne Claimant
for perjury. But he made a sufficient job out of
that, for the reports filled six columns a day and
he usually postponed the scrap-booking until Sunday;
then he had forty-two columns to cut out and paste
in—a proper labor for Hercules. He did his work
well, but if he had been older and feebler it would
have killed him once a week. Without doubt he
does his literary lectures well, but also without doubt
he prepares them fifteen minutes before he is due
on his platform and thus gets into them a freshness

and sparkle which they might lack if they underwent the staling process of overstudy.

He was good company when he was awake. He was refined, sensitive, charming, gentle, generous, honest himself and unsuspicious of other people's honesty, and I think he was the purest male I have known, in mind and speech. George Dolby was something of a contrast to him, but the two were very friendly and sociable together, nevertheless. Dolby was large and ruddy, full of life and strength and spirits, a tireless and energetic talker, and always overflowing with good nature and bursting with jollity. It was a choice and satisfactory menagerie, this pensive poet and this gladsome gorilla. An indelicate story was a sharp distress to Stoddard; Dolby told him twenty-five a day. Dolby always came home with us after the lecture, and entertained Stoddard till midnight. Me, too. After he left I walked the floor and talked, and Stoddard went to sleep on the sofa. I hired him for company.

Dolby had been agent for concerts, and theaters, and Charles Dickens, and all sorts of shows and "attractions," for many years. He had known the human being in many aspects, and he didn't much believe in him. But the poet did. The waifs and estrays found a friend in Stoddard; Dolby tried to persuade him that he was dispensing his charities unworthily, but he was never able to succeed. One night a young American got access to Stoddard at the Concert Rooms and told him a moving tale. He said he was living on the Surrey side, and for some strange reason his remittances had failed to arrive from home; he had no money, he was out of employment and friendless; his girl wife and his new baby were actually suffering for food. For the love of Heaven could he lend him a sovereign until his remittance should resume? Stoddard was deeply touched, and gave him a sovereign on my account. Dolby scoffed, but Stoddard stood his ground. Each told me his story later in the evening, and I backed Stoddard's judgment. Dolby said we were women in disguise, and not a sane kind of woman, either. The next week the young man came again. His wife was ill with the pleurisy, the baby had the botts or something—I am not sure of the name of the disease; the doctor and the drugs had eaten up the money; the poor little family were starving. If Stoddard, "in the kindness of his heart, could only spare him another sovereign," etc., etc. Stoddard was much moved, and spared him a sovereign for me. Dolby was outraged. He spoke up and said to the customer:

"Now, young man, you are going to the hotel with us and state your case to the other member of the family. If you don't make him believe in you I shan't honor this poet's drafts in your interest any longer, for I don't believe in you myself."

The young man was quite willing. I found no fault in him. On the contrary, I believed in him at once and was solicitous to heal the wounds inflicted by Dolby's too frank incredulity; therefore I did everything I could think of to cheer him up and entertain him and make him feel at home and comfortable. I spun many yarns; among others the tale of "Jim Wolf and the Cats." Learning that he had done something in a small way in literature, I offered to try to find a market for him in that line. His face lighted joyfully at that, and he said that if I could only sell a small manuscript to Tom Hood's *Annual* for him it would be the happiest event of his sad life and he would hold me in grateful remembrance always. That was a most pleasant night for three of us, but Dolby was disgusted and sarcastic.

Next week the baby died. Meantime I had spoken to Tom Hood and gained his sympathy. The young man had sent his manuscript to him, and the very day the child died the money for the MS. came—three guineas. The young man came with a poor little strip of crape around his arm and thanked me, and said that nothing could have been more timely than that money and that his poor little wife was grateful beyond words for the service I had rendered. He wept, and in fact Stoddard and I wept with him, which was but natural. Also Dolby wept. At least he wiped his eyes and wrung out his handkerchief, and sobbed stertorously and made other exaggerated shows of grief. Stoddard and I were ashamed of Dolby and tried to make the young man understand that he meant no harm, it was only his way. The young man said sadly that he was not minding it, his grief was too deep for other hurts; that he was only thinking of the funeral and the heavy expenses which——

We cut that short and told him not to trouble

about it, leave it all to us; send the bills to Mr. Dolby and——

"Yes," said Dolby, with a mock tremor in his voice, "send them to me and I will pay them. What, are you going? You must not go alone in your worn and broken condition. Mr. Stoddard and I will go with you. Come, Stoddard. We will comfort the bereaved mamma and get a lock of the baby's hair."

It was shocking. We were ashamed of him again, and said so. But he was not disturbed. He said:

"Oh, I know this kind; the woods are full of them. I'll make this offer: if he will show me his family I will give him twenty pounds. Come!"

The young man said he would not remain to be insulted, and he said good-night and took his hat. But Dolby said he would go with him and stay by him until he found the family. Stoddard went along to soothe the young man and modify Dolby. They drove across the river and all over Southwork, but did not find the family. At last the young man confessed that there wasn't any.

The thing he sold to Tom Hood's *Annual* for three guineas was "Jim Wolf and the Cats." And he did not put my name to it.

So that small tale was sold three times. I am selling it again now. It is one of the best properties I have come across.

[*Written about 1898*

MACFARLANE

WHEN I was turned twenty I wandered to Cincinnati, and was there several months. Our boarding-house crew was made up of commonplace people of various ages and both sexes. They were full of bustle, frivolity, chatter, and the joy of life, and were good-natured, clean-minded, and well-meaning; but they were oppressively uninteresting, for all that —with one exception. This was Macfarlane, a Scotchman. He was forty years old—just double my age—but we were opposite in most ways and comrades from the start. I always spent my evenings by the wood fire in his room, listening in comfort to his tireless talk and to the dulled complainings of the winter storms, until the clock struck ten. At that hour he grilled a smoked herring, after the fashion of an earlier friend in Philadelphia, the Englishman Sumner. His herring was his nightcap and my signal to go.

He was six feet high and rather lank, a serious and sincere man. He had no humor, nor any comprehension of it. He had a sort of smile, whose office was to express his good nature, but if I ever heard him laugh, the memory of it is gone from me. He was intimate with no one in the house but me, though he was courteous and pleasant with all. He had two or three dozen weighty books—philosophies, histories, and scientific works—and at the head of this procession were his Bible and his dictionary. After his herring he always read two or three hours in bed.

Diligent talker as he was, he seldom said anything about himself. To ask him a personal question gave him no offense—nor the asker any information; he merely turned the matter aside and flowed

placidly on about other things. He told me once
that he had had hardly any schooling, and that such
learning as he had, he had picked up for himself.
That was his sole biographical revelation, I believe.
Whether he was bachelor, widower, or grass widower, remained his own secret. His clothes were
cheap, but neat and caretakingly preserved. Ours
was a cheap boarding house; he left the house at
six, mornings, and returned to it toward six, evenings; his hands were not soft, so I reasoned that
he worked at some mechanical calling ten hours a
day, for humble wages—but I never knew. As a
rule, technicalities of a man's vocation, and figures
and metaphors drawn from it, slip out in his talk
and reveal his trade; but if this ever happened in
Macfarlane's case I was none the wiser, although
I was constantly on the watch during half a year
for those very betrayals. It was mere curiosity, for
I didn't care what his trade was, but I wanted to
detect it in true detective fashion and was annoyed
because I couldn't do it. I think he was a remarkable man, to be able to keep the shop out of his
talk all that time.

There was another noteworthy feature about him:
he seemed to know his dictionary from beginning
to end. He claimed that he did. He was frankly
proud of this accomplishment and said I would not
find it possible to challenge him with an English
word which he could not promptly spell and define.
I lost much time trying to hunt up a word which
would beat him, but those weeks were spent in vain
and I finally gave it up; which made him so proud

and happy that I wished I had surrendered earlier.

He seemed to be as familiar with his Bible as he was with his dictionary. It was easy to see that he considered himself a philosopher and a thinker. His talk always ran upon grave and large questions; and I must do him the justice to say that his heart and conscience were in his talk and that there was no appearance of reasoning and arguing for the vain pleasure of hearing himself do it.

Of course his thinking and reasoning and philosophizings were those of a but partly taught and wholly untrained mind, yet he hit by accident upon some curious and striking things. For instance. The time was the early part of 1856—fourteen or fifteen years before Mr. Darwin's *Descent of Man* startled the world—yet here was Macfarlane talking the same idea to me, there in the boarding house in Cincinnati.

The same general idea, but with difference. Macfarlane considered that the animal life in the world was developed in the course of æons of time from a few microscopic seed germs, or perhaps *one* microscopic seed germ deposited upon the globe by the Creator in the dawn of time, and that this development was progressive upon an ascending scale toward ultimate perfection until *man* was reached; and that then the progressive scheme broke pitifully down and went to wreck and ruin!

He said that man's heart was the only bad heart in the animal kingdom; that man was the only animal capable of feeling malice, envy, vindictiveness, revengefulness, hatred, selfishness, the only animal that loved drunkenness, almost the only animal that could endure personal uncleanliness and a filthy habitation, the sole animal in whom was fully developed the base instinct called *patriotism,* the sole animal that robs, persecutes, oppresses, and kills members of his own immediate tribe, the sole animal that steals and enslaves the members of any *tribe.*

He claimed that man's intellect was a brutal addition to him and degraded him to a rank far below the plane of the other animals, and that there was never a man who did not use his intellect daily all his life to advantage himself at other people's expense. The divinest divine reduced his domestics to humble servitude under him by advantage of his superior intellect, and those servants in turn were above a still lower grade of people by force of brains that were still a little better than theirs.

[Written in 1898

OLD LECTURE DAYS IN BOSTON

Nasby, and others of Redpath's Lecture Bureau

I REMEMBER Petroleum Vesuvius Nasby (Locke) very well. When the Civil War began he was on the staff of the Toledo *Blade,* an old and prosperous and popular weekly newspaper. He let fly a Nasby letter and it made a fine strike. He was famous at once. He followed up his new lead, and gave the Copperheads and the Democratic party a most admirable hammering every week, and his letters were copied everywhere, from the Atlantic to the Pacific, and read and laughed over by everybody—at least everybody except particularly dull and prejudiced Democrats and Copperheads. For suddenness, Nasby's fame was an explosion; for universality it was atmospheric. He was soon offered a company; he accepted and was straightway ready to leave for the front; but the Governor of the state was a wiser man than were the political masters of Körner and Petöfi; for he refused to sign Nasby's commission and ordered him to stay at home. He said that in the field Nasby would be only one soldier, handling one sword, but at home with his pen he was an army—with artillery! Nasby obeyed and went on writing his electric letters.

I saw him first when I was on a visit to Hartford; I think it was three or four years after the war. The Opera House was packed and jammed with people to hear him deliver his lecture on "Cussed be Canaan." He had been on the platform with that same lecture—and no other—during two or three years, and it had passed his lips several hundred times, yet even now he could not deliver any sentence of it without his manuscript—except the opening one. His appearance on the stage was welcomed with a prodigious burst of applause, but he did not stop to bow or in any other way acknowledge the greeting, but strode straight to the reading desk, spread his portfolio open upon it, and immediately petrified himself into an attitude which he never changed during the hour and a half occupied by his performance, except to turn his leaves—his body bent over the desk, rigidly supported by his left arm, as by a stake, the right arm lying across his back. About once in two minutes his right arm swung forward, turned a leaf, then swung to its resting-place on his back again—just the action of a machine, and suggestive of one; regular, recurrent, prompt, exact. You might imagine you heard it *clash*. He was a great, burly figure, uncouthly and provincially clothed, and he looked like a simple old farmer.

I was all curiosity to hear him begin. He did not keep me waiting. The moment he had crutched himself upon his left arm, lodged his right upon his back, and bent himself over his manuscript he raised his face slightly, flashed a glance upon the audience, and bellowed this remark in a thundering bull-voice:

"We are all descended from grandfathers!"

Then he went right on roaring to the end, tearing his ruthless way through the continuous applause and laughter, and taking no sort of account of it. His lecture was a volleying and sustained discharge of bull's-eye hits, with the slave power and its Northern apologists for target, and his success was due to his matter, not his manner; for his delivery was destitute of art, unless a tremendous and inspiring earnestness and energy may be called by that name. The moment he had finished his piece he turned his back and marched off the stage with the seeming of being not personally concerned with the applause that was booming behind him.

He had the constitution of an ox and the strength and endurance of a prize-fighter. Express trains were not very plenty in those days. He missed a connection, and in order to meet this Hartford engagement he had traveled two-thirds of a night and a whole day in a *cattle car*—it was midwinter. He went from the cattle car to his reading desk without dining; yet on the platform his voice was powerful and he showed no signs of drowsiness or fatigue. He sat up talking and supping with me until after midnight, and then it was I that had to give up, not he. He told me that in his first season he read his "Cussed be Canaan" twenty-five nights a month for nine successive months. No other lecturer ever matched that record, I imagine.

He said that as one result of repeating his lecture 225 nights straight along, he was able to say its opening sentence without glancing at his manuscript; and sometimes even *did* it, when in a daring mood. And there was another result: he reached home the day after his long campaign, and was sitting by the fire in the evening, musing, when the clock broke into his revery by striking eight. Habit is habit, and before he realized where he was he had thundered out, *"We are all descended from grand-fathers!"*

I began as a lecturer in 1866, in California and Nevada; in 1867 lectured in New York once and in the Mississippi Valley a few times; in 1868 made the whole Western circuit; and in the two or three following seasons added the Eastern circuit to my route. We had to bring out a new lecture every season, now (Nasby with the rest), and expose it in the "Star Course," Boston, for a first verdict, before an audience of 2,500 in the old Music Hall; for it was by that verdict that all the lyceums in the country determined the lecture's commercial value. The campaign did not really *begin* in Boston, but in the towns around. We did not appear in Boston until we had rehearsed about a month in those towns and made all the necessary corrections and revisings.

This system gathered the whole tribe together in the city early in October, and we had a lazy and sociable time there for several weeks. We lived at Young's Hotel; we spent the days in Redpath's Bureau, smoking and talking shop; and early in the evenings we scattered out among the towns and made them indicate the good and poor things in the new lectures. The country audience is the difficult audience; a passage which it will approve with a ripple will bring a crash in the city. A fair success in the country means a triumph in the city. And so, when we finally stepped on to the great stage at the Music Hall we already had the verdict in our pocket.

But sometimes lecturers who were "new to the business" did not know the value of "trying it on the dog," and these were apt to come to the Music Hall with an untried product. There was one case of this kind which made some of us very anxious when we saw the advertisement. De Cordova—humorist—he was the man we were troubled about. I think he had another name, but I have forgotten what it was. He had been printing some dismally humorous things in the magazines; they had met with a deal of favor and given him a pretty wide name; and now he suddenly came poaching upon our preserve and took us by surprise. Several of us felt pretty unwell—too unwell to lecture. We got outlying engagements postponed and remained in town. We took front seats in one of the great galleries—Nasby, Billings, and I—and waited. The house was full. When De Cordova came on he was received with what we regarded as a quite overdone and almost indecent volume of welcome. I think we were not jealous, nor even envious, but it made us sick, anyway. When I found he was going to read a humorous *story*—from manuscript—I felt better and hopeful, but still anxious. He had a Dickens arrangement of tall gallows frame adorned with upholsteries, and he stood behind it under its overhead row of hidden lights. The whole thing had a quite stylish look and was rather impressive. The audience was so sure that he was going to be funny that they took a dozen of his first utterances on trust and laughed cordially—so cordially, indeed, that it was very hard for us to bear—and we felt very much disheartened. Still, I tried to believe he would fail, for I saw that he didn't know how to read. Presently the laughter began to relax; then it began to shrink in area; and next to lose spontaneity; and next to show gaps between; the gaps widened; they widened more; more yet; still more. It was getting to be almost all gaps and silence, with that untrained and unlively voice droning through them. Then the house sat dead and emotionless for a whole ten minutes. We drew a deep sigh; it ought to have been a sigh of pity for a defeated fellow craftsman, but it was not—for we were mean and selfish, like all the human race, and it was a sigh of satisfaction to see our unoffending brother fail.

He was laboring now, and distressed; he constantly mopped his face with his handkerchief, and his voice and his manner became a humble appeal for compassion, for help, for charity, and it was a pathetic thing to see. But the house remained cold and still, and gazed at him curiously and wonderingly.

There was a great clock on the wall, high up; presently the general gaze forsook the reader and fixed itself upon the clock face. We knew by dismal experience what that meant; we knew what was going to happen, but it was plain that the reader had not been warned and was ignorant. It was approaching nine now—half the house watching the clock, the reader laboring on. At five minutes to nine, twelve hundred people rose, with one impulse, and swept like a wave down the aisles toward the doors! The reader was like a person stricken with a paralysis; he stood choking and gasping for a few minutes, gazing in a white horror at that retreat, then he turned drearily away and wandered from the stage with the groping and uncertain step of one who walks in his sleep.

The management were to blame. They should have told him that the last suburban cars left at nine and that half the house would rise and go then, no matter who might be speaking from the platform. I think De Cordova did not appear again in public,

[*Written about 1898*

Ralph Keeler

He was a Californian. I probably knew him in San Francisco in the early days—about 1865—when I was a newspaper reporter, and Bret Harte, Ambrose Bierce, Charles Warren Stoddard and Prentice Mulford were doing young literary work for Mr. Joe Lawrence's weekly periodical, the *Golden Era*. At any rate, I knew him in Boston a few years later, where he comraded with Howells, Aldrich, Boyle O'Reilly, and James T. Fields, and was greatly liked by them. I say he comraded with them, and that is the proper term, though he would not have given the relationship so familiar a name himself, for he was the modestest young fellow that ever was and looked humbly up to those distinguished men from his lowly obscurity, and was boyishly grateful for the friendly notice they took of him, and frankly grateful for it; and when he got a smile and a nod from Mr. Emerson and Mr. Whittier and Holmes and Lowell and Longfellow, his happiness was the prettiest thing in the world to see. He was not more than twenty-four at this time; the native sweetness of his disposition had not been marred by cares and disappointments; he was buoyant and hopeful, simple-hearted, and full of the most engaging and unexacting little literary ambitions. Whomsoever he met became his friend and—by some natural and unexplained impulse—took him under protection.

He probably never had a home or a boyhood.

He had wandered to California as a little chap from somewhere or other, and had cheerfully achieved his bread in various humble callings, educating himself as he went along, and having a good and satisfactory time. Among his various industries was clog-dancing in a "nigger" show. When he was about twenty years old he scraped together eighty-five dollars— in greenbacks, worth about half that sum in gold— and on this capital he made the tour of Europe and published an account of his travels in the *Atlantic Monthly.* When he was about twenty-two he wrote a novel called *Gloverson and His Silent Partners;* and not only that, but found a publisher for it. But that was not really a surprising thing, in his case, for not even a publisher is hard-hearted enough to be able to say no to some people—and Ralph was one of those people. His gratitude for a favor granted him was so simple and sincere and so eloquent and touching that a publisher would recognize that if there was no money in the book there was still a profit to be had out of it beyond the value of money and above money's reach. There *was* no money in that book, not a single penny; but Ralph Keeler always spoke of his publisher as other people speak of divinities. The publisher lost two or three hundred dollars on the book, of course, and knew he would lose it when he made the venture, but he got much more than the worth of it back in the author's adoring admiration of him.

Ralph had little or nothing to do, and he often went out with me to the small lecture towns in the neighborhood of Boston. These lay within an hour

of town, and we usually started at six or thereabouts,
and returned to the city in the morning.   It took
about a month to do these Boston annexes, and that
was the easiest and pleasantest month of the four
or five which constituted the "lecture season."   The
"lyceum system" was in full flower in those days, and
James Redpath's Bureau in School Street, Boston,
had the management of it throughout the Northern
States and Canada.   Redpath farmed out the lectures in groups of six or eight to the lyceums all
over the country at an average of about $100 a
night for each lecture.   His commission was 10 per
cent; each lecture appeared about 110 nights in the
season.   There were a number of good drawing
names in his list: Henry Ward Beecher; Anna Dickinson; John B. Gough; Horace Greeley; Wendell
Phillips; Petroleum V. Nasby; Josh Billings; Hayes,
the Arctic Explorer; Vincent, the English astron-
omer; Parsons, Irish orator; Agassiz; *et al.* He had
in his list twenty or thirty men and women of light
consequence and limited reputation who wrought for
fees ranging from twenty-five dollars to fifty dollars.
Their names have perished long ago.   Nothing but
art could find them a chance on the platform.   Redpath furnished that art.   All the lyceums wanted
the big guns, and wanted them yearningly, longingly,
strenuously.   Redpath granted their prayers—on
this condition: for each house-filler allotted them
they must hire several of his house-emptiers.   This
arrangement permitted the lyceums to get through
alive for a few years, but in the end it killed them
all and abolished the lecture business.

Beecher, Gough, Nasby, and Anna Dickinson were the only lecturers who knew their own value and exacted it. In towns their fee was $200 and $250; in cities, $400. The lyceum always got a profit out of these four (weather permitting), but generally lost it again on the house-emptiers.

There were two women who should have been house-emptiers—Olive Logan and Kate Field—but during a season or two they were not. They charged $100, and were recognized house-fillers for certainly two years. After that they were capable emptiers and were presently shelved. Kate Field had made a wide, spasmodic notoriety in 1867 by some letters which she sent from Boston—by telegraph—to the *Tribune* about Dickens's readings there in the beginning of his triumphant American tour. The letters were a frenzy of praise—praise which approached idolatry—and this was the right and welcome key to strike, for the country was itself in a frenzy of enthusiasm about Dickens. Then the idea of *telegraphing* a newspaper letter was new and astonishing, and the wonder of it was in every one's mouth. Kate Field became a celebrity at once. By and by she went on the platform; but two or three years had elapsed and her subject—Dickens—had now lost its freshness and its interest. For a while people went to see *her,* because of her name; but her lecture was poor and her delivery repellently artificial; consequently, when the country's desire to look at her had been appeased, the platform forsook her.

She was a good creature, and the acquisition of a perishable and fleeting notoriety was the disaster of her life. To her it was infinitely precious, and she tried hard, in various ways, during more than a quarter of a century, to keep a semblance of life in it, but her efforts were but moderately successful. She died in the Sandwich Islands, regretted by her friends and forgotten of the world.

Olive Logan's notoriety grew out of—only the initiated knew what. Apparently it was a manufactured notoriety, not an earned one. She *did* write and publish little things in newspapers and obscure periodicals, but there was no talent in them, and nothing resembling it. In a century they would not have made her known. Her name was really built up out of newspaper paragraphs set afloat by her husband, who was a small-salaried minor journalist. During a year or two this kind of paragraphing was persistent; one could seldom pick up a newspaper without encountering it.

It is said that Olive Logan has taken a cottage at Nahant, and will spend the summer there.

Olive Logan has set her face decidedly against the adoption of the short skirt for afternoon wear.

The report that Olive Logan will spend the coming winter in Paris is premature. She has not yet made up her mind.

Olive Logan was present at Wallack's on Saturday evening, and was outspoken in her approval of the new piece.

Olive Logan has so far recovered from her alarming illness that if she continues to improve her physicians will cease from issuing bulletins to-morrow.

The result of this daily advertising was very curious. Olive Logan's name was as familiar to the simple public as was that of any celebrity of the time, and people talked with interest about her doings and movements and gravely discussed her opinions. Now and then an ignorant person from the backwoods would proceed to inform himself, and then there were surprises in store for all concerned:

"Who *is* Olive Logan?"

The listeners were astonished to find that they couldn't answer the question. It had never occurred to them to inquire into the matter.

"What has she *done*?"

The listeners were dumb again. They didn't know. They hadn't inquired.

"Well, then, how does she come to be celebrated?"

"Oh, it's about *something,* I don't know what. I never inquired, but I supposed everybody knew."

For entertainment I often asked these questions myself, of people who were glibly talking about that celebrity and her doings and sayings. The questioned were surprised to find that they had been taking this fame wholly on trust and had no idea who Olive Logan was or what she had done—if anything.

On the strength of this oddly created notoriety Olive Logan went on the platform, and for at least two seasons the United States flocked to the lecture halls to look at her. She was merely a name and some rich and costly clothes, and neither of these properties had any lasting quality, though for a while

they were able to command a fee of $100 a night.
She dropped out of the memories of men a quarter
of a century ago.

Ralph Keeler was pleasant company on my lecture flights out of Boston, and we had plenty of
good talks and smokes in our rooms after the committee had escorted us to the inn and made their
good-night. There was always a committee, and
they wore a silk badge of office; they received us
at the station and drove us to the lecture hall; they
sat in a row of chairs behind me on the stage,
minstrel fashion, and in the earliest days their chief
used to introduce me to the audience; but these introductions were so grossly flattering that they made
me ashamed, and so I began my talk at a heavy
disadvantage. It was a stupid custom. There was
no occasion for the introduction; the introducer was
almost always an ass, and his prepared speech a
jumble of vulgar compliments and dreary effort to
be funny; therefore after the first season I always
introduced myself—using, of course, a burlesque of
the time-worn introduction. This change was not
popular with committee chairmen. To stand up
grandly before a great audience of his townsmen
and make his little devilish speech was the joy of
his life, and to have that joy taken from him was
almost more than he could bear.

My introduction of myself was a most efficient
"starter" for a while, then it failed. It had to be
carefully and painstakingly worded, and very ear-
nestly spoken, in order that all strangers present
might be deceived into the supposition that I was

only the introducer and not the lecturer; also that the flow of overdone compliments might sicken those strangers; then, when the end was reached and the remark casually dropped that I was the lecturer and had been talking about myself, the effect was very satisfactory. But it was a good card for only a little while, as I have said; for the newspapers printed it, and after that I could not make it go, since the house knew what was coming and retained its emotions.

Next I tried an introduction taken from my Californian experiences. It was gravely made by a slouching and awkward big miner in the village of Red Dog. The house, very much against his will, forced him to ascend the platform and introduce me. He stood thinking a moment, then said:

"I don't know anything about this man. At least I know only two things; one is, he hasn't been in the penitentiary, and the other is [after a pause, and almost sadly], *I don't know why.*"

That worked well for a while, then the newspapers printed it and took the juice out of it, and after that I gave up introductions altogether.

Now and then Keeler and I had a mild little adventure, but none which couldn't be forgotten without much of a strain. Once we arrived late at a town and found no committee in waiting and no sleighs on the stand. We struck up a street in the gay moonlight, found a tide of people flowing along, judged it was on its way to the lecture hall—a correct guess—and joined it. At the hall I tried to press in, but was stopped by the ticket-taker.

"Ticket, please."

I bent over and whispered: "It's all right. I am the lecturer."

He closed one eye impressively and said, loud enough for all the crowd to hear: "No you don't. Three of you have got in, up to now, but the next lecturer that goes in here to-night *pays*."

Of course we paid; it was the least embarrassing way out of the trouble. The very next morning Keeler had an adventure. About eleven o'clock I was sitting in my room, reading the paper, when he burst into the place all atremble with excitement and said:

"Come with me—quick!"

"What is it? What's happened?"

"Don't wait to talk. Come with me."

We tramped briskly up the main street three or four blocks, neither of us speaking, both of us excited, I in a sort of panic of apprehension and horrid curiosity; then we plunged into a building and down through the middle of it to the farther end. Keeler stopped, put out his hand, and said:

"Look!"

I looked, but saw nothing except a row of books.

"What is it, Keeler?"

He said, in a kind of joyous ecstasy, "Keep on looking—to the right; farther—farther to the right. There—see it? *Gloverson and His Silent Partners!*"

And there it was, sure enough.

"This is a library! Understand? Public library. And they've got it!"

His eyes, his face, his attitude, his gestures, his whole being spoke his delight, his pride, his happiness. It never occurred to me to laugh; a supreme joy like that moves one the other way. I was stirred almost to the crying point to see so perfect a happiness.

He knew all about the book, for he had been cross-examining the librarian. It had been in the library two years and the records showed that it had been taken out three times.

"And read, too!" said Keeler. "See—the leaves are all cut!"

Moreover, the book had been *"bought,* not given —it's on the record." I think *Gloverson* was published in San Francisco. Other copies had been sold, no doubt, but this present sale was the only one Keeler was certain of. It seems unbelievable that the sale of an edition of one book could give an author this immeasurable peace and contentment, but I was there and I saw it.

Afterward Keeler went out to Ohio and hunted out one of Osawatomie Brown's brothers on his farm and took down in longhand his narrative of his adventures in escaping from Virginia after the tragedy of 1859—the most admirable piece of reporting, I make no doubt, that was ever done by a man destitute of a knowledge of shorthand writing. It was published in the *Atlantic Monthly,* and I made three attempts to read it, but was frightened off each time before I could finish. The tale was so vivid and so real that I seemed to be living those adventures myself and sharing their intolerable perils, and the torture of it was so sharp that I was never able to follow the story to the end.

By and by the *Tribune* commissioned Keeler to go to Cuba and report the facts of an outrage or an insult of some sort which the Spanish authorities had been perpetrating upon us according to their well-worn habit and custom. He sailed from New York in the steamer and was last seen alive the night before the vessel reached Havana. It was said that he had not made a secret of his mission, but had talked about it freely, in his frank and innocent way. There were some Spanish military men on board. It may be that he was not flung into the sea; still, the belief was general that that was what had happened.

[Written in 1898. Vienna

BEAUTIES OF THE GERMAN LANGUAGE

February 3.—Lectured for the benefit of a charity last night, in the Börsendorfersaal. Just as I was going on the platform a messenger delivered to me an envelope with my name on it, and this written under it: "Please read one of these to-night." Inclosed were a couple of newspaper clippings—two versions of an anecdote, one German, the other English. I was minded to try the German one on those people, just to see what would happen, but my courage weakened when I noticed the formidable look of the closing word, and I gave it up. A pity, too, for it ought to read well on the platform and get an encore. That or a brickbat. There is never any telling what a new audience will do; their tastes are capricious. The point of this anecdote is a justifiable gibe at the German long word, and is not as much of an exaggeration as one might think. The German long word is not a legitimate construction, but an ignoble artificiality, a sham. It has no recognition by the dictionary and is not found there. It is made by jumbling a lot of words into one, in a quite unnecessary way; it is a lazy device of the vulgar and a crime against the language. Nothing can be gained, no valuable amount of space saved, by jumbling the following words together on a visiting card: "Mrs. Smith, widow of the late Commander-in-chief of the Police Department," yet a German widow can persuade herself to do it, without much trouble: "Mrs.-late-commander-in-chief-of-the-police-department's-widow-Smith." This is the English version of the anecdote:

A Dresden paper, the *Weidmann,* which thinks that there are kangaroos (Beutelratte) in South Africa, says the Hottentots (Hottentoten) put them in cages (kotter) provided with covers (lattengitter) to protect them from the rain. The cages are therefore called lattengitterwetterkotter, and the imprisoned kangaroo lattengitterwetterkotter-beutelratte. One day an assassin (attentäter) was arrested who had killed a Hottentot woman (Hottentotenmutter), the mother of two stupid and stuttering children in Strättertrotel. This woman, in the German language is entitled Hottentotenstrottertrottelmutter, and her assassin takes the name Hottentotenstrottermutterattentäter. The

murderer was confined in a kangaroo's cage—
Beutelrattenlattengitterwetterkotter—whence a few
days later he escaped, but fortunately he was re-
captured by a Hottentot, who presented himself at
the mayor's office with beaming face. "I have captured the Beutelratte," said he. "Which one?" said
the mayor; "we have several." "The Attentäter-
lattengitterwetterkotterbeutelratte." "Which attentäter are you talking about?" "About the Hot-
tentotenstrottertrottelmutterattentäter." "Then
why don't you say at once the Hottentotenstrot-
telmutterattentäterlattengitterwetterkotterbeutel-
ratte?"

[*Written Sunday, June 26, 1898. Kaltenleutgeben*

A VIENNESE PROCESSION

I WENT in the eight-o'clock train to Vienna, to
see the procession. It was a stroke of luck, for at
the last moment I was feeling lazy and was minded
not to go. But when I reached the station, five
minutes late, the train was still there, a couple of
friends were there also, and so I went. At Liesing,
half an hour out, we changed to a very long train
and left for Vienna, with every seat occupied. That
was no sign that this was a great day, for these
people are not critical about shows; they turn out for
anything that comes along. Half an hour later we
were driving into the city. No particular bustle
anywhere—indeed, less than is usual on an Austrian
Sunday; bunting flying, and a decoration here and
there—a quite frequent thing in this jubilee year;

but as we passed the American Embassy I saw a
couple of our flags out and the minister and his
menservants arranging to have another one added.
This woke me up—it seemed to indicate that something really beyond the common was to the fore.

As we neared the bridge which connects the First
Bezirk with the Third, a pronounced and growing
life and stir were noticeable—and when we entered
the wide square where the Schwarzenberg palace is,
there was something resembling a jam. As far as
we could see down the broad avenue of the Park
Ring both sides of it were packed with people in
their holiday clothes. Our cab worked its way across
the square, and then flew down empty streets, all
the way, to Liebenberggasse No. 7—the dwelling
we were aiming for. It stands on the corner of that
street and the Park Ring, and its balconies command a mile stretch of the latter avenue. By a
trifle after nine we were in the shade of the awn-
ings of the first-floor balcony, with a dozen other
guests, and ready for the procession. Ready, but
it would not start for an hour yet, and would not
reach us for half an hour afterward. As to numbers, it would be a large matter, for by report
it would march 25,000 strong. But it isn't numbers
that make the interest of a procession; I have seen
a vast number of long processions which didn't pay.
It is clothes that make a procession; where you have
those of the right pattern you can do without length.
Two or three months ago I saw one with the Emperor and an archbishop in it, and the archbishop
was being carried along under a canopied arrange-

ment and had his skullcap on, and the venerable
Emperor was following him on foot and bareheaded.
Even if that had been the entire procession, it would
have paid.   I am old, now, and may never be an
emperor at all; at least in this world.   I have been
disappointed so many times that I am growing more
and more doubtful and resigned every year; but
if it ever should happen, the procession will have
a fresh interest for the archbishop, for he will
walk.

The wait on the balcony was not dull.   There was
the spacious avenue stretching into the distance, right
and left, to look at, with its double wall of massed
humanity, an eager and excited lot, broiling in the
sun, and a comforting spectacle to contemplate from
the shade.   That is, on our side of the street they
were in the sun, but not on the other side, where
the park is; there was dense shade there.   They
were good-natured people, but they gave the policemen plenty of trouble, for they were constantly surg-
ing into the roadway and being hustled back again.
They were in fine spirits, yet it was said that the
most of them had been waiting there in the jam three
or four hours—and two-thirds of them were women
and girls.

At last a mounted policeman came galloping down
the road in solitary state—first sign that pretty soon
the show would open.   After five minutes he was
followed by a man on a decorated bicycle.   Next,
a marshal's assistant sped by on a polished and
shiny black horse.   Five minutes later, distant strains
of music.   Five more, and far up the street the head

of the procession twinkles into view. That *was* a procession! I wouldn't have missed it for anything. According to my understanding, it was to be composed of shooting-match clubs from all over the Austrian Empire, with a club or two from France and Germany as guests. What I had in my imagination was 25,000 men in sober dress, drifting monotonously by, with rifles slung to their backs—a New York target excursion on a large scale. In my fancy I could see the colored brothers toting the ice pails and targets and swabbing off perspiration.

But this was a different matter. One of the most engaging spectacles in the world is a Wagner opera force marching on to the stage, with its music braying and its banners flying. This was that spectacle infinitely magnified, and with the glories of the sun upon it and a countless multitude of excited witnesses to wave the handkerchiefs and do the hurrahing. It was grand and beautiful and sumptuous; and no tinsel, no shams, no tin armor, no cotton velvet, no make-believe silk, no Birmingham Oriental rugs; everything was what it professed to be. It is the clothes that make a procession, and for these costumes all the centuries were drawn upon, even from times which were already ancient when Kaiser Rudolph himself was alive.

There were bodies of spearmen with plain steel casques of a date a thousand years ago; other bodies in more ornamental casques of a century or two later, and with breastplates added; other bodies with chain-mail elaborations, some armed with crossbows, some with the earliest crop of matchlocks; still other bodies clothed in the stunningly picturesque plate armor and plumed great helmets of the middle of the sixteenth century. And then there were bodies of men-at-arms in the darling velvets of the Middle Ages, and nobles on horseback in the same—doublets with huge puffed sleeves, wide brigand hats with great plumes; and the rich and effective colors—old gold, black, and scarlet; deep yellow, black, and scarlet; brown, black, and scarlet. A portly figure clothed like that, with a two-handed sword as long as a billiard cue, and mounted on a big draft horse finely caparisoned, with the sun flooding the splendid colors—a figure like that, with fifty duplicates marching in his rear, is procession enough, all by itself.

Yet that was merely a detail. All the centuries were passing by; passing by in glories of color and multiplicities of strange and quaint and curious and beautiful costumes not to be seen in this world now outside the opera and the picture books. And now and then, in the midst of this flowing tide of splendors appeared a sharply contrasting note—a mounted committee in evening dress—swallow-tails, white kids, and shiny new plug hats; and right in their rear, perhaps, a hundred capering clowns in thunder-and-lightning dress, or a band of silken pages out of ancient times, plumed and capped and daggered, dainty as rainbows, and mincing along in flesh-colored tights; and as handy at it, too, as if they had been born and brought up to it.

At intervals there was a great platform car bethroned and grandly canopied, upholstered in silks, carpeted with Oriental rugs, and freighted with girls clothed in gala costumes. There were several military companies dressed in uniforms of various by-gone periods—among others, one dating back a century and a half, and another of Andreas Hofer's time and region; following this latter was a large company of men and women and girls dressed in the society fashions of a period stretching from the Directory down to about 1840—a thing worth seeing. Among the prettiest and liveliest and most picturesque costumes in the pageant were those worn by regiments and regiments of peasants, from the Tyrol and Bohemia and everywhere in the Empire. They are of ancient origin, but are still worn to-day.

I have seen no procession which evoked more enthusiasm than this one brought out. It would have made any country deliver its emotions, for it was a most stirring sight to see. At the end of this year I shall be sixty-three—if alive—and about the same if dead. I have been looking at processions for sixty years, and, curiously enough, all my really wonderful ones have come in the last three years—one in India in '96, the Queen's Record procession in London last year, and now this one. As an appeal to the imagination—an object-lesson synopsizing the might and majesty and spread of the greatest empire the world has seen—the Queen's procession stands first; as a picture for the eye, this one beats it; and in this regard it even falls no very great way short, perhaps, of the Jeypore pageant—and that was a dream of enchantment.

[*Written 1898. Vienna*

COMMENT ON TAUTOLOGY AND GRAMMAR

May 6. . . . I do not find that the repetition of an important word a few times—say, three or four times—in a paragraph troubles my ear if clearness of meaning is best secured thereby. But tautological repetition which has no justifying object, but merely exposes the fact that the writer's balance at the vocabulary bank has run short and that he is too lazy to replenish it from the thesaurus—that is another matter. It makes me feel like calling the writer to account. It makes me want to remind him that he is not treating himself and his calling with right respect, and, incidentally, that he is not treating me with proper reverence. At breakfast, this morning, a member of the family read aloud an interesting review of a new book about Mr. Gladstone in which the reviewer used the strong adjective "delightful" thirteen times. Thirteen times in a short review, not a long one. In five of the cases the word was distinctly the right one, the exact one, the best one our language can furnish, therefore it made no discord; but in the remaining cases it was out of tune. It sharped or flatted, one or the other, every time, and was as unpleasantly noticeable as is a false note in music. I looked in the thesaurus, and under a single head I found four words which would replace with true notes the false ones uttered by four of the misused "delightfuls"; and of course if I had hunted under related heads for an hour and made an exhaustive search I should have found right words, to a shade, wherewith to replace the remaining delinquents.

I suppose we all have our foibles. I like the exact word, and clarity of statement, and here and there a touch of good grammar for picturesqueness; but that reviewer cares for only the last mentioned of these things. His grammar is foolishly correct, offensively precise. It flaunts itself in the reader's face all along, and struts and smirks and shows off, and is in a dozen ways irritating and disagreeable. To be serious, I write good grammar myself, but not in that spirit, I am thankful to say. That is to say, my grammar is of a high order, though not at the top. Nobody's is. Perfect grammar—persistent, continuous, sustained—is the fourth dimension, so to speak; many have sought it, but none has found it. Even this reviewer, this purist, with all his godless airs, has made two or three slips. At least, I think he has. I am almost sure, by witness of my ear, but cannot be positive, for I know grammar by ear only, not by note, not by the rules. A generation ago I knew the rules—knew them by heart, word for word, though not their meanings —and I still know one of them: the one which says —which says—but never mind, it will come back to me presently. This reviewer even seems to know (or seems even to know, or seems to know even) how to put the word "even" in the right place; and the word "only," too. I do not like that kind of persons. I never knew one of them that came to any good. A person who is as self-righteous as that

will do other things. I know this, because I have
noticed it many a time. I would never hesitate to
injure that kind of a man if I could. When a man
works up his grammar to that altitude, it is a sign.
It shows what he will do if he gets a chance; it shows
the kind of disposition he has; I have noticed it
often. I knew one once that did a lot of things.
They stop at nothing.

But, anyway, this grammatical coxcomb's review
is interesting, as I said before. And there is one
sentence in it which tastes good in the mouth, so
perfectly do the last five of its words report a something which we have all felt after sitting long over
an absorbing book. The matter referred to is Mr.
Gladstone's boswellized conversations and his felicitous handling of his subject.

One facet of the brilliant talker's mind flashes out on
us after another till we tire with interest.

That is clearly stated. We recognize that feeling. In the morning paper I find a sentence of another breed.

There had been no death before the case of Cornelius
Lean which had arisen and terminated in death since the
special rules had been drawn up.

By the context I know what it means, but you are
without that light and will be sure to get out of it
a meaning which the writer of it was not intending
to convey.

[*Written in 1900*

PRIVATE HISTORY OF A MS. THAT CAME TO GRIEF

IT happened in London; not recently, and yet not very many years ago. An acquaintance had proposed to himself a certain labor of love, and when he told me about it I was interested. His idea was to have a fine translation made of the evidence given in the *Joan of Arc Trials and Rehabilitation,* and placed before the English-speaking world. A translation had been made and published a great many years before, but had achieved no currency, and in fact was not entitled to any, for it was a piece of mere shoemaker-work. But we should have the proper thing, now; for this acquaintance of mine was manifestly a Joan enthusiast, and as he had plenty of money and nothing to do but spend it, I took at par his remark that he had employed the most competent person in Great Britain to open this long-neglected mine and confer its riches upon the public. When he asked me to write an Introduction for the book, my pleasure was complete, my vanity satisfied.

At this moment, by good fortune, there chanced to fall into my hands a biographical sketch of me of so just and laudatory a character—particularly as concerned one detail—that it gave my spirit great contentment; and also set my head to swelling—I will not deny it. For it contained praises of the very thing which I most loved to hear praised—*the good quality of my English;* moreover, they were uttered by four English and American literary experts of high authority.

I am as fond of compliments as another, and as hard to satisfy as the average; but these satisfied me. I was as pleased as you would have been if they had been paid to you.

It was under the inspiration of that great several-voiced verdict that I set about that Introduction for Mr. X's book; and I said to myself that I would put a quality of English into it which would establish the righteousness of that judgment. I said I would treat the subject with the reverence and dignity due it; and would use plain, simple English words, and a phrasing undefiled by meretricious artificialities and affectations.

I did the work on those lines; and when it was finished I said to myself very privately . . .

But never mind. I delivered the MS. to Mr. X, and went home to wait for the praises. On the way I met a friend. Being in a happy glow over this pleasant matter, I could not keep my secret. I wanted to tell somebody, and I told him. For a moment he stood curiously measuring me up and down with his eye, without saying anything; then he burst into a rude, coarse laugh, which hurt me very much. He followed this up by saying:

"*He* is going to edit the translations of the *Trials* when it is finished? *He?*"

"He said he would."

"Why, what does he know about editing?"

"I don't know; but that is what he said. Do you think he isn't competent?"

"Competent? He is innocent, vain, ignorant, good-hearted, red-headed, and all that—there isn't a better-meaning man; but he doesn't know anything about literature and has had no literary training or experience; *he* can't edit anything."

"Well, all I know is, he is going to try."

"Indeed he will! He is quite unconscious of his incapacities; he would undertake to edit Shakespeare, if invited—and improve him, too. The world cannot furnish his match for guileless self-complacency; yet I give you my word he doesn't know enough to come in when it rains."

This gentleman's ability to judge was not to be questioned. Therefore, by the time I reached home I had concluded to ask Mr. X not to edit the translation, but to turn that work over to some expert whose name on the title page would be valuable.

Three days later Mr. X brought my Introduction to me, neatly typecopied. He was in a state of considerable enthusiasm, and said:

"Really I find it quite good—quite, I assure you."

There was an airy and patronizing complacency about this damp compliment which affected my head and healthfully checked the swelling which was going on there.

I said, with cold dignity, that I was glad the work had earned his approval.

"Oh, it has, I assure you!" he answered, with large cheerfulness. "I assure you it quite has. I have gone over it very thoroughly, yesterday and

last night and to-day, and I find it quite creditable
—quite.   I have made a few corrections—that is,
suggestions, and——"

"Do you mean to say that you have been ed——"

"Oh, nothing of consequence, nothing of consequence, I assure you," he said, patting me on the
shoulder and genially smiling; "only a few little
things that needed just a mere polishing touch—
nothing of consequence, I assure you.   Let me have
it back as soon as you can, so that I can pass it on
to the printers and let them get to work on it while
I am editing the translation."

I sat idle and alone, a time, thinking grieved
thoughts, with the edited Introduction unopened in
my hand.   I could not look at it yet awhile.   I had
no heart for it, for my pride was deeply wounded.
It was the only time I had been edited in thirty-two
years, except by Mr. Howells, and he did not intrude
his help, but furnished it at my request.   "And now
here is a half-stranger, obscure, destitute of literary
training, destitute of literary experience, destitute
of——"

But I checked myself there; for that way lay
madness.   I must seek calm; for my self-respect's
sake I must not descend to unrefined personalities.
I must keep in mind that this person was innocent
of injurious intent and was honorably trying to do
me a service.   To feel harshly toward him, speak
harshly of him—this was not the right Christian
spirit.   These just thoughts tranquillized me and restored to me my better self, and I opened the Introduction at the middle.

I will not deny it, my feelings rose to 104 in the shade:

"The idea! That this long-eared animal—this literary kangaroo—this illiterate hostler, with his skull full of axle grease—this . . ."

But I stopped there, for this was not the right Christian spirit.

I subjected myself to an hour of calming meditation, then carried the raped Introduction to that friend whom I have mentioned above and showed it to him. He fluttered the leaves over, then broke into another of those ill-bred laughs which are such a mar to him.

"I knew he would!" he said—as if gratified. "Didn't I tell you he would edit Shakespeare?"

"Yes, I know; but I did not suppose he would edit *me*."

"Oh, you didn't! Well, now you see that he is even equal to *that*. I tell you there are simply no bounds to that man's irreverence."

"I realize it, now," I said.

"Well, what are you going to do? Let him put it in his book—either edited or *un*edited?"

"Of course not!"

"That is well. You are becoming rational again. But what are your plans? You are not going to stop where you are, are you? You will write him a letter and give him Hark from the Tomb?"

"No, I shall write him a letter, but not in that spirit, I trust."

"*Why* shan't you?"

"Because he has meant me a kindness, and I

hope I am not the man to reward him for it in that way."

The friend looked me over awhile, pensively, then said——

"Mark, I am ashamed of you. This is mere school-girl sentimentality. You ought to baste him—you know it yourself."

I said I had no such feeling in my heart and should put nothing of the kind in my letter.

"I shall point out his errors to him in gentleness and in the unwounding language of persuasion. Many a literary beginner has been disheartened and defeated by the uncharitable word wantonly uttered; this one shall get none such from me. It is more Christian-like to do a good turn than an ill one, and you ought to encourage me in my attitude, not scoff at it. This man shall not be my enemy; I will make him my lasting and grateful friend."

I felt that I was in the right, and I went home and began the letter and found pleasure and contentment in the labor, for I had the encouragement and support of an approving conscience.

The letter will be found in its proper place in this chapter of my *Autobiography*; it follows:

THE LETTER

Dear Mr. X:

I find on my desk the first two pages of Miss Z's translation, with your emendations marked in them. Thank you for sending them.

I have examined the first page of my amended Introduction and will begin now and jot down some notes upon your corrections. If I find any changes which shall not seem to me to be improvements, I will point out my reasons for thinking so. In this way I may chance to be helpful to you and thus profit you, perhaps, as much as you have desired to profit me.

Notes

Section I. *First Paragraph.* "Jeanne d'Arc." This is rather cheaply pedantic, and is not in very good taste. Joan is not known by that name among plain people of our race and tongue. I notice that the name of the Deity occurs several times in the brief installment of the *Trials* which you have favored me with; to be consistent, it will be necessary that you strike out "God" and put in "Dieu." Do not neglect this.

First line. What is the trouble with *"at the"?* And why *"Trial?"* Has some uninstructed person deceived you into the notion that there was but one, instead of half a dozen?

Amongst. Wasn't *"among"* good enough?

Next half-dozen Corrections. Have you failed to perceive that by taking the word *"both"* out of its proper place you have made foolishness of the sentence? And don't you see that your smug *"of which"* has turned *that* sentence into reporter's English? *"Quite."* Why do you intrude that shopworn favorite of yours where there is nothing useful for it to do? Can't you rest easy in your literary grave without it?

Next sentence. You have made no improvement in it. Did you change it merely to *be* changing something?

Second Paragraph. Now you have begun on my punctuation. Don't you realize that you ought not to intrude your help in a delicate art like that, with your limitations? And do you think you have added just the right smear of polish to the closing clause of the sentence?

Second Paragraph. How do you know it was his "own" sword? It could have been a borrowed one. I am cautious in matters of history, and you should not put statements in my mouth for which you cannot produce vouchers. **Your** other corrections are rubbish.

Third Paragraph. Ditto.

Fourth Paragraph. Your word "directly" is misleading; it could be construed to mean "at once." Plain clarity is better than ornate obscurity. I note your sensitive marginal remark: *"Rather unkind to French feelings—referring to Moscow."* Indeed, I have not been concerning myself about French feelings, but only about stating the facts. I have said several uncourteous things about the French— calling them a "nation of ingrates," in one place—but you have been so busy editing commas and semicolons that you overlooked them and failed to get scared at them. The next paragraph ends with a slur at the French, but I have reasons for thinking you mistook it for a compliment. It is discouraging to try to penetrate a mind like yours. You ought to get it out and dance on it. That would take some of the rigidity out of it. And you ought to use it sometimes; that would help. If you had done this every now and then along through life, it would not have petrified.

Fifth Paragraph. Thus far, I regard this as your master- piece! You are really perfect in the great art of reducing simple and dignified speech to clumsy and vapid common- place.

Sixth Paragraph. You have a singularly fine and aristo- cratic disrespect for homely and unpretending English. Every time I use "go back" you get out your polisher and slick it up to "return." "Return" is suited only to the drawing-room—it is ducal, and says itself with a simper and a smirk.

Seventh Paragraph. "Permission" is ducal. Ducal and affected. "Her" great days were *not* "over"; they were only half over. Didn't you know that? Haven't you read anything at all about Joan of Arc? The truth is, you do not pay any attention; I told you on my very first page that the public part of her career lasted two years, and you have forgotten it already. You really must get your mind out and have it repaired; you see, yourself, that it is all caked together.

Eighth Paragraph. She "rode away *to* assault and capture a stronghold." Very well; but you do not tell us whether she succeeded or not. You should not worry the reader with uncertainties like that. I will remind you once more that clarity is a good thing in literature. An apprentice cannot do better than keep this useful rule in mind. *Closing Sentences.* Corrections which are not corrections.

Ninth Paragraph. "Known" history. That word is a polish which is too delicate for me; there doesn't seem to be any sense in it. This would have surprised me, last week.

Second Sentence. It cost me an hour's study before I found out what it meant. I see, now, that it is intended to mean what it meant before. It really does accomplish its intent, I think, though in a most intricate and slovenly fashion. What was your idea in reframing it? Merely in order that you might add this to your other editorial contributions and be able to say to people that the most of the Introduction was your work? I am afraid that that was really your sly and unparliamentary scheme. Certainly we do seem to live in a very wicked world.

Closing Sentence. There is your empty "however" again. I cannot think what makes you so flatulent.

II. *In Captivity.* "Remainder." It is curious and interesting to notice what an attraction a fussy, mincing, nickel-plated artificial word has for you. This is not well.

Third Sentence. But she *was* held to ransom; it wasn't a case of "should have been" and it wasn't a case of *"if it* had been offered"; it *was* offered, and also accepted, as the second paragraph shows. You ought never to edit except when awake.

Fourth Sentence. Why do you wish to change that? It was more than "demanded"; it was *required.* Have you no sense of shades of meaning in words?

Fifth Sentence. Changing it to "benefactress" takes the dignity out of it. If I had called her a braggart, I suppose you would have polished her into a braggartess, with your curious and random notions about the English tongue.

Closing Sentence. "Sustained" is sufficiently nickel-plated to meet the requirements of your disease, I trust. "Wholly" adds nothing; the sentence means just what it meant before. In the rest of the sentence you sacrifice simplicity to airy fussiness.

Second Paragraph. It was not blood money, unteachable ass, any more than is the money that buys a house or a horse; it was an ordinary business transaction of the time, and was not dishonorable. "With her hands, feet and neck *both* chained," etc. The restricted word "both" cannot be applied to three things, but only to two. *"Fence:"* You "lifted" that word from further along—and with what valuable result? The next sentence—after your doctoring of it—has no meaning. The one succeeding it—after your doctoring of it—refers to nothing, wanders around in space, has no meaning and no reason for existing, and is by a shade or two more demented and twaddlesome than anything hitherto ground out of your strange and interesting editorial mill.

Closing Sentence. "Neither" for "either." Have you now debauched the grammar to your taste?

Third Paragraph. It was sound English before you decayed it. Sell it to the museum.

Fourth Paragraph. I note the compliment you pay yourself, margined opposite the closing sentence: *"Easier trans-*

lation." But it has two defects. In the first place it is a *mis*translation, and in the second place it translates half of the grace out of Joan's remark.

Fifth Paragraph. Why are you so prejudiced against fact and so indecently fond of fiction? Her generalship was *not* "that of a tried and trained military experience," for she hadn't had any, and no one swore that she had had any. I had stated the facts; you should have reserved your fictions.

Note: To be intelligible, that whole paragraph must consist of a single sentence; in breaking it up into several, you have knocked the sense all out of it.

Eighth Paragraph. "When the flames leapt up and enveloped her frail form" is handsome, very handsome, even elegant, but it isn't yours; you hooked it out of "The Costermonger's Bride; or The Fire Fiend's Foe." To take other people's things is not right, and God will punish you. *"Parched"* lips? How do you know they were? Why do you make statements which you cannot verify, when you have no motive for it but to work in a word which you think is nobby?

III. *The Rehabilitation.* "Their statements were taken down *as evidence."* Wonderful! If you had failed to mention that particular, many persons might have thought they were taken down as entertainment.

IV. *The Riddle of All Time.* I note your marginal remark: "Riddle—Anglice?" Look in your spelling book. "We can understand how the genius was created," etc., "by steady and congenial growth." We can't understand anything of the kind; genius is not "created" by any farming process—it is *born.* You are thinking of potatoes. *Note:* Whenever I say "circumstances" you change it to "environment"; and you persistently change my thats into whiches and my whiches into thats. This is merely silly, you know.

Second Paragraph. I note your marginal remark, "2 *comprehends."* I suppose some one has told you that repetition is tautology, and then has left you to believe that repetition is always tautology. But let it go; with your limitations one would not be able to teach you how to distinguish between the repetition which isn't tautology and the repetition which is.

Closing Sentence. Your tipsy emendation, when straightened up on its legs and examined, is found to say this: "We fail to see her issue thus equipped, and we cannot understand why." That is to say, she did *not* issue so equipped, and you cannot make out why she didn't. *That* is the riddle that defeats you, labor at it as you may? Why, if that had happened, it wouldn't be a riddle at all—except to you—but a thing likely to happen to nearly anybody, and not matter for astonishment to any intelligent person standing by at the time—or later. There *is* a riddle, but you have mistaken the nature of it, I cannot tell how, labor at it as I may; and I will try to point it out to you so that you can see some of it. We do *not* fail to see her issue so equipped, we *do* see her. That is the whole marvel, mystery, riddle. That she, an ignorant country girl, sprang upon the world equipped with amazing natural gifts is not the riddle—it could have happened to you if you had been some one else; but the fact that those talents were instantly and effectively usable *without previous training* is the mystery which we cannot master, the riddle which we cannot solve. Do you get it?

Third Paragraph. Drunk.

V. *As Prophet.* "And in *every case* realized the complete fulfillment." How do you know she did that? There is no testimony to back up that wild assertion. I was particular not to claim that all her prophecies came true; for that would have been to claim that we have her whole list, whereas it is likely that she made some that failed and did not get upon the record. People do not record prophecies that failed. Such is not the custom.

VI. *Her Character.* "Comforted" is a good change, and quite sane. But you are not playing fair; you are getting some sane person to help you. *Note:* When I wrote "counselled her, advised her," *that* was tautology; the "2 comprehends" was a case of repetition which was *not* tautological. But I am sure you will never be able to learn the difference. *Note:* "But she, Jeanne d'Arc, when presently she found," etc. That is the funniest yet, and the commonplacest. But it isn't original, you got it out of "How to Write Literary Without Any Apprenticeship," sixpence to the trade; retail, sevenpence farthing. *Erased Passage.* I note with admiration your marginal remark explaining your objection to it: *"Is it warrantable to assert that she bragged? Is it in good taste? It was assuredly foreign to her character."* I will admit that my small effort at playfulness was not much of a pearl; but such as it was, I realize that I threw it into the wrong trough.

VII. *Her Face and Form.* You have misunderstood me again. I did not mean that the artist had several ideas and one prevailing one; I meant that he had only *one* idea. In that same sentence, "omits" and "forgets" have just the same meaning; have you any clear idea, then, why you made the change? Is it your notion that "gross" is an improvement on "big," "perform" an improvement on "do," "inquiring" an improvement on "asking," and "in such wise" an improvement on "then," or have you merely been seduced by the fine, large sounds of those words? Are you incurably hostile to simplicity of speech? And finally, do you not see that you have edited all the dignity out of the paragraph and substituted simpering commonplace for it, and that your addition at the end is a deliciously flat and funny anticlimax? Still, I note your command in the margin, *"Insert this remark,"* and I dutifully obey.

Second Paragraph. "Exploited" was worth a shilling, there; you have traded it for a word not worth tuppence ha'-penny, and got cheated, and serves you right. Read "rightly," if it shocks you.

Close of Paragraph. You have exploited another anti-climax—and in the form, too, of an impudent advertisement of your book. It seems to me that for a person of your elegance of language you are curiously lacking in certain other delicacies.

Third Paragraph. I must reserve my thanks. "Moreover" is a parenthesis, when interjected in that fashion; a parenthesis is evidence that the man who uses it does not know how to write English or is too indolent to take the trouble to do it; a parenthesis usually throws the emphasis upon the wrong word, and has done it in this instance; a man who will wantonly use a parenthesis will steal. For these reasons I am unfriendly to the parenthesis. When a man puts one into my mouth his life is no longer safe. "Break another lance" is a knightly and sumptuous phrase, and I honor it for its hoary age and for the faithful service it has done in the prize-composition of the schoolgirl, but I have ceased from employing it since I got my puberty, and must solemnly object to fathering it here. And besides, it makes me hint that I have broken one of those things before, in honor of the Maid, an intimation not justified by the facts. I did not break any lances or other furniture, I only wrote a book about her.

Truly yours,

MARK TWAIN.

It cost me something to restrain myself and say these smooth and half-flattering things to this immeasurable idiot, but I did it and have never regretted it. For it is higher and nobler to be kind to

even a shad like him than just. If we should deal
out justice only, in this world, who would escape?
No, it is better to be generous, and in the end more
profitable, for it gains gratitude for us, and love,
and it is far better to have the love of a literary
strumpet like this than the reproaches of his
wounded spirit. Therefore I am glad I said no
harsh things to him, but spared him, the same as I
would a tapeworm. It is reward enough for me
to know that my children will be proud of their
father for this, when I am gone. I could have said
hundreds of unpleasant things about this tadpole,
but I did not even feel them.[1]

---

[1] The letter was not sent, after all. The temptation was strong,
but pity for the victim prevailed. The MS. was, however, re-
called and later published in *Harper's Magazine* and in book
form as *St. Joan of Arc*.

CHAPTERS ADDED IN FLORENCE

— 1904 —

AUTHOR'S NOTE

FINALLY in Florence, in 1904, I hit upon the right way to do an Autobiography: Start it at no particular time of your life; wander at your free will all over your life; talk only about the thing which interests you for the moment; drop it the moment its interest threatens to pale, and turn your talk upon the new and more interesting thing that has intruded itself into your mind meantime.

Also, make the narrative a combined Diary *and* Autobiography. In this way you have the vivid thing of the present to make a contrast with memories of like things in the past, and these contrasts have a charm which is all their own. No talent is required to make a Combined Diary and Autobiography interesting.

And so, I have found the right plan. It makes my labor amusement—mere amusement, play, pastime, and wholly effortless.[1]

---

[1] [The reader will realize, even if the author did not, that this had been his plan from the beginning.]

[Florence, January, 1904

VILLA QUARTO

THIS villa is situated three or four miles from
Florence, and has several names. Some call it the
Villa Reale di Quarto, some call it the Villa Principessa, some call it the Villa Granduchessa; this
multiplicity of names was an inconvenience to me
for the first two or three weeks, for as I had heard
the place called by only one name, when letters
came for the servants directed to the care of one
or the other of the other names, I supposed a mistake had been made and remailed them. It has been
explained to me that there is reason for these several
names. Its name Quarto it gets from the district
which it is in, it being in the four-mile radius from
the center of Florence. It is called Reale because
the King of Würtemberg occupied it at one time;
Principessa and Granduchessa because a Russian
daughter of the Imperial house occupied it at another. There is a history of the house somewhere,
and some time or other I shall get it and see if
there are any details in it which could be of use
in this chapter. I should like to see that book, for
as an evolutionist I should like to know the beginning
of this dwelling and the several stages of its evolu-
tion. Baedeker says it was built by Cosimo I, as-
sisted by an architect. I have learned this within
the past three minutes, and it wrecks my development scheme. I was surmising that the house began
in a small and humble way, and was the production

of a poor farmer whose idea of home and comfort
it was; that following him a generation or two later
came a successor of better rank and larger means
who built an addition; that successor after successor
added more bricks and more bulk as time dragged
on, each in his turn leaving a detail behind him
of paint or wallpaper to distinguish his reign from
the others; that finally in the last century came the
three that precede me, and added their specialties.
The King of Würtemberg broke out room enough
in the center of the building—about a hundred feet
from each end of it—to put in the great staircase,
a cheap and showy affair, almost the only wooden
thing in the whole edifice, and as comfortable and
sane and satisfactory as it is out of character with
the rest of the asylum. The Russian princess, who
came with native superstitions about cold weather,
added the hot-air furnaces in the cellar and the vast
green majolica stove in the great hall where the
king's staircase is—a stove which I thought might
possibly be a church—a nursery church for children,
so imposing is it for size and so richly adorned
with basso relievos of an ultra-pious sort. It is
loaded and fired from a secret place behind the
partition against which it is backed. Last of all
came Satan also, the present owner of the house,
an American product, who added a cheap and stingy
arrangement of electric bells, inadequate acetylene
gas plant, obsolete waterclosets, perhaps a dozen
pieces of machine-made boarding-house furniture,
and some fire-auction carpets which blaspheme the

standards of color and art all day long, and never quiet down until the darkness comes and pacifies them.

However, if the house was built for Cosimo four hundred years ago and with an architect on deck, I suppose I must dismiss those notions about the gradual growth of the house in bulk. Cosimo would want a large house, he would want to build it himself so that he could have it just the way he wanted it. I think he had his will. In the architecture of this barrack there has been no development. There was no architecture in the first place and none has been added, except the king's meretricious staircase, the princess's ecclesiastical stove, and the obsolete water-closets. I am speaking of art-architecture; there is none.

There is no more architecture of that breed discoverable in this long stretch of ugly and ornamentless three-storied house front than there is about a rope walk or a bowling alley. The shape and proportions of the house suggest those things, it being two hundred feet long by sixty wide. There is no art-architecture inside the house, there is none outside.

We arrive now at practical architecture—the useful, the indispensable, which plans the inside of a house and by wisely placing and distributing the rooms, or by studiedly and ineffectually distributing them, makes the house a convenient and comfortable and satisfactory abiding place or the reverse. The inside of the house is evidence that Cosimo's architect was not in his right mind. And it seems to me that it is not fair and not kind in Baedeker to keep on exposing him and his crime down to this late date. I am nobler than Baedeker, and more humane, and I suppress it. I don't remember what it was, anyway.

I shall go into the details of this house, not because I imagine it differs much from any other old-time palace or new-time palace on the continent of Europe, but because every one of its crazy details interests me, and therefore may be expected to interest others of the human race, particularly women. When they read novels they usually skip the weather, but I have noticed that they read with avidity all that a writer says about the furnishings, decorations, conveniences, and general style of a home.

The interior of this barrack is so chopped up and systemless that one cannot deal in exact numbers when trying to put its choppings-up into statistics.

In the basement or cellar there are as follows:

Stalls and boxes for many horses—right under the principal bedchamber. The horses noisily dance to the solicitations of the multitudinous flies all night.

Feed stores.

Carriage house.

Acetylene-gas plant.

A vast kitchen. Put out of use years ago.

Another kitchen.

Coal rooms.

Coke rooms.

Peat rooms.

Wood rooms.

3 furnaces.

Wine rooms.

Various storerooms for all sorts of domestic supplies.

Lot of vacant and unclassified rooms.

Labyrinth of corridors and passages, affording the stranger an absolute certainty of getting lost.

A vast cesspool! It is cleaned out every thirty years.

Couple of dark stairways leading up to the ground floor.

About twenty divisions, as I count them.

This cellar seems to be of the full dimension of the house's foundation—say two hundred feet by sixty.

The ground floor, where I am dictating—is cut up into twenty-three rooms, halls, corridors, and so forth. The next floor above contains eighteen divisions of the like sort, one of which is the billiard room and another the great drawing-room.

The top story consists of twenty bedrooms and a furnace. Large rooms they necessarily are, for they are arranged ten on a side, and they occupy that whole space of two hundred feet long by sixty wide, except that there is a liberal passage, or hallway, between them. There are good fireplaces up there, and they would make charming bedchambers if handsomely and comfortably furnished and decorated. But there would need to be a lift—not a European lift, with its mere stand-up space and its imperceptible movement, but a roomy and swift American one.

These rooms are reached now by the same process by which they were reached in Cosimo's time—by leg power. Their brick floors are bare and unpainted, their walls are bare and painted the favorite European color, which is now and always has been an odious stomach-turning yellow. It is said that these rooms were intended for servants only and that they were meant to accommodate two or three servants apiece. It seems certain that they have not been occupied by any but servants in the last fifty or one hundred years, otherwise they would exhibit some remains of decoration.

If, then, they have always been for the use of servants only, where did Cosimo and his family sleep? Where did the King of Würtemberg bestow his dear ones? For below that floor there are not any more than three good bedchambers and five devilish ones. With eighty cut-ups in the house and with but four persons in my family, this large fact is provable: that we can't invite a friend to come and stay a few days with us, because there is not a bedroom unoccupied by ourselves that we could offer him without apologies. In fact, we have no friend whom we love so little and respect so moderately as to be willing to stuff him into one of those vacant cells.

Yes—where did the vanished aristocracy sleep? I mean the real aristocracy, not the American successor who required no room to speak of. To go

on with my details: this little room where I am
dictating these informations on this eighth day of
January, 1904, is on the east side of the house.
It is level with the ground and one may step from
its nine- or ten-feet-high vast door into the terrace
garden, which is a great, square, level space sur-
rounded by an ornamental iron railing with vases of
flowers distributed here and there along its top. It
is a pretty terrace with abundant green grass, with
handsome trees, with a great fountain in the middle,
and with roses of various tints nodding in the balmy
air and flashing back the rays of the January sun.
Beyond the railing to the eastward stretches the
private park, and through its trees curves the road
to the far-off iron gate on the public road, where
there is neither porter nor porter's lodge nor any way
to communicate with the mansion. Yet from time
immemorial the Italian villa has been a fortress
hermetically sealed up in high walls of masonry and
with entrance guarded by locked iron gates. The
gates of Italy have always been locked at nightfall
and kept locked the night through. No Italian
trusted his contadini neighbors in the old times, and
his successor does not trust them now. There are
bells and porters for the convenience of outsiders
desiring to get in at other villas, but it is not the
case with this one, and apparently never has been.
Surely it must have happened now and then that
these kings and nobilities got caught out after the
gates were locked. Then how did they get in? We
shall never know. The question cannot be answered.
It must take its place with the other unsolved mys-

tery of where the aristocracies slept during those centuries when they occupied this fortress.

To return to that glass door. Outside it are exceedingly heavy and coarse Venetian shutters, a fairly good defense against a catapult.

These, like the leaves of the glass door, swing open in the French fashion, and I will remark in passing that to my mind the French window is as rational and convenient as the English-American window is the reverse of this. Inside the glass door (three or four inches inside of it) are solid doors made of boards, good and strong and ugly. The shutters, the glass door, and these wooden-door defenses against intrusion of light and thieves are all armed with strong and heavy bolts which are shot up and down by the turning of a handle. These house walls being very thick, these doors and shutters and things do not crowd one another, there is plenty of space between them, and there is room for more in case we should get to feeling afraid. This shuttered glass door, this convenient exit to the terrace and garden, is not the only one on this side of the house from which one can as handily step upon the terrace. There is a procession of them stretching along, door after door, along the east, or rear, front of the house, from its southern end to its northern end—eleven in the procession. Beginning at the south end they afford exit from a parlor; a large bedroom (mine); this little twelve-by-twenty reception room where I am now at work; and a ten-by-twelve ditto, which is in effect the beginning of a corridor forty feet long by twelve

wide, with three sets of triple glass doors for exit
to the terrace. The corridor empties into a dining
room, and the dining room into two large rooms
beyond, all with glass-door exits to the terrace.
When the doors which connect these seven rooms
and the corridor are thrown open the two-hundred-
foot stretch of variegated carpeting with its warring
and shouting and blaspheming tumult of color makes
a fine and almost contenting, receding, and diminish-
ing perspective, and one realizes that if some sane
person could have the privilege and the opportunity
of burning the existing carpets and instituting har-
monies of color in their place, the reformed perspective would be very beautiful. Above each of the
eleven glass doors is a duplicate on the next floor—
ten feet by six, of glass. And above each of these
on the topmost floor is a smaller window—thirty-
three good openings for light on this eastern front,
the same on the western front, and nine of ampler
size on each end of the house. Fifty-six of these
eighty-four windows contain double enough glass to
equip the average window of an American dwelling,
yet the house is by no means correspondingly light.
I do not know why; perhaps it is because of the
dismal upholstering of the walls.

Villa di Quarto is a palace; Cosimo built it for
that, his architect intended it for that, it has always
been regarded as a palace, and an old resident of
Florence told me the other day that it was a good
average sample of the Italian palace of the great
nobility, and that its grotesqueness and barbarities,
incongruities and destitution of conveniences, are to

be found in the rest. I am able to believe this because I have seen some of the others.

I think there is not a room in this huge confusion
of rooms and halls and corridors and cells and
waste spaces which does not contain some memento
of each of its illustrious occupants, or at least two
or three of them.

We will examine the parlor at the head of that
long perspective which I have been describing. The
arched ceiling is beautiful both in shape and in decoration. It is finely and elaborately frescoed. The
ceiling is a memento of Cosimo. The doors are
draped with heavy pale-blue silk, faintly figured;
that is the King of Würtemberg relic. The gleam-
ing-white brass-banded porcelain pagoda which contains an open fireplace for wood is a relic of the
Russian princess and a remembrancer of her native
experiences of cold weather. The light-gray wallpaper figured with gold flowers is anybody's—we
care not to guess its pedigree. The rest of the room
is manifestly a result of the present occupation.
The floor is covered with a felt-like filling of strenuous red; one can almost see Pharaoh's host floun-
dering in it. There are four rugs scattered about
like islands, violent rugs whose colors swear at one
another and at the Red Sea. There is a sofa upholstered in a coarse material, a frenzy of green
and blue and blood, a cheap and undeceptive imitation of Florentine embroidery. There is a sofa
and two chairs upholstered in pale-green silk, figured;
the wood is of three different breeds of American
walnut, flimsy, cheap, machine-made. There is a

French-walnut sofa upholstered in figured silk of a
fiendish crushed-strawberry tint of a faded aspect,
and there is an armchair which is a mate to it.
There is a plain and naked black-walnut table without a cover to modify its nudity; under it is a large
round ottoman covered with the palest of pale-green
silk, a sort of glorified mushroom which curses with
all its might at the Red Sea and the furious rugs
and the crushed-strawberry relics. Against the wall
stands a tall glass-fronted bookcase, machine-made
—the material, American butternut. It stands near
enough to the King of Würtemberg's heavy silken
door-drapery to powerfully accent its cheapness and
ugliness by contrast. Upon the walls hang three
good water-colors, six or eight very bad ones, a
pious-looking portrait, and a number of photographs, one of them a picture of a count, who has
a manly and intelligent face and looks like a gentleman.

The whole literature of this vast house is contained in that fire-auction American bookcase.
There are four shelves. The top one is made up of
indiscriminate literature of good quality; the next
shelf is made up of cloth-covered books devoted to
Christian Science and spiritualism—forty thin books;
the two remaining shelves contain fifty-four bound
volumes of Blackwood, in date running backward
from about 1870. This bookcase and its contents
were probably imported from America.

The room just described must be dignified with
that imposing title, library, on account of the presence in it of that butternut bookcase and its indigent

contents. It does duty, now, as a private parlor
for Mrs. Clemens during those brief and widely separated occasions when she is permitted to leave for
an hour the bed to which she has been so long
condemned. We are in the extreme south end of the
house, if there is any such thing as a south end to
a house, where orientation cannot be determined
by me, because I am incompetent in all cases where
an object does not point directly north or south.
This one slants across between, and is therefore a
confusion to me. This little private parlor is in
one of the two corners of what I call the south
end of the house. The sun rises in such a way that
all the morning it is pouring its light in through
the thirty-three glass doors or windows which pierce
the side of the house which looks upon the terrace
and garden, as already described; the rest of the
day the light floods this south end of the house;
as I call it; at noon the sun is directly above Florence
yonder in the distance in the plain—directly above
those architectural features which have been so familiar to the world in pictures for some centuries:
the Duomo, the Campanile, the Tomb of the Medici,
and the beautiful tower of the Palazzo Vecchio;
above Florence, but not very high above it, for it
never climbs quite halfway to the zenith in these
winter days; in this position it begins to reveal the
secrets of the delicious blue mountains that circle
around into the west, for its light discovers, un-
covers, and exposes a white snowstorm of villas and
cities that you cannot train yourself to have confidence in, they appear and disappear so mysteriously

and so as if they might be not villas and cities at all, but the ghosts of perished ones of the remote and dim Etruscan times; and late in the afternoon the sun sinks down behind those mountains somewhere, at no particular time and at no particular place, so far as I can see.

This "library," or boudoir, or private parlor, opens into Mrs. Clemens's bedroom, and it and the bedroom together stretch all the way across the south end of the house. The bedroom gets the sun before noon, and is prodigally drenched and deluged with it the rest of the day. One of its windows is particularly well calculated to let in a liberal supply of sunshine, for it contains twelve great panes, each of them more than two feet square. The bedroom is thirty-one feet long by twenty-four wide, and there had been a time when it and the "library" had no partition between, but occupied the whole breadth of the south end of the house in an unbroken stretch. It must have been a ballroom or banqueting room at that time. I suggest this merely because perhaps not even Cosimo would need so much bedroom, whereas it would do very well indeed as a banqueting room because of its proximity to the cooking arrangements, which were not more than two or three hundred yards away, down cellar, a very eligible condition of things indeed in the old times. Monarchs cannot have the conveniences which we plebeians are privileged to luxuriate in—they can't, even to-day. If I were invited to spend a week in Windsor Castle it would gladden me and make me feel proud; but if there was any hint about regular

boarders I should let on that I didn't hear. As a
palace Windsor Castle is great; great for show, spa-
ciousness, display, grandeur, and all that; but the
bedrooms are small, uninviting, and inconvenient,
and the arrangements for delivering food from the
kitchen to the table are so clumsy and waste so much
time, that a meal there probably suggests recent cold
storage. This is only conjecture; I did not eat there.
In Windsor Castle the courses are brought up by
dumb waiter from the profound depth where the
vast kitchen is; they are then transferred by rail on a
narrow little tramway to the territory where the
dinner is to have place. This trolley was still being
worked by hand when I was there four years ago;
still it was without doubt a great advance upon
Windsor Castle transportation of any age before
Queen Victoria's. It is startling to reflect that what
we call convenience in a dwelling house, and which
we regard as necessities, were born so recently that
hardly one of them existed in the world when Queen
Victoria was born. The valuable part—to *my* thinking the valuable part—of what we call civilization
had no existence when she emerged upon the planet.
She sat in her chair in that venerable fortress and
saw it grow from its mustard seed to the stupendous
tree which it had become before she died. She saw
the whole of the new creation, she saw everything
that was made, and without her witness was not
anything made that was made. A very creditable
creation indeed, taking all things into account; since
man, quite unassisted, did it all out of his own head.
I jump to this conclusion because I think that if

Providence had been minded to help him, it would have occurred to Providence to do this some hundred thousand centuries earlier. We are accustomed to seeing the hand of Providence in everything. Accustomed, because if we missed it, or thought we missed it, we had discretion enough not to let on. We are a tactful race. We have been prompt to give Providence the credit of this fine and showy new civilization and we have been quite intemperate in our praises of this great benefaction; we have not been able to keep still over this splendid five-minute attention; we can only keep still about the ages of neglect which preceded it and which it makes so conspicuous. When Providence washes one of his worms into the sea in a tempest, then starves him and freezes him on a plank for thirty-four days, and finally wrecks him again on an uninhabited island, where he lives on shrimps and grasshoppers and other shell-fish for three months, and is at last rescued by some old whisky-soaked, profane, and blasphemous infidel of a tramp captain, and carried home gratis to his friends, the worm forgets that it was Providence that washed him overboard, and only remembers that Providence rescued him. He finds no fault, he has no sarcasms for Providence's crude and slow and labored ingenuities of invention in the matter of life-saving, he sees nothing in these delays and ineffectiveness but food for admiration; to him they seem a marvel, a miracle; and the longer they take and the more ineffective they are, the greater the miracle; meantime he never allows himself to break out in any good hearty unhandicapped thanks for the tough old shipmaster who really saved him, he damns him with faint praise as "the instrument," his rescuer "under Providence."

VILLA QUARTO (*Continued*)

To get to that corner room with its bookcase freighted with twenty dollars' worth of ancient Blackwood and modern spiritualistic literature, I have passed through—undescribed—a room that is my bedroom. Its size is good, its shape is good—thirty feet by twenty-two. Originally it was fifty feet long, stretching from one side of the house to the other, in the true Italian fashion which makes everybody's bedroom a passageway into the next room—kings, nobles, serfs, and all; but this American countess, the present owner, cut off twenty feet of the room and reattached ten feet of it to the room as a bathroom, and devoted the rest to a hallway. This bedroom is lighted by one of those tall glass doors, already described, which give upon the terrace. It is divided across the middle by some polished white pillars as big as my body, with Doric capitals, supporting a small arch at each end and a long one in the middle; this is indeed grandeur and is quite imposing. The fireplace is of a good size, is of white marble, and the carvings upon it are of the dainty and graceful sort proper to its age, which is probably four hundred years. The fireplace and the stately columns are aristocratic, they recognize their kinship, and they smile at each other. That is, when they are not swearing at the rest of the room's belongings. The front half of the room is aglare with a paper loud of pattern, atrocious in color, and cheap beyond the dreams of avarice. The rear half is painted from floor to ceiling a dull, dead and repulsive yellow. It seems strange that yellow should be the favorite in Europe whereby to undecorate a wall; I have never seen the yellow wall which did not depress me and make me unhappy. The floor of the room is covered with a superannuated nightmare of a carpet whose figures are vast and riotous and whose indignant reds and blacks and yellows quarrel day and night and refuse to be reconciled. There is a door opening into the bathroom, and at that same end of the room is a door opening into a small box of a hall which leads to another convenience. Those two doors strictly follow the law of European dwellings, whether built for the prince or for the pauper. That is to say they are rude, thin, cheap planks, flimsy; the sort of door which in the South the negro attaches to his chicken coop. These doors, like all such doors on the Continent, have a gimlet handle in place of a door knob. It wrenches from the socket a bolt which has no springs and which will not return to that socket except upon compulsion. You can't slam a door like that; it would simply rebound. That gimlet handle catches on any garment that tries to get by; if tearable it tears it; if not tearable it stops the wearer with a suddenness and a violence and an unexpectedness which break down all his religious reserves, no matter who he may be.

The bedroom has a door on each side of the front end, so that anybody may tramp through that wants to at any time of the day or night, this being the only way to get to the room beyond, where the precious library is bookcased. Furniture: a salmon-colored silk sofa, a salmon-colored silk chair, a pair of ordinary wooden chairs, and a stuffed chair whose upholstery is of a species unknown to me but devilish; in the corner, an ordinary thin-legged kitchen table; against one wall a wardrobe and a dressing bureau; on the opposite side a rickety chest of drawers made of white pine painted black and ornamented with imitation brass handles; brass double bedstead. One will concede that this room is not over-embarrassed with furniture. The two clapboard doors already spoken of are mercifully concealed by parti-colored hangings of unknown country and origin; the three other doors already mentioned are hooded with long curtains that descend to the floor and are caught apart in the middle to permit the passage of people and light. These curtains have a proud and ostentatious look which deceives no one, it being based upon a hybrid silk with cotton for its chief ingredient. The color is a solid yellow, and deeper than the yellow of the rearward half of the walls; and now here is a curious thing: one may look from one of these colors to the other fifty times, and each time he will think that the one he is looking at is the ugliest. It is a most curious and interesting effect. I think that if one could get himself toned down to where he could look upon these curtains without passion he would then perceive that it takes both of them together to be the ugliest color known to art.

We have considered these two yellows, but they do not exhaust the matter; there is still another one in the room. This is a lofty and sumptuous canopy over the brass bedstead, made of brilliant and shiny and shouting lemon-colored satin—genuine satin, almost the only genuine thing in the whole room. It is of the nobility, it is of the aristocracy, it belongs with the majestic white pillars and the dainty old marble fireplace; all the rest of the room's belongings are profoundly plebeian, they are exiles, they are sorrowful outcasts from their rightful home, which is the poorhouse.

On the end wall of the yellow half of the room hang a couple of framed engravings, female angels engaged in their customary traffic of transporting departed persons to heaven over a distant prospect of city and plain and mountain.

The discords of this room, in colors, in humble poverty and showy and self-complacent pretentiousness, are repeated everywhere one goes in the huge house.

I am weary of particulars. One may travel two hundred feet down either side of the house, through an aimless jumble of useless little reception rooms and showy corridors, finding nothing sane or home-like till he reaches the dining room at the end.

On the next floor, over the Blackwood library, there is a good bedroom well furnished, and with a fine stone balcony and the majestic view, just mentioned, enlarged and improved, thence northward two hundred feet, cut up in much the same disarray as is that ground floor. But in the midst is a great drawing-room about forty feet square and perhaps as many high, handsomely and tastefully hung with brocaded silk and with a very beautifully frescoed ceiling. But the place has a most angry look, for scattered all about it are divans and sofas and chairs and lofty window hangings of that same fierce lemon-colored satin heretofore noted as forming the canopy of the brass bedstead downstairs. When one steps suddenly into that great place on a splendid Florentine day it is like entering hell on a Sunday morning when the brightest and yellowest brimstone fires are going.

I think I have said that the top floor has twenty rooms. They are not furnished, they are spacious, and from all of them one has a wide and charming view. Properly furnished they would be pleasant, homelike, and in every way satisfactory.

End of March. Now that we have lived in this house four and one-half months, my prejudices have fallen away one by one and the place has become very homelike to me. Under certain conditions I should like to go on living in it indefinitely. Indeed, I could reduce the conditions to two and be quite satisfied. I should wish the owner to move out of Italy; out of Europe; out of the planet.

I realize that there is no way of realizing this and so after two and a half months I have given it up and have been house hunting ever since. House hunting in any country is difficult and depressing; in the regions skirting Florence it leads to despair, and if persisted in will end in suicide. Professor Willard Fiske, the scholar, who bought the Walter

Savage Landor villa fourteen or fifteen years ago,
tells me that he examined three hundred villas before
he found one that would suit him; yet he was a
widower without child or dependent and merely
needed a villa for his lone self. I was in it twelve
years ago and it seemed to me that he had not
bought a villa, but only a privilege—the privilege
of building it over again and making it humanly
habitable. During the first three weeks of February
I climbed around over and prowled through an
average of six large villas a week, but found none
that would answer, in the circumstances. One of the
circumstances, and the most important of all, being
that we are in Italy by the command of physicians
in the hope that in this mild climate Mrs. Clemens
will get her health back. She suddenly lost it nineteen months ago, being smitten helpless by nervous
prostration complicated with an affection of the
heart of several years' standing, and the times since
this collapse that she has been able to stand on her
feet five minutes at a time have been exceedingly
rare. I have examined two villas that were about
as large as this one, but the interior architecture was
so ill contrived that there was not comfortable room
in them for my family of four persons. As a rule
the bedchambers served as common hallways, which
means that for centuries Tom, Dick, and Harry of
both sexes and all ages have moved in procession
to and fro through those ostensibly private rooms.

Every villa I examined had a number of the details which I was ordered to find; four possessed
almost every one of them. In the case of the four

the altitudes were not satisfactory to the doctors; two of them were too high, the other pair too low. These fifteen or twenty villas were all furnished. The reader of these notes will find that word in the dictionary, and it will be defined there; but that definition can have no value to a person who is desiring to know what the word means over here when it is attached to an advertisement proposing to let a dwelling house. Here it means a meager and scattering array of cheap and rickety chairs, tables, sofas, etc., upholstered in worn and damaged fragments of somber and melancholy hue that suggest the grave and compel the desire to retire to it. The average villa is properly a hospital for ailing and superannuated furniture. In its best days this furniture was never good nor comely nor attractive nor comfortable. When that best day was, was too long ago for anyone to be able to date it now.

Each time that I have returned from one of these quests I have been obliged to concede that the insurrection of color in this Villa di Quarto is a rest to the eye after what I had been sighing and sorrowing over in those others, and that this is the only villa in the market so far as I know that has furniture enough in it for the needs of the occupants. Also I will concede that I was wrong in thinking this villa poverty-stricken in the matter of conveniences; for by contrast with those others this house is rich in conveniences.

Some time ago a lady told me that she had just returned from a visit to the country palace of a princess, a huge building standing in the midst of a great and beautiful and carefully kept flower garden, the garden in its turn being situated in a great and beautiful private park. She was received by a splendid apparition of the footman species, who ushered her into a lofty and spacious hall richly garnished with statuary, pictures, and other ornaments, fine and costly, and thence down an immensely long corridor which shone with a similar garniture, superb and showy to the last degree; and at the end of this enchanting journey she was delivered into the princess's bedchamber and received by the princess, who was ailing slightly and in bed. The room was very small, it was without bric-à-brac or prettinesses for the comfort of the eye and spirit, the bedstead was iron, there were two wooden chairs and a small table, and in the corner stood an iron tripod which supported a common white washbowl. The costly glories of the house were all for show; no money had been wasted on its mistress's comfort. I had my doubts about this story when I first acquired it; I am more credulous now.

A word or two more concerning the furnishings of the Villa di Quarto. The rooms contain an average of four pictures each, say two photographs or engravings and two oil- or water-color paintings of chromo degree.

High up on the walls of the great entrance hall hang several of those little shiny white cherubs which one associates with the name of Della Robbia. The walls of this hall are further decorated, or at least relieved, by the usual great frameless oval oil portraits of long-departed aristocrats which one custom-

arily finds thus displayed in all Florentine villas.
In the present case the portraits were painted by
artists of chromo rank, with the exception of one.
As I have had no teaching in art, I cannot decide
what is a good picture and what isn't, according to
the established standards; I am obliged to depend on
my own crude standards. According to these the picture which I am now considering sets forth a most
noble, grave, and beautiful face, faultless in all details and with beautiful and faultless hands; and if it
belonged to me I would never take a lesson in art lest
the picture lose for me its finished, complete, and
satisfying perfection.

　　.　　　.　　　.　　　.　　　.　　　.　　　.

We have lived in a Florentine villa before. This
was twelve years ago. This was the Villa Viviani,
and was pleasantly and commandingly situated on a
hill in the suburb of Settignano, overlooking Florence and the great valley. It was secured for us and
put in comfortable order by a good friend, Mrs.
Ross, whose stately castle was a twelve minutes'
walk away. She still lives there, and had been a
help to us more than once since we established relations with the titled owner of the Villa di Quarto.
The year spent in the Villa Viviani was something of
a contrast to the five months which we have now
spent in this ducal barrack. Among my old manu-
scripts and random and spasmodic diaries I find
some account of that pleasantly remembered year,
and will make some extracts from the same and
introduce them here.

When we were passing through Florence in the

spring of '92 on our way to Germany, the diseased-world's bathhouse, we began negotiations for a villa, and friends of ours completed them after we were gone. When we got back three or four months later, everything was ready, even to the servants and the dinner. It takes but a sentence to state that, but it makes an indolent person tired to think of the planning and work and trouble that lie concealed in it. For it is less trouble and more satisfaction to bury two families than to select and equip a home for one.

The situation of the villa was perfect. It was three miles from Florence, on the side of a hill. The flowery terrace on which it stood looked down upon sloping olive groves and vineyards; to the right, beyond some hill spurs, was Fiesole, perched upon its steep terraces; in the immediate foreground was the imposing mass of the Ross castle, its walls and turrets rich with the mellow weather stains of forgotten centuries; in the distant plain lay Florence, pink and gray and brown, with the rusty huge dome of the cathedral dominating its center like a captive balloon, and flanked on the right by the smaller bulb of the Medici chapel and on the left by the airy tower of the Palazzo Vecchio; all around the horizon was a billowy rim of lofty blue hills, snowed white with innumerable villas. After nine months of familiarity with this panorama, I still think, as I thought in the beginning, that this is the fairest picture on our planet, the most enchanting to look upon, the most satisfying to the eye and the spirit. To see the sun sink down, drowned on his pink and

purple and golden floods, and overwhelm Florence
with tides of color that make all the sharp lines
dim and faint and turn the solid city to a city of
dreams, is a sight to stir the coldest nature and
make a sympathetic one drunk with ecstasy.

Sept. 26, '92.—Arrived in Florence. Got my head
shaved. This was a mistake. Moved to the villa
in the afternoon. Some of the trunks brought up
in the evening by the contadino—if that is his title.
He is the man who lives on the farm and takes
care of it for the owner, the marquis. The contadino
is middle-aged and like the rest of the peasants—
that is to say, brown, handsome, good-natured, courteous, and entirely independent without making any
offensive show of it. He charged too much for the
trunks, I was told. My informant explained that
this was customary.

Sept. 27.—The rest of the trunks brought up this
morning. He charged too much again, but I was
told that this also was customary. It is all right,
then. I do not wish to violate the customs. Hired
landau, horses, and coachman. Terms, four hundred
and eighty francs a month and a *pourboire* to the
coachman, I to furnish lodging for the man and
the horses, but nothing else. The landau has seen
better days and weighs thirty tons. The horses are
feeble and object to the landau; they stop and turn
around every now and then and examine it with
surprise and suspicion. This causes delay. But it
entertains the people along the road. They came
out and stood around with their hands in their
pockets and discussed the matter with one another.

I was told they said that a forty-ton landau was not the thing for horses like those—what they needed was a wheelbarrow.

I will insert in this place some notes made in October concerning the villa:

This is a two-story house. It is not an old house —from an Italian standpoint, I mean. No doubt there has always been a nice dwelling on this eligible spot since a thousand years B.C., but this present one is said to be only two hundred years old. Outside, it is a plain square building like a box, and is painted a light yellow and has green window shutters. It stands in a commanding position on an artificial terrace of liberal dimensions which is walled around with strong masonry. From the walls the vineyards and olive orchards of the estate slant away toward the valley; the garden about the house is stocked with flowers and a convention of lemon bushes in great crockery tubs; there are several tall trees— stately stone pines—also fig trees and trees of breeds not familiar to me; roses overflow the retaining walls and the battered and mossy stone urns on the gateposts in pink and yellow cataracts, exactly as they do on the drop curtains of theaters; there are gravel walks shut in by tall laurel hedges. A back corner of the terrace is occupied by a dense grove of old ilex trees. There is a stone table in there, with stone benches around it. No shaft of sunlight can penetrate that grove. It is always deep twilight in there, even when all outside is flooded with the intense sun glare common to this region. The carriage road leads from the inner gate eight hundred feet to the public road, through the vineyard, and there one may take the horse car for the city, and will find it a swifter and handier convenience than a sixty-ton landau. On the east (or maybe it is the south) front of the house is the Viviani coat of arms in plaster, and near it a sun dial which keeps very good time.

The house is a very fortress for strength. The main walls—of brick covered with plaster—are about three feet thick; the partitions of the rooms, also of brick, are nearly the same thickness. The ceilings of the rooms on the ground floor are more than twenty feet high; those of the upper floors are also higher than necessary. I have several times tried to count the rooms in the house, but the irregularities baffle me. There seem to be twenty-eight.

The ceilings are frescoed, the walls are papered. All the floors are of red brick covered with a coating of polished and shining cement which is as hard as stone and looks like it; for the surfaces have been painted in patterns, first in solid colors and then snowed over with varicolored freckles of paint to imitate granite and other stones. Sometimes the body of the floor is an imitation of gray granite with a huge star or other ornamental pattern of imitation fancy marbles in the center; with a two-foot band of imitation red granite all around the room, whose outer edge is bordered with a six-inch stripe of imitation lapis-lazuli; sometimes the body of the floor is red granite, then the gray is used as a bordering stripe. There are plenty of windows, and worlds of sun and light; these floors are slick and shiny and full of reflections, for each is a mirror in its way, softly imaging all objects after the subdued fashion of forest lakes.

There is a tiny family chapel on the main floor, with benches for ten or twelve persons, and over the little altar is an ancient oil painting which seems to me to be as beautiful and as rich in tone as any of those old-master performances down yonder in the galleries of the Pitti and the Uffizi. Botticelli, for instance; I wish I had time to make a few remarks about Botticelli—whose real name was probably Smith.

The curious feature of the house is the *salon*. This is a spacious and lofty vacuum which occupies the center of the house; all the rest of the house is built around it; it extends up through both stories and its roof projects some feet above the rest of the building. That vacuum is very impressive. The sense of its vastness strikes you the moment you step into it and cast your eyes around it and aloft. I tried many names for it: the Skating Rink, the Mammoth Cave, the Great Sahara, and so on, but none exactly answered. There are five divans distributed along its walls; they make little or no show, though their aggregate length is fifty-seven feet. A piano in it is a lost object. We have tried to reduce the sense of desert space and emptiness with tables and things, but they have a defeated look and do not do any good. Whatever stands or moves under that soaring painted vault is belittled.

Over the six doors are huge plaster medallions which are supported by great naked and handsome

plaster boys, and in these medallions are plaster portraits in high relief of some grave and beautiful
men in stately official costumes of a long-past day—
Florentine senators and judges, ancient dwellers here
and owners of this estate. The date of one of them
is 1305—middle-aged, then, and a judge—he could
have known, as a youth, the very creators of Italian
art; he could have walked and talked with Dante,
and probably did. The date of another is 1343
—he could have known Boccaccio and spent his
afternoons yonder in Fiesole gazing down on plague-
reeking Florence and listening to that man's improper tales, and he probably did. The date of another is 1463—he could have met Columbus, and
he knew the Magnificent Lorenzo, of course. These
are all Cerretanis—or Cerretani-Twains, as I may
say, for I have adopted myself into their family
on account of its antiquity, my origin having been
heretofore too recent to suit me.

But I am forgetting to state what it is about that
Rink that is so curious—which is, that it is not really
vast, but only seems so. It is an odd deception,
and unaccountable; but a deception it is. Measured
by the eye it is sixty feet square and sixty high;
but I have been applying the tape line, and find it
to be but forty feet square and forty high. These
are the correct figures; and what is interestingly
strange is that the place continues to look as big
now as it did before I measured it.

This is a good house, but it cost very little and
is simplicity itself, and pretty primitive in most of
its features. The water is pumped to the ground

floor from a well by hand labor, and then carried upstairs by hand. There is no drainage; the cesspools are right under the windows. This is the case with everybody's villa.

The doors in this house are like the doors of the majority of the houses and hotels of Italy—plain, thin, unpaneled boards painted white. This makes the flimsiest and most unattractive door known to history. The knob is not a knob, but a thing like the handle of a gimlet—you can get hold of it only with your thumb and forefinger. Still, even that is less foolish than our American door knob, which is always getting loose and turning futilely round and round in your hand, accomplishing nothing.

The windows are all of the rational continental breed; they open apart, like doors; and when they are bolted for the night they don't rattle and a person can go to sleep.

There are cunning little fireplaces in the bedrooms and sitting rooms, and lately a big, aggressive-looking German stove has been set up on the south frontier of the Great Sahara.

The stairs are made of granite blocks, the hallways of the second floor are of red brick. It is a safe house. Earthquakes cannot shake it down, fire cannot burn it. There is absolutely nothing burnable but the furniture, the curtains, and the doors. There is not much furniture; it is merely summer furniture—or summer bareness, if you like. When a candle set fire to the curtains in a room over my head the other night where samples of the family slept, I was wakened out of my sleep by shouts and

screams, and was greatly terrified until an answer
from the window told me what the matter was—
that the window curtains and hangings were on fire.
In America I should have been more frightened
than ever, then, but this was not the case here.
I advised the samples to let the fire alone and go
to bed; which they did, and by the time they got
to sleep there was nothing of the attacked fabrics
left. We boast a good deal in America of our fire
departments, the most efficient and wonderful in the
world, but they have something better than that to
boast of in Europe—a rational system of building
which makes human life safe from fire and renders
fire departments needless. We boast of a thing
which we ought to be ashamed to require.

This villa has a roomy look, a spacious look;
and when the sunshine is pouring in and lighting
up the bright colors of the shiny floors and walls
and ceilings there is a large and friendly suggestion
of welcome about the aspects, but I do not know
that I have ever seen a continental dwelling which
quite met the American standard of a home in all
the details. There is a trick about an American
house that is like the deep-lying untranslatable
idioms of a foreign language—a trick uncatchable
by the stranger, a trick incommunicable and inde-
scribable; and that elusive trick, that intangible
something, whatever it is, is just the something that
gives the home look and the home feeling to an
American house and makes it the most satisfying
refuge yet invented by men—and women, mainly
women. The American house is opulent in soft and

varied colors that please and rest the eye, and in surfaces that are smooth and pleasant to the touch, in forms that are shapely and graceful, in objects without number which compel interest and cover nakedness; and the night has even a higher charm than the day, there, for the artificial lights do really give light instead of merely trying and failing; and under their veiled and tinted glow all the snug coziness and comfort and charm of the place is at best and loveliest. But when night shuts down on the continental home there is no gas or electricity to fight it, but only dreary lamps of exaggerated ugliness and of incomparable poverty in the matter of effectiveness.

Sept. 29, '92.—I seem able to forget everything except that I have had my head shaved. No matter how closely I shut myself away from draughts it seems to be always breezy up there. But the main difficulty is the flies. They like it up there better than anywhere else; on account of the view, I suppose. It seems to me that I have never seen any flies before that were shod like these. These appear to have talons. Wherever they put their foot down they grab. They walk over my head all the time and cause me infinite torture. It is their park, their club, their summer resort. They have garden parties there, and conventions, and all sorts of dissipation. And they fear nothing. All flies are daring, but these are more daring than those of other nationalities. These cannot be scared away by any device. They are more diligent, too, than the other kinds; they come before daylight and stay till after dark.

But there are compensations. The mosquitoes are not a trouble. There are very few of them, they are not noisy, and not much interested in their calling. A single unkind word will send them away; if said in English, which impresses them because they do not understand it, they come no more that night. We often see them weep when they are spoken to harshly. I have got some of the eggs to take home. If this breed can be raised in our climate they will be a great advantage. There seem to be no fleas here. This is the first time we have struck this kind of an interregnum in fifteen months. Everywhere else the supply exceeds the demand.

Oct. 1.—Finding that the coachman was taking his meals in the kitchen, I reorganized the contract to include his board, at thirty francs a month. That is what it would cost him up above us in the village, and I think I can feed him for two hundred, and save thirty out of it. Saving thirty is better than not saving anything.

That passage from the diary reminds me that I did an injudicious thing along about that time which bore fruit later. As I was to give the coachman, Vittorio, a monthly *pourboire,* of course I wanted to know the amount. So I asked the coachman's *padrone* (master), instead of asking somebody else— anybody else. He said thirty francs a month would be about right. I was afterward informed that this was an overcharge, but that it was customary, there being no customary charges except overcharges. However, at the end of that month the coachman demanded an extra *pourboire* of fifteen francs.

When I asked why, he said his padrone had taken his other *pourboire* away from him. The padrone denied this in Vittorio's presence, and Vittorio seemed to retract. The padrone *said* he did, and he certainly had that aspect, but I had to take the padrone's word for it as interpreter of the coachman's Italian. When the padrone was gone the coachman resumed the charge, and as we liked him—and also believed him—we made his aggregate *pourboire* forty-five francs a month after that, and never doubted that the padrone took two-thirds of it. We were told by citizens that it was customary for the padrone to seize a considerable share of his dependent's *pourboire,* and also the custom for the padrone to deny it. That padrone is an accommodating man and a most capable and agreeable talker, speaking English like an archangel, and making it next to impossible for a body to be dissatisfied with him; yet his seventy-ton landau has kept us supplied with lame horses for nine months, whereas we were entitled to a light carriage suited to hill-climbing, and fastidious people would have made him furnish it.

The Cerretani family, of old and high distinction in the great days of the Republic, lived on this place during many centuries. Along in October we began to notice a pungent and suspicious odor which we were not acquainted with and which gave us some little apprehension, but I laid it on the dog, and explained to the family that that kind of a dog always smelled that way when he was up to windward of the subject, but privately I knew it was

not the dog at all. I believed it was our adopted
ancestors, the Cerretanis. I believed they were preserved under the house somewhere and that it would
be a good scheme to get them out and air them.
But I was mistaken. I made a secret search and
had to acquit the ancestors. It turned out that the
odor was a harmless one. It came from the wine
crop, which was stored in a part of the cellars to
which we had no access. This discovery gave our
imaginations a rest and it turned a disagreeable
smell into a pleasant one. But not until we had
so long and lavishly flooded the house with odious
disinfectants that the dog left and the family had to
camp in the yard most of the time. It took two
months to disinfect the disinfectants and persuade
our wealth of atrocious stenches to emigrate. When
they were finally all gone and the wine fragrance
resumed business at the old stand, we welcomed it
with effusion and have had no fault to find with
it since.

Oct. 6.—I find myself at a disadvantage here.
Four persons in the house speak Italian and nothing
else, one person speaks German and nothing else,
the rest of the talk is in the French, English, and
profane languages. I am equipped with but the
merest smattering in these tongues, if I except one
or two. Angelo speaks French—a French which he
could get a patent on, because he invented it himself;
a French which no one can understand, a French
which resembles no other confusion of sounds heard
since Babel, a French which curdles the milk. He
prefers it to his native Italian. He loves to talk

it; loves to listen to himself; to him it is music; he will not let it alone. The family would like to get their little Italian savings into circulation, but he will not give change. It makes no difference what language he is addressed in, his reply is in French, his peculiar French, his grating, uncanny French, which sounds like shoveling anthracite down a coal chute. I know a few Italian words and several phrases, and along at first I used to keep them bright and fresh by whetting them on Angelo; but he partly couldn't understand them and partly didn't want to, so I have been obliged to withdraw them from the market for the present. But this is only temporary. I am practicing, I am preparing. Some day I shall be ready for him, and not in ineffectual French, but in his native tongue. I will seethe this kid in its mother's milk.

Oct. 27.—The first month is finished. We are wonted, now. It is agreed that life at a Florentine villa is an ideal existence. The weather is divine, the outside aspects lovely, the days and the nights tranquil and reposeful, the seclusion from the world and its worries as satisfactory as a dream. There is no housekeeping to do, no plans to make, no marketing to superintend—all these things do themselves, apparently. One is vaguely aware that somebody is attending to them, just as one is aware that the world is being turned over and the constellations worked and the sun shoved around according to the schedule, but that is all; one does not feel personally concerned, or in any way responsible. Yet there is no head, no chief executive; each servant minds his or her own department, requiring no supervision and having none. They hand in elaborately itemized bills once a week; then the machinery goes silently on again, just as before. There is no noise, or fussing, or quarreling, or confusion—upstairs. I don't know what goes on below. Late in the afternoons friends come out from the city and drink tea in the open air, and tell what is happening in the world; and when the great sun sinks down upon Florence and the daily miracle begins, they hold their breaths and look. It is not a time for talk.

A Memory of John Hay

A quarter of a century or so ago I was visiting John Hay, now Secretary of State, at Whitelaw Reid's house in New York, which Hay was occupying for a few months while Reid was absent on a holiday in Europe. Temporarily, also, Hay was editing Reid's paper, the New York *Tribune*. I remember two incidents of that Sunday visit particularly well, and I think I shall use them presently to illustrate something which I intend to say. One of the incidents is immaterial, and I hardly know why it is that it has stayed with me so many years. I must introduce it with a word or two. I had known John Hay a good many years; I had known him when he was an obscure young editorial writer on the *Tribune* in Horace Greeley's time, earning three or four times the salary he got, considering the high character of the work which came from his pen. In those earlier days he was a picture to look at, for beauty of feature, perfection of form, and grace of carriage and movement. He had a charm about him of a sort quite unusual to my Western ignorance and inexperience—a charm of manner, intonation, apparently native and unstudied elocution, and all that—the groundwork of it, native, the ease of it, the polish of it, the winning naturalness of it, acquired in Europe, where he had been *chargé d'affaires* some time at the Court of Vienna. He was joyous, cordial, a most pleasant comrade.

Now I am coming to it. John Hay was not afraid of Horace Greeley.

I will leave that remark in a paragraph by itself; it cannot be made too conspicuous. John Hay was the only man who ever served Horace Greeley on the *Tribune* of whom that can be said. In the past few years, since Hay has been occupying the post of Secretary of State, with a succession of foreign difficulties on his hands such as have not fallen to the share of any previous occupant of that chair, perhaps, when we consider the magnitude of the matters involved, we have seen that that courage of his youth is his possession still and that he is not any more scarable by kings and emperors and their fleets and armies than he was by Horace Greeley.

I arrive at the application now. That Sunday morning, twenty-five years ago, Hay and I had been chatting and laughing and carrying on almost like our earlier selves of '67, when the door opened and Mrs. Hay, gravely clad, gloved, bonneted, and just from church, and fragrant with the odors of Presbyterian sanctity, stood in it. We rose to our feet at once, of course—rose through a swiftly fall-

ing temperature—a temperature which at the beginning was soft and summer-like, but which was
turning our breath and all other damp things to
frost crystals by the time we were erect—but we
got no opportunity to say the pretty and polite thing
and offer the homage due; the comely young matron
forestalled us. She came forward, smileless, with
disapproval written all over her face, said most
coldly, "Good morning, Mr. Clemens," and passed
on and out.

There was an embarrassed pause—I may say a
very embarrassed pause. If Hay was waiting for
me to speak, it was a mistake; I couldn't think of a
word. It was soon plain to me that the bottom had
fallen out of his vocabulary, too. When I was able
to walk I started toward the door, and Hay, grown
gray in a single night, so to speak, limped feebly
at my side, making no moan, saying no word. At
the door his ancient courtesy rose and bravely flick-
ered for a moment, then went out. That is to say,
he tried to ask me to call again, but at that point
his ancient sincerity rose against the fiction and
squelched it. Then he tried another remark, and
that one he got through with. He said, pathetically
and apologetically:

"She is very strict about Sunday."

More than once in these past years I have heard
admiring and grateful people say, and have said it
myself:

"He is not afraid of this whole nation of eighty
millions when his duty requires him to do an unpopular thing."

Twenty-five years have gone by since then, and

through manifold experiences I have learned that no courage is absolutely perfect; that there is always some one who is able to modify his pluck.

Another incident of that visit was this: in trading remarks concerning our ages I confessed to forty-two and Hay to forty. Then he asked if I had begun to write my autobiography, and I said I hadn't. He said that I ought to begin at once and that I had already lost two years. Then he said in substance this:

"At forty a man reaches the top of the hill of life and starts down on the sunset side. The ordinary man, the average man, not to particularize too closely and say the commonplace man, has at that age succeeded or failed; in either case he has lived all of his life that is likely to be worth recording; also in either case the life lived is worth setting down, and cannot fail to be interesting if he comes as near to telling the truth about himself as he can. And he *will* tell the truth in spite of himself, for his facts and his fictions will work loyally together for the protection of the reader; each fact and each fiction will be a dab of paint, each will fall in its right place, and together they will paint his portrait; not the portrait *he* thinks they are painting, but his real portrait, the inside of him, the soul of him, his character. Without intending to lie, he will lie all the time; not bluntly, consciously, not dully unconsciously, but half-consciously—consciousness in twilight; a soft and gentle and merciful twilight which makes his general form comely, with his virtuous prominences and projections discernible and his ungracious ones in shadow. His truths will be recognizable as truths, his modifications of facts which would tell against him will go for nothing, the reader will see the fact through the film and know his man. There is a subtle devilish something or other about autobiographical composition that defeats all the writer's attempts to paint his portrait *his* way."

Hay meant that he and I were ordinary average commonplace people, and I did not resent my share of the verdict, but nursed my wound in silence. His idea that we had finished our work in life, passed the summit, and were westward bound downhill, with me two years ahead of him and neither of us with anything further to do as benefactors to mankind, was all a mistake. I had written four books then, possibly five. I have been drowning the world in literary wisdom ever since, volume after volume; he has been the historian of Mr. Lincoln, and his book will never perish; he has been ambassador, brilliant orator, competent and admirable Secretary of State, and would be President next year if we were a properly honest and grateful nation instead of an ungrateful one, a nation which has usually not been willing to have a Chief Magistrate of gold when it could get one of tin.

I had lost two years, but I resolved to make up that loss. I resolved to begin my autobiography at once. I did begin it, but the resolve melted away and disappeared in a week and I threw my beginning away. Since then, about every three or four years I have made other beginnings and thrown them away. Once I tried the experiment of a diary, intending to inflate that into an autobiography when its accumulation should furnish enough material, but that experiment lasted only a week; it took me half of every night to set down the history of the day, and at the week's end I did not like the result.

Within the last eight or ten years I have made several attempts to do the autobiography in one way or another with a pen, but the result was not satisfactory; it was too literary. With the pen in one's hand, narrative is a difficult art; narrative should flow as flows the brook down through the hills and the leafy woodlands, its course changed by every bowlder it comes across and by every grass-clad gravelly spur that projects into its path; its surface broken, but its course not stayed by rocks and gravel on the bottom in the shoal places; a brook that never goes straight for a minute, but *goes,* and goes briskly, sometimes ungrammatically, and sometimes fetching a horseshoe three-quarters of a mile around, and at the end of the circuit flowing within a yard of the path it traversed an hour before; but always *going,* and always following at least one law, always loyal to that law, the law of *narrative,* which *has no law.* Nothing to do but make the trip; the how of it is not important, so that the trip is made.

With a pen in the hand the narrative stream is a canal; it moves slowly, smoothly, decorously, sleepily, it has no blemish except that it is all blemish. It is too literary, too prim, too nice; the gait and style and movement are not suited to narrative. That canal stream is always reflecting; it is its nature, it can't help it. Its slick shiny surface is interested in everything it passes along the banks—cows, foliage, flowers, everything. And so it wastes a lot of time in reflections.

[Florence, April, 1904

NOTES ON "INNOCENTS ABROAD"

I WILL begin with a note upon the dedication. I wrote the book in the months of March and April, 1868, in San Francisco. It was published in August, 1869. Three years afterward Mr. Goodman of Virginia City, Nevada, on whose newspaper I had served ten years before and of whom I have had much to say in the book called *Roughing It*—I seem to be overloading the sentence and I apologize—came East, and we were walking down Broadway one day when he said:

"How did you come to steal Oliver Wendell Holmes's dedication and put it in your book?"

I made a careless and inconsequential answer, for I supposed he was joking. But he assured me that he was in earnest. He said:

"I'm not discussing the question of whether you stole it or didn't—for that is a question that can be settled in the first bookstore we come to. I am only asking you *how* you came to steal it, for that is where my curiosity is focalized."

I couldn't accommodate him with this information, as I hadn't it in stock. I could have made oath that I had not stolen anything, therefore my vanity was not hurt nor my spirit troubled. At bottom I supposed that he had mistaken another book for mine, and was now getting himself into an untenable place and preparing sorrow for himself and triumph for me. We entered a bookstore and he asked for *The Innocents Abroad* and for the dainty little blue-and-gold edition of Dr. Oliver Wendell Holmes's poems. He opened the books, exposed their dedications, and said:

"Read them. It is plain that the author of the second one stole the first one, isn't it?"

I was very much ashamed and unspeakably astonished. We continued our walk, but I was not able to throw any gleam of light upon that original question of his. I could not remember ever having seen Doctor Holmes's dedication. I knew the poems, but the dedication was new to me.

I did not get hold of the key to that secret until months afterward; then it came in a curious way, and yet it was a natural way; for the natural way provided by nature and the construction of the human mind for the discovery of a forgotten event is to employ another forgotten event for its resurrection.

I received a letter from the Reverend Doctor Rising, who had been rector of the Episcopal church in Virginia City in my time, in which letter Doctor Rising made reference to certain things which had happened to us in the Sandwich Islands six years before; among other things he made casual mention of the Honolulu Hotel's poverty in the matter of literature. At first I did not see the bearing of the remark; it called nothing to my mind. But presently

it did—with a flash! There was but one book in
Mr. Kirchhof's hotel, and that was the first volume
of Doctor Holmes's blue-and-gold series. I had had
a fortnight's chance to get well acquainted with its
contents, for I had ridden around the big island
(Hawaii) on horseback and had brought back so
many saddle boils that if there had been a duty on
them it would have bankrupted me to pay it. They
kept me in my room, unclothed and in persistent
pain, for two weeks, with no company but cigars
and the little volume of poems. Of course I read
them almost constantly; I read them from beginning to end, then began in the middle and read
them both ways. In a word, I read the book to
rags, and was infinitely grateful to the hand that
wrote it.

Here we have an exhibition of what repetition
can do when persisted in daily and hourly over a
considerable stretch of time, where one is merely
reading for entertainment, without thought or intention of preserving in the memory that which is
read. It is a process which in the course of years
tries all the juice out of a familiar verse of Scripture,
leaving nothing but a dry husk behind. In that case
you at least know the origin of the husk, but in the
case in point I apparently preserved the husk, but
presently forgot whence it came. It lay lost in some
dim corner of my memory a year or two, then came
forward when I needed a dedication, and was
promptly mistaken by me as a child of my own happy
fancy.

I was new, I was ignorant, the mysteries of the

human mind were a sealed book to me as yet, and I stupidly looked upon myself as a tough and unforgivable criminal. I wrote to Doctor Holmes and told him the whole disgraceful affair, implored him in impassioned language to believe that I never intended to commit this crime, and was unaware that I had committed it until I was confronted with the awful evidence. I have lost his answer. I could better have afforded to lose an uncle. Of these I had a surplus, many of them of no real value to me, but that letter was beyond price and unsparable. In it Doctor Holmes laughed the kindest and healingest laugh over the whole matter, and at considerable length and in happy phrase assured me that there was no crime in unconscious plagiarism; that I committed it every day, that he committed it every day, that every man alive on the earth who writes or speaks commits it every day, and not merely once or twice, but every time he opens his mouth; that all our phrasings are spiritualized shadows cast multitudinously from our readings: that no happy phrase of ours is ever quite original with us; there is nothing of our own in it except some slight change born of our temperament, character, environment, teachings, and associations; that this slight change differentiates it from another man's manner of saying it, stamps it with our special style, and makes it our own for the time being; all the rest of it being old, moldy, antique, and smelling of the breath of a thousand generations of them that have used it before!

In the thirty-odd years which have elapsed since

then I have satisfied myself that what Doctor Holmes said was true.

I wish to make a note upon the preface of the *Innocents.* In the last paragraph of that brief preface I speak of the proprietors of the *Daily Alta Californian* having "waived their rights" in certain letters which I wrote for that journal while absent on the *Quaker City* trip. I was young then, I am white-headed now, but the insult of that word rankles yet, now that I am reading that paragraph for the first time in many years, reading that paragraph for the first time since it was written, perhaps. There were rights, it is true—such rights as the strong are able to acquire over the weak and the absent. Early in '66 George Barnes invited me to resign my reportership on his paper, the San Francisco *Morning Call,* and for some months thereafter I was without money or work; then I had a pleasant turn of fortune. The proprietors of the Sacramento *Union,* a great and influential daily journal, sent me to the Sandwich Islands to write four letters a month at twenty dollars apiece. I was there four or five months, and returned to find myself about the best known man on the Pacific coast. Thomas McGuire, proprietor of several theaters, said that now was the time to make my fortune—strike while the iron was hot—break into the lecture field! I did it. I announced a lecture on the Sandwich Islands, closing the advertisement with the remark: "Admission one dollar; doors open at half past seven, the trouble begins at eight." A true prophecy. The trouble certainly did begin at eight, when I found myself in front of the only audience I had ever faced, for the fright which pervaded me from head to foot was paralyzing. It lasted two minutes and was as bitter as death; the memory of it is indestructible, but it had its compensations, for it made me immune from timidity before audiences for all time to come. I lectured in all the principal Californian towns and in Nevada, then lectured once or twice more in San Francisco, then retired from the field rich—for me —and laid out a plan to sail westward from San Francisco and go around the world. The proprietors of the *Alta* engaged me to write an account of the trip for that paper—fifty letters of a column and a half each, which would be about 2,000 words per letter, and the pay to be twenty dollars per letter.

I went east to St. Louis to say good-by to my mother, and then I was bitten by the prospectus of Captain Duncan of the *Quaker City* excursion, and I ended by joining it. During the trip I wrote and sent the fifty letters; six of them miscarried and I wrote six new ones to complete my contract. Then I put together a lecture on the trip and delivered it in San Francisco at great and satisfactory pecuniary profit; then I branched out into the country and was aghast at the result: I had been entirely forgotten, I never had people enough in my houses to sit as a jury of inquest on my lost reputation! I inquired into this curious condition of things and found that the thrifty owners of that prodigiously rich Alta newspaper had *copyrighted* all those poor little twenty-dollar letters and had threatened with prosecution any journal which should venture to copy a paragraph from them.

And there I was! I had contracted to furnish a large book, concerning the excursion, to the American Publishing Co. of Hartford, and I supposed I should need all those letters to fill it out with. I was in an uncomfortable situation—that is, if the proprietors of this stealthily acquired copyright should refuse to let me use the letters. That is what they did; Mr. Mac—something—I have forgotten the rest of his name[1]—said his firm were going to make a book out of the letters in order to get back the thousand dollars which they had paid for them. I said that if they had acted fairly and honorably, and had allowed the country press to use the letters or portions of them, my lecture skirmish on the coast would have paid me ten thousand dollars, whereas the *Alta* had lost me that amount. Then he offered a compromise: he would publish the book and allow me 10-per-cent royalty on it. The compromise did not appeal to me, and I said so. The book sale would be confined to San Francisco, and my royalty would not pay me enough to board me three months, whereas my Eastern contract, if carried out, could be profitable to me, for I had a sort of reputation on the Atlantic seaboard, acquired through the publication of six excursion letters in the New York *Tribune* and one or two in the *Herald*.

In the end Mr. Mac agreed to suppress his book, on certain conditions: in my preface I must thank the *Alta* for waiving its "rights" and granting me

---

[1] May 20, 1906. I recall it now—MacCrellish.—M. T.

permission. I objected to the thanks. I could not with any large degree of sincerity thank the *Alta* for bankrupting my lecture raid. After considerable debate my point was conceded and the thanks left out.

Noah Brooks was editor of the *Alta* at the time, a man of sterling character and equipped with a right heart, also a good historian where facts were not essential. In biographical sketches of me written many years afterward (1902) he was quite eloquent in praises of the generosity of the *Alta* people in giving to me without compensation a book which, as history had afterward shown, was worth a fortune. After all the fuss, I did not levy heavily upon the *Alta* letters. I found that they were newspaper matter, not book matter. They had been written here and there and yonder, as opportunity had given me a chance working moment or two during our feverish flight around about Europe or in the furnace heat of my stateroom on board the *Quaker City,* therefore they were loosely constructed and needed to have some of the wind and water squeezed out of them. I used several of them—ten or twelve, perhaps. I wrote the rest of *The Innocents Abroad* in sixty days, and I could have added a fortnight's labor with the pen and gotten along without the letters altogether. I was very young in those days, exceedingly young, marvelously young, younger than I am now, younger than I shall ever be again, by hundreds of years. I worked every night from eleven or twelve until broad day in the morning, and as I did 200,000 words in the sixty days the average was more than 3,000 words a day—nothing for Sir Walter Scott, nothing for Louis Stevenson, nothing for plenty of other people, but quite handsome for me. In 1897, when we were living in Tedworth Square, London, and I was writing the book called *Following the Equator,* my average was 1,800 words a day; here in Florence (1904), my average seems to be 1,400 words per sitting of four or five hours.[1]

I was deducing from the above that I have been slowing down steadily in these thirty-six years, but I perceive that my statistics have a defect: 3,000 words in the spring of 1868, when I was working seven or eight or nine hours at a sitting, has little or no advantage over the sitting of to-day, covering half the time and producing half the output. Figures often beguile me, particularly when I have the arranging of them myself; in which case the remark attributed to Disraeli would often apply with justice and force:

"There are three kinds of lies: lies, damned lies, and statistics."

[*Florence, April, 1904*

STEVENSON, ALDRICH, ETC.

. . . [2] BUT it was on a bench in Washington Square that I saw the most of Louis Stevenson. It was an outing that lasted an hour or more and

---

[1] With the pen, I mean. This Autobiography is dictated, **not** written.

[2] Nothing is omitted from the MS. here, whatever may have been the thought in the author's mind.

was very pleasant and sociable. I had come with him from his house, where I had been paying my respects to his family. His business in the square was to absorb the sunshine. He was most scantily furnished with flesh, his clothes seemed to fall into hollows as if there might be nothing inside but the frame for a sculptor's statue. His long face and lank hair and dark complexion and musing and melancholy expression seemed to fit these details justly and harmoniously, and the altogether of it seemed especially planned to gather the rags of your observation and focalize them upon Stevenson's special distinction and commanding feature, his splendid eyes. They burned with a smoldering rich fire under the penthouse of his brows, and they made him beautiful.

.   .   .   .

I said I thought he was right about the others, but mistaken as to Bret Harte; in substance I said that Harte was good company and a thin but pleasant talker; that he was always bright, but never brilliant; that in this matter he must not be classed with Thomas Bailey Aldrich, nor must any other man, ancient or modern; that Aldrich was always witty, always brilliant, if there was anybody present capable of striking his flint at the right angle; that Aldrich was as sure and prompt and unfailing as the red-hot iron on the blacksmith's anvil—you had only to hit it competently to make it deliver an explosion of sparks. I added:

"Aldrich has never had his peer for prompt and pithy and witty and humorous sayings. None has equaled him, certainly none has surpassed him, in the felicity of phrasing with which he clothed these children of his fancy. Aldrich was always brilliant, he couldn't help it; he is a fire opal set round with rose diamonds; when he is not speaking, you know that his dainty fancies are twinkling and glimmering around in him; when he speaks the diamonds flash. Yes, he was always brilliant; he will always be brilliant; he will be brilliant in hell—you will see."

Stevenson, smiling a chuckly smile, "I hope not."

"Well, you will, and he will dim even those ruddy fires and look like a blond Venus backed against a pink sunset."

.   .   .   .   .   .

There on that bench we struck out a new phrase— one, or the other of us, I don't remember which— "submerged renown." Variations were discussed: submerged fame, submerged reputation, and so on, and a choice was made; submerged renown was elected, I believe. This important matter rose out of an incident which had been happening to Stevenson in Albany. While in a bookshop or bookstall there he had noticed a long rank of small books cheaply but neatly gotten up and bearing such titles as *Davis's Selected Speeches, Davis's Selected Poetry,* Davis's this and Davis's that and Davis's the other thing; compilations every one of them, each with a brief, compact, intelligent, and useful introductory chapter by this same Davis, whose first name I have forgotten. Stevenson had begun the matter with this question:

"Can you name the American author whose fame

and acceptance stretch widest and furthest in the States?"

I thought I could, but it did not seem to me that it would be modest to speak out, in the circumstances. So I diffidently said nothing. Stevenson noticed, and said:

"Save your delicacy for another time—you are not the one. For a shilling you can't name the American author of widest note and popularity in the States. But I can."

Then he went on and told about that Albany incident. He had inquired of the shopman, "Who is this Davis?"

The answer was, "An author whose books have to have freight trains to carry them, not baskets. Apparently you have not heard of him?"

Stevenson said no, this was the first time. The man said:

"Nobody has heard of Davis; you may ask all round and you will see. You never see his name mentioned in print, not even in advertisements; these things are of no use to Davis, not any more than they are to the wind and the sea. You never see one of Davis's books floating on top of the United States, but put on your diving armor and get yourself lowered away down and down and down till you strike the dense region, the sunless region of eternal drudgery and starvation wages—there you will find them by the million. The man that gets that market, his fortune is made, his bread and butter are safe, for those people will never go back on him. An author may have a reputation which is confined to the surface, and lose it and become pitied, then despised, then forgotten, entirely forgotten—the frequent steps in a surface reputation. A surface reputation, however great, is always mortal, and always killable if you go at it right—with pins and needles, and quiet slow poison, not with the club and the tomahawk. But it is a different matter with the submerged reputation—down in the deep water; once a favorite there, always a favorite; once beloved, always beloved; once respected, always respected, honored, and believed in. For what the reviewer says never finds its way down into those placid deeps, nor the newspaper sneers, nor any breath of the winds of slander blowing above. Down there they never hear of these things. Their idol may be painted clay, up there at the surface, and fade and waste and crumble and blow away, there being much weather there; but down below he is gold and adamant and indestructible.

[Florence, April, 1904

Henry H. Rogers

Mr. Rogers has been visiting the witness stand periodically in Boston for more than a year now. For eleven years he has been my closest and most valuable friend. His wisdom and steadfastness saved my copyrights from being swallowed up in the wreck and ruin of Charles L. Webster & Co., and his commercial wisdom has protected my pocket ever since in those lucid intervals wherein I have been willing to listen to his counsels and abide by his advice—a thing which I do half the time and half the time I don't.

He is four years my junior; he is young in spirit, and in looks, complexion, and bearing, easy and graceful in his movements, kind-hearted, attractive, winning, a natural gentleman, the best-bred gentleman I have met on either side of the ocean in any rank of life from the Kaiser of Germany down to the bootblack. He is affectionate, endowed with a fine quality of humor, and with his intimates he is a charming comrade. I am his principal intimate and that is my idea of him. His mind is a bewildering spectacle to me when I see it dealing with vast business complexities like the affairs of the prodigious Standard Oil Trust, the United States Steel, and the rest of the huge financial combinations of our time—for he and his millions are in them all, and his brain is a very large part of the machinery which keeps them alive and going. Many a time in the past eleven years my small and troublesome affairs have forced me to spend days and weeks of waiting time down in the city of New York, and my waiting refuge has been his private office in the Standard Oil Building, stretched out on a sofa behind his chair, observing his processes, smoking, reading, listening to his reasonings with the captains of industry, and intruding my advice where it was not invited, not desired, and in no instance adopted, so far as I remember. A patient man, I can say that for him.

The private office was a spacious, high-ceiled chamber on the eleventh floor of the Standard Oil

Building, with large windows which looked out upon the moving life of the river, with the Colossus of Liberty enlightening the world holding up her torch in the distance. When I was not there it was a solitude, since in those intervals no one occupied the place except Mr. Rogers and his brilliant private secretary, Miss Katherine I. Harrison, whom he once called in on an emergency thirteen or fourteen years ago from among the 750 clerks laboring for the Standard Oil in the building. She was nineteen or twenty years old then and did stenographic work and typewriting at the wage of that day, which was fifteen or twenty dollars a week. He has a sharp eye for capacity, and after trying Miss Harrison for a week he promoted her to the post of chief of his private secretaries and raised her wages. She has held the post ever since; she has seen the building double its size and increase its clerical servants to 1,500, and her own salary climb to ten thousand dollars a year. She is the only private secretary who sits in the sanctum; the others are in the next room and come at the bell call. Miss Harrison is alert, refined, well read in the good literature of the day, is fond of paintings and buys them; she is a cyclopædia in whose head is written down the multitudinous details of Mr. Rogers's business; order and system are a native gift with her; Mr. Rogers refers to her as he would to a book, and she responds with the desired information with a book's confidence and accuracy. Several times I have heard Mr. Rogers say that she is quite able to conduct his affairs, substantially without his help.

Necessarily Mr. Rogers's pecuniary aid was sought by his full share of men and women without capital who had ideas for sale—ideas worth millions if their exploitation could be put in charge of the right man. Mr. Rogers's share of these opportunities was so large that if he had received and conversed with all his applicants of that order he might have made many millions per hour, it is true, but he would not have had half an hour left in the day for his own business. He could not see all of these people, therefore he saw none of them, for he was a fair and just man. For his protection, his office was a kind of fortress with outworks, these outworks being several communicating rooms into which no one could get access without first passing through an outwork where several young colored men stood guard and carried in the cards and requests and brought back the regrets. Three of the communicating rooms were for consultations, and they were seldom unoccupied. Men sat in them waiting—men who were there by appointment— appointments not loosely specified, but specified by the minute hand of the clock. These rooms had ground-glass doors and their privacy was in other ways protected and secured. Mr. Rogers consulted with a good many men in those rooms in the course of his day's work of six hours; and whether the matter in hand was small and simple or great and complicated, it was discussed and dispatched with marvelous celerity. Every day these consultations supplied a plenty of vexations and exasperations for Mr. Rogers—I know this quite well—but if ever

they found revealment in his face or manner it could
have been for only a moment or two, for the signs
were gone when he re-entered his private office and
he was always his brisk and cheerful self again and
ready to be chaffed and joked, and reply in kind. His
spirit was often heavily burdened, necessarily, but
it cast no shadow, and those about him sat always
in the sunshine.

Sometimes the value of his securities went down
by the million, day after day, sometimes they went
up as fast, but no matter which it was, the face and
bearing exhibited by him were only proper to a
rising market. Several times every day Miss Harrison had to act in a diplomatic capacity. Men
called whose position in the world was such that they
could not be dismissed with the formula "engaged"
along with Mr. Rogers's regrets, and to these Miss
Harrison went out and explained, pleasantly and
tactfully, and sent them away comfortable. Mr.
Rogers transacted a vast amount of business during
his six hours daily, but there always seemed time
enough in the six hours for it.

That Boston gas lawsuit came on at a bad time
for Mr. Rogers, for his health was poor and remained so during several months. Every now and
then he had to stay in his country house at Fair
Haven, Massachusetts, a week or two at a time,
leaving his business in Miss Harrison's hands and
conferring with her once or twice daily by long-
distance telephone. To prepare himself for the witness stand was not an easy thing, but the materials
for it were to be had, for Mr. Rogers never de-

stroyed a piece of paper that had writing on it, and, as he was a methodical man, he had ways of tracing out any paper he needed, no matter how old it might be. The papers needed in the gas suit, wherein Mr. Rogers was sued for several millions of dollars, went back in date a good many years and were numberable by the hundreds; but Miss Harrison ferreted them all out from the stacks and bales of documents in the Standard Oil vaults and caused them to be listed and annotated by the other secretaries. This work cost weeks of constant labor, but it left Mr. Rogers in shape to establish for himself an unsurpassable reputation as a witness.

I wish to make a momentary digression here and call up an illustration of what I have been saying about Mr. Rogers's habits in the matter of order and system. When he was a young man of twenty-four, out in the oil regions of Pennsylvania and straitened in means, he had some business relations with another young man; time went on, they separated and lost sight of each other. After a lapse of twenty years this man's card came in one day and Mr. Rogers had him brought into the private office. The man showed age, his clothes showed that he was not prosperous, and his speech and manner indicated that hard luck had soured him toward the world and the fates. He brought a bill against Mr. Rogers, oral in form, for $1,500—a bill thirty years old. Mr. Rogers drew the check and gave it to him, saying he could not allow him to lose it, though he almost deserved to lose it for risking the claim thirty years without presenting it. When he was gone Mr. Rogers said:

"My memory is better than his. I paid the money at the time; knowing this, I know I took a receipt, although I do not remember that detail. To satisfy myself that I have not been careless, I will have that receipt searched out."

It took a day or two, but it was found and I saw it; then it was sent back to its place again among the archives.

[Added in 1909

HENRY H. ROGERS *(Continued)*

The value of his advice.—His beautiful nature.

SINCE he passed from life many months have gone by, and still I have not found myself competent to put into words my feelings for him and my estimate of him. For he is as yet too near, the restraint of his spirit too effective.

All through my life I have been the easy prey of the cheap adventurer. He came, he lied, he robbed, and went his way, and the next one arrived by the next train and began to scrape up what was left. I was in the toils of one of these creatures sixteen years ago, and it was Mr. Rogers who got me out. We were strangers when we met, and friends when we parted, half an hour afterward. The meeting was accidental and unforeseen, but it had memorable and fortunate consequences for me. He dragged me out of that difficulty, and also out of the next one—a year or two later—which was still more formidable than its predecessor. He did these saving things at no cost to my self-love, no hurt to my pride; indeed, he did them with so delicate an art that I almost seemed to have done them myself. By no sign, no hint, no word did he ever betray any consciousness that I was under obligations to him. I have never been so great as that, and I have not known another who was. I have never approached it; it belongs among the loftiest of human attributes. This is a world where you get nothing for nothing; where you pay value for everything you get and 50 per cent over; and when it is gratitude you owe, you have to pay a thousand. In fact, gratitude is a debt which usually goes on accumulating, like blackmail; the more you pay, the more is exacted. In time you are made to realize that the kindness done you is become a curse and you wish it had not happened. You find yourself situated as was Mr. W., a friend of friends of mine, years ago. He was rich and good-hearted and appreciative. His wife's life was saved by a grocer's young man, who stopped her runaway horses. Her husband was grateful beyond words. For he supposed gratitude was a sentiment; he did not know it had a price and that *he* was not the one to determine the rate. But by and by he was educated. Then he said to the grocer's young man, "Take this five hundred dollars and vanish; I have had you and your tribe on my back three years, and if ever another man saves my wife's life, let him buy a coffin, for he will need it."

Mr. Rogers was a great man. No one denies him that praise. He was great in more ways than one—ways in which other men are great, ways in which he had not a monopoly; but in that fine trait which I have mentioned he was uniquely great; he held that high place almost alone, almost without a sharer. If nobilities of character were accorded decorations symbolizing degrees of merit and distinction, I think this one could claim rank, unchallenged, with the Garter and the Golden Fleece.

But what I am trying to place before unfamiliar eyes is the heart of him.

When the publishing house of Webster & Company failed, in the early '90's, its liabilities exceeded its assets by 66 per cent. I was morally bound for the debts, though not legally. The panic was on, business houses were falling to ruin everywhere, creditors were taking the assets—when there were any—and letting the rest go. Old business friends of mine said: "Business is business, sentiment is sentiment—and this is business. Turn the assets over to the creditors and compromise on that; other creditors are not getting 33 per cent." My wife said, "No, you will pay a hundred cents on the dollar." Mr. Rogers was certainly a business man— no one doubts that. People who know him only by printed report will think they know what his attitude would be in the matter. And they will be mistaken. He sided with my wife. He was the only man who had a clear eye for the situation, and could see that it differed from other apparently parallel situations. In substance he said this: "Business has its laws and customs, and they are justified; but a literary man's reputation is his life; he can afford to be money poor, but he cannot afford to be character poor; you must earn the cent per cent, and pay it." My nephew, the late Samuel E. Moffett—himself a literary man—felt in the same way, naturally enough; but I only mention him to recall and revivify a happy remark which he made, and which traveled around the globe: "Honor knows no statute of limitations."

So it was decided. I must cease from idling and take up work again. I must write a book; also I must return to the lecture platform. My wife said I could clear off the load of debt in four years. Mr. Rogers was more cautious, more conservative, more liberal. He said I could have as many years as I wanted—seven to start with. That was his joke. When he was not in the humor for pleasantry, it was because he was asleep. Privately I was afraid his seven might be nearer the mark than Mrs. Clemens's four.

One day I got a shock—a shock which disturbed me a good deal. I overheard a brief conversation between Mr. Rogers and a couple of other seasoned men of affairs.

First Man of Affairs. "How old is Clemens?"

Mr. Rogers. "Fifty-eight."

First Man of Affairs. "Ninety-five per cent of the men who fail at fifty-eight never get up again."

Second Man of Affairs. "You can make it ninety-eight per cent and be nearer right."

Those sayings haunted me for several days,

troubling me with melancholy forebodings, and would not be reasoned away by me. There wasn't any room for reasoning, anyway, so far as I could see. If, at fifty-eight, ninety-eight men in a hundred who fail never get up again, what chance had I to draw No. 99 or No. 100? However, the depression did not last; it soon passed away, because Mrs. Clemens took her always-ready pencil and paper, when she learned my trouble, and clearly and convincingly ciphered out the intake of the four years and the resultant success. I could see that she was right. Indeed, she was always right. In foresight, wisdom, accurate calculation, good judgment, and the ability to see all sides of a problem, she had no match among people I have known, except Mr. Rogers.

Necessarily it took a good while to arrange the details and make the engagements for a lecture trip around the globe, but this labor was completed at last, and we made our start in the middle of July, 1895, booked ahead for twelve months.

Meantime he was in command, in the matter of the creditors—and had been from the beginning. There were ninety-six creditors. He had meetings with them, discussions, arguments, persuasions, but no quarrels. Mrs. Clemens wanted to turn over to the creditors the house she had built in Hartford, and which stood in her name, but he would not allow it. Neither would he allow my copyrights to go to them. Mrs. Clemens had lent the Webster firm $65,000 upon its notes, in its perishing days, in the hope of saving its life, and Mr. Rogers insisted upon making her a preferred creditor and letting her have the copyrights in liquidation of the notes. He would not budge from this position, and the creditors finally yielded the point.

Mr. Rogers insisted upon just two things besides the relinquishment of the copyrights: the creditors must be content with the Webster assets, for the present, and give me time to earn the rest of the firm's debt. He won them over. There were a clarity about his reasonings, and a charm about his manner, his voice, and the kindness and sincerity that looked out of his eyes, that could win anybody that had brains in his head and a heart in his body. Of the ninety-six creditors, only three or four stood out for rigorous and uncompromising measures against me and refused to relent. The others said I could go free and take my own time. They said they would obstruct me in no way and would bring no actions; and they kept their word. As to the three or four, I have never resented their animosity, except in my Autobiography. And even there, not in spite, not in malice, but only frankly and in only a brief chapter—a chapter which can never wound them, for I have every confidence that they will be in hell before it is printed.

The long, long head that Mr. Rogers carried on his shoulders! When he was so strenuous about my copyrights, and so determined to keep them in the family, I was not able to understand why he should think the matter so important. He insisted that they were a great asset. I said they were not an asset at all; I couldn't even *give* them away. He

said, wait—let the panic subside and business re-
vive, and I would see; they would be worth more
than they had ever been worth before.

That was his idea—the idea of a financier, familiar with finance; of a capitalist, deep in railroads,
oil, banks, iron, copper, telegraphs, and so on, and
familiar with those things, but what could he know
about books? What was his opinion about copyright values worth, if it clashed with the opinion of
experienced old publishers? Which it did. The
Webster failure threw seven of my books on my
hands. I had offered them to three first-class publishers; they didn't want them. If Mr. Rogers had
let Mrs. Clemens and me have our way, the copyrights would have been handed over to the publishers.

I am grateful to his memory for many a kindness
and many a good service he did me, but gratefulest
of all for the saving of my copyrights—a service
which saved me and my family from want and assured us permanent comfort and prosperity.

How could he look into the future and see all
that, when the men whose trade and training it was
to exercise that technical vision were forecast blind
and saw no vestige of it? This is only one example
of the wonders of his mind; his intimates could cite
many others, products of that rich treasury.

I was never able to teach him anything about
finance, though I tried hard and did the best I could.
I was not able to move him. Once I had hopes for
a little while. The Standard Oil declared one of its
customary fury-breeding 40- or 50-per-cent dividends

on its $100,000,000 capital, and the storm broke out, as usual. To the unposted public a 40- or 50-per-cent dividend could mean only one thing—the giant Trust was squeezing an utterly and wickedly unfair profit out of the helpless people; whereas in truth the giant Trust was not doing anything of the kind, but was getting only 5 or 6 per cent on the money actually invested in its business, which was eight or ten times a hundred millions. In my quality of uneducated financial expert I urged that the nominal capital be raised to $1,000,000,000; then next year's dividend would drop to 4 or 5 per cent, the year's profit would be the same as usual, but the usual storm would not happen. If I remember rightly, I think he offered the objection that the tenfold increase of taxes would be too heavy, and I rejoined that by the ill-veiled exultation in his eye I knew he regarded my suggestion as of vast value and was trying to invent some plausible way of getting out of paying a commission on it. I often gave him fresh financial ideas, quite uninvited; and in return—uninvited—he told me how to write my literature better; but nothing came of it, both of us remained as poor as ever.

Unconsciously we all have a standard by which we measure other men, and if we examine closely we find that this standard is a very simple one, and is this: we admire them, we envy them, for great qualities which we ourselves lack. Hero worship consists in just that. Our heroes are the men who do things which we recognize, with regret, and sometimes with a secret shame, that we cannot do. We find not much in ourselves to admire, we are always privately wanting to be like somebody else. If everybody was satisfied with himself, there would be no heroes.

Mr. Rogers was endowed with many great qualities; but the one which I most admired, and which was to me a constant reproach because I lacked it, was his unselfishness where a friend or a cause that was near his heart was concerned, and his native readiness to come forward and take vigorous hold of the difficulty involved and abolish it. I was born to indolence, idleness, procrastination, indifference —the qualities that constitute a shirk; and so he was always a wonder to me, and a delight—he who never shirked anything, but kept his master brain and his master hands going all day long, and every day, and was happiest when he was busiest, and apparently lightest of heart when his burden of labor and duty was heaviest.

He could take trouble; I could not take trouble, either for myself or for anyone else. I dreaded anything that might disturb my ease and comfort, and would put that thing from me even when it cost me shame to do it; and so to see him take trouble, no end of trouble, days and days of trouble, and take it so patiently, so placidly, so interestedly— and so affectionately, too, if it was for somebody else —was to me a strange and marvelous thing, and beautiful. It probably never occurred to him to admire it; no, he would be occupied in admiring some quality in some one else which was lacking in his own composition.

The question of what is a gentleman was being thrashed out in the newspapers shortly after Mr. Rogers's death, and many definitions were furnished, but no decision reached. The larger part of the definitions were in substance alike, differing only in small details and delicate shadings. They painted a lofty and charming and lovable personality. Mr. Rogers could have sat for that portrait.

INTERVAL OF TWO YEARS

The final dictation, beginning January 9, 1906.
Present Mr. Clemens, Mr. Paine,
Miss Hobby, stenographer.

Mr. Clemens (to Mr. Paine):

The more I think of this [the biography], the more nearly impossible the project seems. The difficulties of it grow upon me all the time. For instance, the idea of blocking out a consecutive series of events which have happened to me, or which I imagine have happened to me—I can see that that is impossible for me. The only thing possible for me is to talk about the thing that something suggests at the moment—something in the middle of my life, perhaps, or something that happened only a few months ago. It is my purpose to extend these notes to 600,000 words, and possibly more. But that is going to take a long time—a long time.

My idea is this: that I write an autobiography. When that autobiography is finished—or before it is finished, but no doubt after it is finished—then you take the manuscript and decide on how much of a biography to make. But this is no holiday excursion—it is a journey.

We will try this—see whether it is dull or interesting—whether it will bore us and we will want to commit suicide. I hate to get at it. I hate to begin, but I imagine if you are here to make suggestions from time to time, we can make it go along, instead of having it drag.

Now let me see, there was something I wanted to talk about, and I supposed it would stay in my head. I know what it is—about the Big Bonanza in Nevada.

I want to read from the commercial columns of the New York *Times*, of a day or two ago, what practically was the beginning of the great Bonanza in Nevada, and these details seem to me to be correct —that in Nevada, during 1871, John Mackay and Fair got control of the Consolidated Virginia Mine for $26,000; that in 1873, two years later, its 108,000 shares sold at $45 per share; and that it was at that time that Fair made the famous silver ore find of the great Bonanza. Also, according to these statistics, in November, '74 the stock went to 115, and in the following month—January, '75— it reached 700. The shares of the companion mine, the California, rose in four months from 37 to 780 —a total property which in 1869 was valued on the Mining Exchange at $40,000, was quoted six years later at $160,000,000. I think those dates are correct. That great Bonanza occupies a rather prominent place in my mind for the reason that I knew persons connected with it. For instance, I knew John Mackay very well—that would be in 1862, '63, and '64, I should say. I don't remember what he was doing when I came to Virginia in 1862, from starving to death down in the so-called mines of Esmeralda, which consisted in that day merely of

silver-bearing quartz—plenty of bearing, and didn't
have much load to carry in the way of silver—and
it was a happy thing for me when I was summoned
to come up to Virginia City to be local editor of
the Virginia City *Enterprise* during three months,
while Mr. William H. Wright (Dan de Quille)
should go east, to Iowa, and visit his family, whom
he hadn't seen for some years. I took the position
of local editor with joy, because there was a salary
of forty dollars a week attached to it and I knew
that that was all of forty dollars more than I was
worth, and I had always wanted a position which
paid in the opposite proportion of value to amount
of work. I took that position with pleasure, not
with confidence—but I had a difficult job—a difficult
job. I was to furnish one column of leaded non-
pareil every day, and as much more as I could get
on paper before the paper should go to press at
two o'clock in the morning. By and by, in the course
of a few months, I met John Mackay, with whom
I had already been well acquainted for some time.
He had established a broker's office on C Street,
in a new frame house, and it was rather sumptuous
for that day and place, for it had part of a carpet
on the floor and two chairs instead of a candle box.
I was envious of Mackay, who had not been in such
very smooth circumstances as this before, and I offered to trade places with him—take his business
and let him have mine—and he asked me how much
mine was worth. I said forty dollars a week. He
said: "I never swindled anybody in my life, and
I don't want to begin on you. This business of mine

is not worth forty dollars a week. You stay where you are and I will try to get a living out of this."

I left Nevada in 1864 to avoid a term in the penitentiary (in another chapter I shall have to explain that) so that it was all of ten years, apparently, before John Mackay developed suddenly into the first of the hundred-millionaires. Apparently his prosperity began in '71—that discovery was made in '71. I know how it was made. I remember those details, for they came across the country to me in Hartford. There was a tunnel 1,700 feet long which struck in from way down on the slope of the mountain and passed under some portion of Virginia City, at a great depth. It was striking for a lode which it did not find, and I think it had been long abandoned. Now it was in groping around in that tunnel that Mr. Fair (afterward U. S. Senator and great multi-millionaire, who was at that time a day laborer working with pick and shovel at five dollars a day)—groping around in that abandoned tunnel to see what he could find— no doubt looking for cross lodes and blind veins— came across a body of rich ore—so the story ran —and he came and reported that to John Mackay. They examined this body of rich ore and found that there was a very great deposit of it. They prospected it in the usual way and proved its magnitude and that it was extremely rich. They thought it was a "chimney," belonging probably to the California, away up on the mountain-side, which had an abandoned shaft—or possibly the Virginia mine

which was not worked then—nobody caring anything about the Virginia, an empty mine. And these
men determined that this body of ore properly belonged to the California mine and by some trick
of nature had been shaken down the mountain-side.
They got O'Brien—who was a silver expert in San
Francisco—to come in as capitalist, and they bought
up a controlling interest in that abandoned mine,
and no doubt got it at that figure—$26,000—six
years later to be worth $160,000,000.

As I say, I was not there. I had been here in
the East, six, seven, or eight years—but friends of
mine were interested. John P. Jones, who has lately
resigned as U. S. Senator after an uninterrupted
term of perhaps thirty years—John P. Jones was
not a Senator yet, but was living in San Francisco.
And he had a great affection for a couple of old
friends of mine—Joseph T. Goodman and Dennis
McCarthy. They had been proprietors of that
paper that I served—the Virginia City *Enterprise*
—and had enjoyed great prosperity in that position.
They were young journeymen printers, typesetting
in San Francisco in 1858, and they went over the
mountains—the Sierras—for they heard of the discovery of silver in that unknown region of Nevada,
to push their fortunes. When they arrived at that
miserable little camp, Virginia City, they had no
money to push their fortunes with. They had only
youth, energy, hope. They found Williams there
("Stud" Williams was his society name), who had
started a weekly newspaper, and he had one journeyman, who set up the paper, and printed it on

a hand press with Williams's help and the help of
a Chinaman—and they all slept in one room—
cooked and slept and worked, and disseminated intelligence in this paper of theirs.   Well, Williams
was in debt fourteen dollars.   He didn't see any
way to get out of it with his newspaper, and so
he sold the paper to Dennis McCarthy and Goodman for two hundred dollars, they to assume the
debt of fourteen dollars and to pay the $200, in
this world or the next—there was no definite promise
about that.   But as Virginia City developed they
discovered new mines, new people began to flock
in, and there was talk of a faro bank and a church
and all those things that go to make a frontier
Christian city, and there was vast prosperity there,
and Goodman and Dennis reaped the advantage of
that.   Their prosperity was so great that they built
a three-story brick building, which was a wonderful thing for that town, and their business increased
so mightily that they would often plant out eleven
columns of new ads on a standing galley and leave
them there to sleep and rest and breed income.
When any man objected, after searching the paper
in the hope of seeing his advertisement, they would
say, "We are doing the best we can."   Now and
then the advertisements would appear, but the
standing galley was doing its work all the time.   But
after a time, when that territory was turned into
a state, in order to furnish office for some people
who needed office, their paper, from paying those
boys twenty to forty thousand dollars a year, had
ceased to pay anything.   I suppose they were very

glad to get rid of it, and probably on the old terms, to some journeyman who was willing to take the old fourteen dollars indebtedness and pay it when he could.

These boys went down to San Francisco, setting type again. They were delightful fellows, always ready for a good time, and that meant that everybody got their money except themselves. And when the Bonanza was about to be discovered Joe Goodman arrived here from somewhere that he'd been —I suppose trying to make business, or a livelihood, or something—and he came to see me to borrow three hundred dollars to take him out to San Francisco. And if I remember rightly he had no prospect in front of him at all, but thought he would be more likely to find it out there among the old friends, and he went to San Francisco. He arrived there just in time to meet Jones (afterwards U. S. Senator), who was a delightful man. Jones met him and said privately, "There has been a great discovery made in Nevada, and I am on the inside." Dennis was setting type in one of the offices there. He was married and was building a wooden house to cost $1,800, and he had paid a part and was building it on installments out of his wages. And Jones said: "I am going to put you and Dennis in privately on the big Bonanza. I am on the inside, I will watch it, and we will put this money up on a margin. Therefore when I say it is time to sell, it will be very necessary to sell." So he put up 20-per-cent margins for those two boys—and that is the time when this great spurt must have happened

which sent that stock up to the stars in one flight—
because, as the history was told to me by Joe Goodman, when that thing happened Jones said to Goodman and Dennis:

"Now then, sell. You can come out $600,000
ahead, each of you, and that is enough. Sell."

"No," Joe objected, "it will go higher."

Jones said: "I am on the inside; you are not.
Sell."

Joe's wife implored him to sell. He wouldn't
do it. Dennis's family implored him to sell. Dennis
wouldn't sell. And so it went on during two weeks.
Each time the stock made a flight Jones tried to
get the boys to sell. They wouldn't do it. They
said, "It is going higher." When he said, "Sell at
$900,000," they said, "No. It will go to million."

Then the stock began to go down very rapidly.
After a little, Joe sold, and he got out with $600,000
cash. Dennis waited for the million, but he never
got a cent. His holding was sold for the "mud"—
so that he came out without anything and had to
begin again setting type.

That is the story as it was told to me many years
ago—I imagine by Joe Goodman; I don't remember now. Dennis, by and by, died poor—never got
a start again.

Joe Goodman immediately went into the broker
business. Six hundred thousand dollars was just
good capital. He wasn't in a position to retire yet.
And he sent me the $300, and said that now he had
started in the broking business and that he was making an abundance of money. I didn't hear any more

then for a long time; then I learned that he had not been content with mere broking, but had speculated on his own account and lost everything he had. And when that happened, John Mackay, who was always a good friend of the unfortunate, lent him $4,000 to buy a grape ranch with, in Fresno County, and Joe went up there. He didn't know anything about the grape culture, but he and his wife learned it in a very little while. He learned it a little better than anybody else, and got a good living out of it until 1886 or '87; then he sold it for several times what he paid for it originally.

He was here a year ago and I saw him. He lives in the garden of California—in Alameda. Before this Eastern visit he had been putting in twelve years of his time in the most unpromising and difficult and stubborn study that anybody has undertaken since Champollion's time; for he undertook to find out what those sculptures mean that they find down there in the forests of Central America. And he did find out and published a great book, the result of his twelve years of study. In this book he furnishes the meanings of those hieroglyphs, and his position as a successful expert in that complex study is recognized by the scientists in that line in London and Berlin and elsewhere. But *he* is no better known than he was before—he is known only to those people. His book was published in about 1901.

This account in the New York *Times* says that in consequence of that strike in the great Bonanza a tempest of speculation ensued, and that the group of mines right around that center reached a value in the stock market of close upon $400,000,000; and six months after that, that value had been reduced by three-quarters; and by 1880, five years later, the stock of the Consolidated Virginia was under $2 a share, and the stock in the California was only $1.75—for the Bonanza was now confessedly exhausted.

[New York, January 10, 1906

I HAVE to make several speeches within the next two or three months, and I have been obliged to make a few speeches during the last two months—and all of a sudden it is borne in upon me that people who go out that way to make speeches at gatherings of one kind or another, and at social banquets particularly, put themselves to an unnecessary amount of trouble, often, in the way of preparation. As a rule, your speech at a social banquet is not an important part of your equipment for that occasion, for the reason that as a rule the banquet is merely given to celebrate some event of merely momentary interest, or to do honor to some guest of distinction—and so there is nothing of large consequence—nothing, I mean, that one should feel bound to concentrate himself upon in talking upon such an occasion, whereas the really important matter, perhaps, is that the speaker make himself reasonably interesting while he is on his feet, and avoid wearying and exasperating the people who are not privileged to make speeches, and also not privileged to get out of the way when other people begin. So, common charity for those people should require that the speaker make some kind of preparation, instead of going to the place absolutely empty.

The person who makes frequent speeches can't afford much time for their preparation, and he probably goes to that place empty (just as I am in the habit of doing), purposing to gather texts from other unprepared people who are going to speak before he speaks. Now it is perfectly true that if you can get yourself located along about number three, and from that lower down on the program, it can be depended on with certainty that one or another of those previous speakers will furnish all the texts needed. In fact, you are likely to have more texts than you do need, and so they can become an embarrassment. You would like to talk to all of those texts, and of course that is a dangerous thing. You should choose one of them and talk to that one— and it is a hundred to one that before you have been on your feet two minutes you will wish you had taken the other one. You will get away from the one you have chosen, because you will perceive that there was another one that was better.

I am reminded of this old, old fact in my experience by what happened the other night at the Players', where twenty-two of my friends of ancient days in the Players' Club gave me a dinner [1] in testimony of their satisfaction in having me back

---

[1] It was at this dinner that the idea of the biography which led to these dictations developed.

again after an absence of three years, occasioned
by the stupidity of the board of management of
that club—a board which had been in office ever
since the founding of the club; and if it were not
the same old board that they had in the beginning
it amounted to the same, because they must have
been chosen, from time to time, from the same
asylum that had furnished the original board. On
this occasion Brander Matthews was chairman, and
he opened the proceedings with an easy and comfortable and felicitous speech. Brander is always
prepared and competent when he is going to make
a speech. Then he called up Gilder, who came
empty, and probably supposed he was going to be
able to fill from Brander's tank, whereas he struck
a disappointment. He labored through and sat
down, not entirely defeated, but a good deal crippled. Frank Millet (painter) was next called up.
He struggled along through his remarks, exhibiting
two things—one, that he had prepared and couldn't
remember the details of his preparation, and the
other that his text was a poor text. In his talk the
main sign of preparation was that he tried to re-
cite two considerable batches of poetry—good poetry
—but he lost confidence and turned it into bad poetry
by bad recitation. Sculpture was to have been rep-
resented, and Saint-Gaudens had accepted and had
promised a speech, but at the last moment he was
not able to come and a man who was thoroughly
unprepared had to get up and make a speech in
Saint-Gaudens's place. He did not hit upon anything original or disturbing in his remarks, and, in

fact, they were so tottering and hesitating and altogether commonplace that really he seemed to have
hit upon something new and fresh when he finished
by saying that he had not been expecting to be called
upon to make a speech! I could have finished his
speech for him, I had heard it so many times.

Those people were unfortunate because they were
thinking—that is Millet and Gilder were—all the
time that Matthews was speaking; they were trying to keep in mind the little preparations which they
had made, and this prevented them from getting
something new and fresh in the way of a text out
of what Brander was saying. In the same way
Millet was still thinking about his preparation while
Gilder was talking, and so he overlooked possible
texts furnished by Gilder. But as I had asked
Matthews to put me last on the list of speakers, I
had all the advantages possible to the occasion. For
I came without a text, and these boys furnished
plenty of texts for me, because my mind was not
absorbed in trying to remember my preparations—
they didn't exist. I spoiled, in a degree, Brander's
speech, because his speech had been prepared with
direct reference to introducing me, the guest of the
occasion—and he had to turn that all around and
get out of it, which he did very gracefully, explaining that his speech was a little lopsided and wrong
end first because I had asked to be placed last in
the list of speakers. I had a plenty good-enough
time, because Gilder had furnished me a text;
Brander had furnished me a text; Millet had furnished me a text. These texts were fresh, hot from

the bat, and they produced the same eager disposition to take hold of them and talk that they would have produced in ordinary conversation around a table in a beer mill.

Now then, I know how banquet speeches should be projected, because I have been thinking over this matter. This is my plan. Where it is merely a social banquet for a good time—such as the one which I am to attend in Washington on the 27th, where the company will consist of the membership of the Gridiron Club (newspaper correspondents exclusively, I think), with as guests the President and Vice-President of the United States and two others—certainly that is an occasion where a person will be privileged to talk about any subject except politics and theology, and even if he is asked to talk to a toast he needn't pay any attention to the toast, but talk about anything. Now then, the idea is this—to take the newspaper of that day, or the newspaper of that evening, and glance over the headings in the telegraphic page—a perfect bonanza of texts, you see! I think a person could pull that day's newspaper out of his pocket and talk that company to death before he would run out of material. If it were to-day, you have the Morris incident. And that reminds me how unexciting the Morris incident will be two or three years from now—maybe six months from now—and yet what an irritating thing it is to-day, and has been for the past few days. It brings home to one this large fact: that the events of life are mainly small events —they only seem large when we are close to them.

By and by they settle down and we see that one doesn't show above another. They are all about one general low altitude, and inconsequential. If you should set down every day, by shorthand, as we are doing now, the happenings of the previous day, with the intention of making out of the massed re-sult an autobiography, it would take from one to two hours—and from that to four hours—to set down the autobiographical matter of that one day, and the result would be a consumption of from five to forty thousand words. It would be a volume. Now one must not imagine that because it has taken all day Tuesday to write up the autobiographical matter of Monday, there will be nothing to write on Wednesday. No, there will be just as much to write on Wednesday as Monday had furnished for Tuesday. And that is because life does not consist mainly—or even largely—of facts and happenings. It consists mainly of the storm of thoughts that is forever blowing through one's head. Could you set them down stenographically? No. Could you set down any considerable fraction of them stenograph-ically? No. Fifteen stenographers hard at work couldn't keep up. Therefore a full autobiography has never been written, and it never will be. It would consist of 365 double-size volumes per year —and so if I had been doing my whole autobio-graphical duty ever since my youth, all the library buildings on the earth could not contain the result.

I wonder what the Morris incident will look like in history fifty years from now. Consider these circumstances: that here at our own doors the mighty

insurance upheaval has not settled down to a level
yet. Even yesterday, and day before, the discredited
millionaire insurance magnates had not all been
flung out and buried from sight under the maledic-
tions of the nation, but some of the McCurdies,
McCalls, Hydes, and Alexanders were still lingering in positions of trust, such as directorships
in banks. Also we have to-day the whole nation's
attention centered upon the Standard Oil corpora-
tion, the most prodigious commercial force existing upon the planet. All the American world are
standing breathless and wondering if the Standard
Oil is going to come out of its Missourian battle
crippled, and if crippled, how much crippled. Also
we have Congress threatening to overhaul the
Panama Canal Commission to see what it has done
with the fifty-nine millions, and to find out what it
proposes to do with the recently added eleven millions. Also there are three or four other matters
of colossal public interest on the board to-day. And
on the other side of the ocean we have Church and
State separated in France; we have a threat of war
between France and Germany upon the Morocco
question; we have a crushed revolution in Russia,
with the Tsar and his family of thieves—the grand
dukes—recovering from their long fright and beginning to butcher the remnants of the revolution-
aries in the old confident way that was the Russian
way in former days for three centuries; we have
China furnishing a solemn and awful mystery. Nobody knows what it is, but we are sending three
regiments in a hurry from the Philippines to China,

under the generalship of Funston, the man who captured Aguinaldo by methods which would disgrace the lowest blatherskite that is doing time in any penitentiary. Nobody seems to know what the Chinese mystery is, but everybody seems to think that a giant convulsion is impending there.

That is the menu as it stands to-day. These are the things which offer themselves to the world's attention to-day. Apparently they are large enough to leave no space for smaller matters, yet *the Morris incident comes up and blots the whole thing out.* The Morris incident is making a flurry in Congress, and for several days now it has been rioting through the imagination of the American nation and setting every tongue afire with excited talk. This autobiography will not see the light of print until after my death. I do not know when that is going to happen, and do not feel a large interest in the matter, anyway. It may be some years yet, but if it does not occur within the next three months I am confident that by that time the nation, encountering the Morris incident in my autobiography, would be trying to remember what the incident was, and not succeeding. That incident, which is so large to-day, will be so small three or four months from now it will then have taken its place with the abortive Russian revolution and these other large matters, and nobody will be able to tell one from the other by difference of size.

This is the Morris incident. A Mrs. Morris, a lady of culture, refinement, and position, called at the White House and asked for a moment's conversation with President Roosevelt. Mr. Barnes, one of the private secretaries, declined to send in her card, and said that she couldn't see the President, that he was busy. She said she would wait. Barnes wanted to know what her errand was, and she said that some time ago her husband had been dismissed from the public service and she wanted to get the President to look into his case. Barnes, finding that it was a military case, suggested that she go to the Secretary of War. She said she had been to the War Office, but could not get admission to the Secretary—she had tried every means she could think of, but had failed. Now she had been advised by the wife of a member of the Cabinet to ask for a moment's interview with the President.

Well, without going into a multiplicity of details, the general result was that Barnes still persisted in saying that she could not see the President, and he also persisted in inviting her, in the circumstances, to go away. She was quiet, but she still insisted on remaining until she could see the President. Then the "Morris incident" happened. At a sign from Barnes a couple of policemen on guard there rushed forward and seized this lady, and began to drag her out of the place. She was frightened and she screamed. Barnes says she screamed repeatedly, and in a way which "aroused the whole White House"—though nobody came to see what was happening. This might give the impression that this was something that was happening six or seven times a day, since it didn't cause any excitement.

But this was not so. Barnes has been a private secretary long enough to work his imagination, probably, and that accounts for most of the screaming—though the lady did *some* of it herself, as she concedes. The woman was dragged out of the White House. She says that in the course of dragging her along the roadway her clothes were soiled with mud and some of them stripped in rags from her back. A negro gathered up her ankles, and so relieved her from contact with the ground. He supporting her by the ankles, and the two policemen carrying her at the other end, they conveyed her to a place—apparently a police station of some kind, a couple of blocks away—and she was dripping portemonnaies and keys, and one thing or another, along the road, and honest people were picking them up and fetching them along. Barnes entered a charge against her of insanity. Apparently the police inspector regarded that as rather a serious charge, and, as he probably had not had one like it before and did not quite know how it ought to be handled, he would not allow her to be delivered to her friends until she had deposited five dollars in his till. No doubt this was to keep her from disappearing from the United States—and he might want to take up this serious charge presently and thresh it out.

That lady still lies in her bed at the principal hotel in Washington, disabled by the shock, and naturally very indignant at the treatment which she has received—but her calm and mild, unexcited, and well-worded account of her adventure is convincing evi-

dence that she was not insane, even to the moderate
extent of five dollars' worth.

There you have the facts. It is as I have said—
for a number of days they have occupied almost the
entire attention of the American nation; they have
swept the Russian revolution out of sight, the China
mystery, and all the rest of it. It is this sort of
thing which makes the right material for an autobiography. You set the incident down which for
the moment is to you the most interesting. If you
leave it alone three or four weeks you wonder why
you ever thought of setting such a thing down—
it has no value, no importance. The champagne
that made you drunk with delight or exasperation
at the time has all passed away; it is stale. But
that is what human life consists of—little incidents
and big incidents, and they are all of the same size
if we let them alone. An autobiography that leaves
out the little things and enumerates only the big ones
is no proper picture of the man's life at all; his life
consists of his feelings and his interests, with here
and there an incident apparently big or little to hang
the feelings on.

That Morris incident will presently have no importance whatever, and yet the biographer of President Roosevelt will find it immensely valuable if he
will consider it—examine it—and be sagacious
enough to perceive that it throws a great deal of
light upon the President's character. Certainly a
biography's chiefest feature is the exhibition of the
character of the man whose biography is being set
forth. Roosevelt's biographer will light up the

President's career step by step, mile after mile, through his life's course, with illuminating episodes and incidents. He should set one of the lamps by the Morris incident, for it indicates character. It is a thing which probably could not have happened in the White House under any other President who has ever occupied those premises. Washington wouldn't call the police and throw a lady out over the fence! I don't mean that Roosevelt would. I mean that Washington wouldn't have any Barneses in his official family. It is the Roosevelts that have the Barneses around. That private secretary was perfectly right in refusing access to the President—the President can't see everybody on everybody's private affairs, and it is quite proper, then, that he should refuse to see anybody on a private affair—treat all the nation alike. That is a thing which has been done, of course, from the beginning until now—people have always been refused admission to the President on private matters, every day, from Washington's time to ours. The secretaries have always carried their point; Mr. Barnes carried his. But, according to the President in office at the time, the methods have varied—one President's secretary has managed it in one way, another President's secretary has managed it in another way—but it never would have occurred to any previous secretary to manage it by throwing the lady over the fence.

Theodore Roosevelt is one of the most impulsive men in existence. That is the reason why he has impulsive secretaries. President Roosevelt prob-

ably never thinks of the right way to do anything.
That is why he has secretaries who are not able to
think of the right way to do anything. We naturally gather about us people whose ways and dis-
positions agree with our own. Mr. Roosevelt is
one of the most likable men that I am acquainted
with. I have known him, and have occasionally met
him, dined in his company, lunched in his company,
for certainly twenty years. I always enjoy his society, he is so hearty, so straightforward, outspoken,
and, for the moment, so absolutely sincere. These
qualities endear him to me when he is acting in his
capacity of private citizen, they endear him to all
his friends. But when he is acting under their impulse as President, they make of him a sufficiently
queer President. He flies from one thing to another with incredible dispatch—throws a somer-
sault and is straightway back again where he was
last week. He will then throw some more somer-
saults and nobody can foretell where he is finally
going to land after the series. Each act of his, and
each opinion expressed, is likely to abolish or con-
trovert some previous act or expressed opinion. This
is what is happening to him all the time as President.
But every opinion that he expresses is certainly his
sincere opinion at that moment, and it is as certainly
not the opinion which he was carrying around in his
system three or four weeks earlier, and which was
just as sincere and honest as the latest one. No, he
can't be accused of insincerity—that is not the
trouble. His trouble is that his newest interest is
the one that absorbs him; absorbs the whole of him

from his head to his feet, and for the time being it annihilates all previous opinions and feelings and convictions. He is the most popular human being that has ever existed in the United States, and that popularity springs from just these enthusiasms of his—these joyous ebullitions of excited sincerity. It makes him so much like the rest of the people. They see themselves reflected in him. They also see that his impulses are not often mean. They are almost always large, fine, generous. He can't stick to one of them long enough to find out what kind of a chick it would hatch if it had a chance, but everybody recognizes the generosity of the intention and admires it and loves him for it.

[New York, January 12, 1906

My seventieth birthday arrived recently—that is to say, it arrived on the 30th of November, but Colonel Harvey [1] was not able to celebrate it on that date because that date had been pre-empted by the President to be used as the usual and perfunctory Thanksgiving Day, a function which originated in New England two or three centuries ago when those people recognized that they really had something to be thankful for—annually, not oftener—if they had succeeded in exterminating their neighbors, the Indians, during the previous twelve months instead of getting exterminated by their neighbors, the In-

---

[1] Col. George Harvey, at the time president of Harper & Brothers, later American Ambassador to the Court of St. James's.

dians. Thanksgiving Day became a habit, for the
reason that in the course of time, as the years drifted
on, it was perceived that the exterminating had
ceased to be mutual and was all on the white man's
side, consequently on the Lord's side; hence it was
proper to thank the Lord for it and extend the
usual annual compliments. The original reason for
a Thanksgiving Day has long ago ceased to exist—
the Indians have long ago been comprehensively and
satisfactorily exterminated and the account closed
with the Lord, with the thanks due. But, from old
habit, Thanksgiving Day has remained with us, and
every year the President of the United States and
the Governors of all the several states and terri-
tories set themselves the task, every November, to
hunt up something to be thankful for, and then they
put those thanks into a few crisp and reverent
phrases, in the form of a proclamation, and this
is read from all the pulpits in the land, the national
conscience is wiped clean with one swipe, and sin
is resumed at the old stand.

The President and the Governors had to have
my birthday—the 30th—for Thanksgiving Day, and
this was a great inconvenience to Colonel Harvey,
who had made much preparation for a banquet to
be given to me on that day in celebration of the
fact that it marked my seventieth escape from the
gallows, according to *his* idea—a fact which he
regarded with favor and contemplated with pleasure,
because he is my publisher and commercially interested. He went to Washington to try to get the
President to select another day for the national

Thanksgiving, and I furnished him with arguments to use which I thought persuasive and convincing, arguments which ought to persuade him even to put off Thanksgiving Day a whole year—on the ground that nothing had happened during the previous twelvemonth except several vicious and inexcusable wars, and King Leopold of Belgium's usual annual slaughters and robberies in the Congo State, together with the insurance revelations in New York, which seemed to establish the fact that if there was an honest man left in the United States, there was *only* one, and we wanted to celebrate his seventieth birthday. But the colonel came back unsuccessful, and put my birthday celebration off to the 5th of December.

In the birthday speech which I made were concealed many facts. I expected everybody to discount those facts 95 per cent, and that is probably what happened. That does not trouble me; I am used to having my statements discounted. My mother had begun it before I was seven years old. But all through my life my facts have had a substratum of truth, and therefore they were not without value. Any person who is familiar with me knows how to strike my average, and therefore knows how to get at the jewel of any fact of mine and dig it out of its blue-clay matrix. My mother knew that art. When I was seven or eight or ten or twelve years old—along there—a neighbor said to her, "Do you ever believe anything that that boy says?" My mother said, "He is the wellspring of truth, but you can't bring up the whole well with one bucket"—

and she added, "I know his average, therefore he
never deceives me. I discount him 90 per cent for
embroidery, and what is left is perfect and priceless
truth, without a flaw in it anywhere."

Now to make a jump of forty years, without
breaking the connection, one of those words was
used again in my presence and concerning me, when
I was fifty years old, one night at Rev. Frank Goodwin's house in Hartford, at a meeting of the Monday Evening Club. The Monday Evening Club still
exists. It was founded about forty-five years ago
by that theological giant, Reverend Doctor Bushnell,
and some comrades of his, men of large intellectual
caliber and more or less distinction, local or national.
I was admitted to membership in it in the fall of
1871, and was an active member thenceforth until I
left Hartford in the summer of 1891. The membership was restricted, in those days, to eighteen—
possibly twenty. The meetings began about the 1st
of October and were held in the private houses
of the members every fortnight thereafter throughout the cold months until the 1st of May. Usually
there were a dozen members present—sometimes as
many as fifteen. There were an essay and a discussion. The essayists followed one another in
alphabetical order through the season. The essayist
could choose his own subject and talk twenty minutes
on it, from MS. or orally, according to his preference. Then the discussion followed, and each member present was allowed ten minutes in which to
express his views. The wives of these people were
always present. It was their privilege. It was also

their privilege to keep still. They were not allowed to throw any light upon the discussion. After the discussion there was a supper, and talk, and cigars. This supper began at ten o'clock promptly, and the company broke up and went away at midnight. At least they did except upon one occasion. In my birthday speech I have remarked upon the fact that I have always bought cheap cigars, and that is true. I have never smoked costly ones, and whenever I go to a rich man's house to dinner I conceal cheap cigars about my person, as a protection against his costly ones. There are enough costly Havana cigars in my house to start a considerable cigar shop with, but I did not buy one of them—I doubt if I have ever smoked one of them. They are Christmas presents from wealthy and ignorant friends, extending back for a long series of years. Among the lot, I found, the other day, a double handful of J. Pierpont Morgan's cigars, which were given to me three years ago by his particular friend, the late William E. Dodge, one night when I was at dinner in Mr. Dodge's house. Mr. Dodge did not smoke, and so he supposed that those were superexcellent cigars, because they were made for Mr. Morgan in Havana out of special tobacco and cost $1.66 apiece. Now whenever I buy a cigar that costs six cents I am suspicious of it. When it costs four and a quarter or five cents I smoke it with confidence. I carried those sumptuous cigars home, after smoking one of them at Mr. Dodge's house to show that I had no animosity, and here they lie ever since. They cannot beguile me. I am waiting for somebody to come along whose lack of education will enable him to smoke them and enjoy them.

Well, that night at the club—as I was saying—George, our colored butler, came to me when the supper was nearly over, and I noticed that he was pale. Normally his complexion was a clear black and very handsome, but now it had modified to old amber. He said:

"Mr. Clemens, what are we going to do? There is not a cigar in the house but those old Wheeling 'long nines.' Can't nobody smoke them but you. They kill at thirty yards. It is too late to telephone —we couldn't get any cigars out from town. What can we do? Ain't it best to say nothing and let on that we didn't think?"

"No," I said, "that would not be honest. Fetch out the 'long nines' "—which he did.

I had just come across those "long nines" a few days or a week before. I hadn't seen a "long nine" for years. When I was a cub pilot on the Mississippi in the late '60's I had had a great affection for them, because they were not only—to my mind— perfect, but you could get a basketful of them for a cent—or a dime—they didn't use cents out there in those days. So when I saw them advertised in Hartford I sent for a thousand at once. They were sent out to me in badly battered and disreputable-looking old square pasteboard boxes, about two hundred in a box. George brought the box, which had caved in on all sides, looking the worst it could, and began to pass them around. The conversation had been brilliantly animated up to that moment—

but now a frost fell upon the company. That is to say, not all of a sudden, but the frost fell upon each man as he took up a cigar and held it poised in the air—and there, in the middle, his sentence broke off. And that kind of thing went all around the table, until, when George had completed his crime the whole place was full of a thick solemnity and silence.

Those men began to light the cigars. Reverend Doctor Parker was the first man to light. He took three or four heroic whiffs—then gave it up. He got up with the excuse that he had to go to the bed-side of a dying parishioner, which I knew was a lie, because if that had been the truth he would have gone earlier. He started out. Reverend Doctor Burton was the next man. He took only one whiff, and followed Parker. He furnished a pretext, and you could see by the sound of his voice that he didn't think much of the pretext, and was vexed with Parker for getting in ahead with a dying client. Rev. Joe Twichell followed, with a good hearty pretext—nothing in it, and he didn't expect anybody to find anything in it, but Twichell is always more or less honest, to this day, and it cost him nothing to say that he had to go now because he must take the midnight train for Boston. Boston was the first place that occurred to him—he would have said Jerusalem if he had thought of it.

It was only a quarter to eleven when they began to hand out pretexts. At five minutes to eleven all those people were out of the house and praying, no doubt, that the pretext might be overlooked, in

consideration of the circumstances. When nobody
was left but George and me I was cheerful—I was
glad—had no compunctions of conscience, no griefs
of any kind. But George was beyond speech, because
he held the honor and credit of the family above
his own, and he was ashamed that this smirch had
been put upon it. I told him to go to bed and try
to sleep it off. I went to bed myself. At breakfast
in the morning, when George was taking a cup of
coffee from Mrs. Clemens's hand, I saw it tremble
in his hand. I knew by that sign there was something on his mind. He brought the cup to me and
asked impressively:

"Mr. Clemens, how far is it from the front door
to the upper gate?"

I said, "It is one hundred and twenty-five steps."

He said, "Mr. Clemens, you know, you can start
at the front door and you can go plumb to the upper
gate and tread on one of them cigars every time."

Now by this roundabout and gradual excursion I
have arrived at that meeting of the club at Rev.
Frank Goodwin's house which I spoke of awhile
back, and where that same word was used in my
presence, and to me, which I mentioned as having
been used by my mother as much as forty years
before. The subject under discussion was dreams.
The talk passed from mouth to mouth in the usual
serene way. The late Charles Dudley Warner delivered his views in the smooth and pleasantly flowing fashion which he had learned in his early
manhood when he was an apprentice to the legal
profession. He always spoke pleasingly, always

smoothly, always choicely, never excitedly, never aggressively, always kindly, gently, and always with a lambent and playful and inconspicuous thread of humor appearing and disappearing along through his talk, like the tinted lights in an opal. To my thinking, there was never much body to what he said, never much juice in it; never anything very substantial to carry away and think about, yet it was always a pleasure to listen to him. Always his art was graceful and charming. Then came the late Colonel Greene, who had been a distinguished soldier in the Civil War and who at the time that I speak of was high up in the Connecticut Mutual and on his way to become its president presently, and in time to die in that harness and leave behind him a blemishless reputation, at a time when the chiefs of the New York insurance companies were approaching the eternal doom of their reputations. Colonel Greene discussed the dream question in his usual way—that is to say, he began a sentence and went on and on, dropping a comma in here and there at intervals of eighteen inches, never hesitating for a word, drifting straight along like a river at half bank with no reefs in it; the surface of his talk as smooth as a mirror; his construction perfect and fit for print without correction, as he went along. And when the hammer fell, at the end of his ten minutes, he dumped in a period right where he was and stopped —and it was just as good there as it would have been anywhere else in that ten minutes' sentence. You could look back over that speech and you'd find it dimly milestoned along with those commas which

he had put in and which could have been left out
just as well, because they merely staked out the
march, and nothing more. They could not call attention to the scenery, because there wasn't any.
His speech was always like that—perfectly smooth,
perfectly constructed; and when he had finished, no
listener could go into court and tell what it was
he had said. It was a curious style. It was impressive—you always thought, from one comma to
another, that he was going to strike something presently, but he never did. But this time that I speak
of, the burly and magnificent Reverend Doctor Burton sat with his eyes fixed upon Greene from the
beginning of the sentence until the end of it. He
looked as the lookout on a whaleship might look who
was watching where a whale had gone down and
was waiting and watching for it to reappear; and
no doubt that was the figure that was in Burton's
mind, because, when at last Greene finished, Burton
threw up his hands and shouted, "There she blows!"

The elder Hammersley took his appointed ten
minutes, easily, comfortably, with good phrasing,
and most entertainingly—and this was always to be
expected of the elder Hammersley.

Then his son, Will Hammersley, a young lawyer,
now this many years a judge of the Connecticut
Supreme Court, took his chance in the dream question. And I can't imagine anything more distressing
than a talk from Will Hammersley—a talk from
the Will Hammersley *of those days*. You *always*
knew that before he got through he would certainly
say something—something that you could carry

away, something that you could consider, something
that you couldn't easily put out of your mind. But
you also knew that you would suffer many a torture
before he got that thing out. He would hesitate and
hesitate, get to the middle of a sentence and search
around and around and around for a word, get the
wrong word, search again, get another wrong one,
search again and again—and so he would go on in
that way till everybody was in misery on his account,
hoping that he would arrive in the course of time,
and yet sinking deeper and deeper toward despair,
with the conviction that this time he was not going
to arrive. He would seem to get so far away from
any possible goal that you would feel convinced that
he could not cover the intervening space and get
there before his ten minutes would come to an end
and leave him suspended between heaven and earth.
But, sure as a gun, before that ten minutes ended
Will Hammersley would arrive at his point and
fetch it out with such a round and complete and
handsome and satisfying unostentatious crash that
you would be lifted out of your chair with admiration and gratitude.

Joe Twichell sometimes took his turn. If he
talked, it was easily perceptible that it was because
he had something to say, and he was always able
to say it well. But almost as a rule, he said nothing,
and gave his ten minutes to the next man. And
whenever he gave it to ——, he ran the risk of
getting lynched on his way home by the rest of
the membership. —— was the dullest white man
in Connecticut—and he probably remains that to

this day; I have not heard of any real competitor.
—— would moon along, and moon along, and
moon along, using the most commonplace, the most
dreary, the most degraded English, with never
an idea in it by any chance. But *he* never gave his
ten minutes to anybody. He always used it up to
the last second. Then there was always a little gap
—had to be for the crowd to recover before the
next man could begin. ——, when he would get
entirely lost in his talk and didn't know where he
was in his idiotic philosophizings, would grasp at
narrative, as the drowning man grasps at a straw.
If a drowning man ever does that—which I doubt.
Then he would tell something in his experiences,
thinking perhaps it had something to do with the
question in hand. It generally hadn't—and this time
he told about a long and arduous and fatiguing
chase which he had had in the Maine woods on a
hot summer's day, after some kind of a wild animal
that he wanted to kill, and how at last, chasing
eagerly after this creature across a wide stream,
he slipped and fell on the ice, and injured his leg—
whereupon a silence and confusion. —— noticed
that something was wrong, and then it occurred
to him that there was a kind of discrepancy in
hunting animals on the ice in summertime, so he
switched off to theology. He always did that. He
was a rabid Christian, and member of Joe Twichell's
church. Joe Twichell could get together the most
impossible Christians that ever assembled in anybody's congregation; and as a usual thing he couldn't
run his church systematically on account of new

deacons who didn't understand the business—the recent deacons having joined their predecessors in the penitentiary down there at Wethersfield. —— would wind up with some very pious remarks— and in fact they all did that. Take the whole crowd—the crowd that was almost always present —and this remark applies to them. There was J. Hammond Trumbull, the most learned man in the United States. He knew everything—everything in detail that had ever happened in this world, and a lot that was going to happen, and a lot that couldn't ever possibly happen. He would close with some piety. Henry C. Robinson—Governor Henry C. Robinson—a brilliant man, a most polished and effective and eloquent speaker, an easy speaker, a speaker who had no difficulties to encounter in delivering himself—always closed with some piety. A. C. Dunham, a man really great in his line— that is to say the commercial line—a great manufacturer, an enterprising man, a capitalist, a most competent and fascinating talker, a man who never opened his mouth without a stream of practical pearls flowing from it—*he* always closed with some piety.

[New York, January 13, 1906

THE piety ending was used also by Franklin and Johnson, and possibly by the rest of the club—most likely by the rest of the club. But I recall that that ending was a custom with Franklin and with Johnson. Franklin was a bluff old soldier. He was

a West Pointer and, I think, had served in the
Mexican War. He commanded one of McClellan's
armies in the Civil War at the time that McClellan
was commander-in-chief. He was an ideal soldier,
simple-hearted, good, kind, affectionate; set in his
opinions, his partialities and his prejudices, believing
everything which he had been taught to believe about
politics, religion, and military matters; thoroughly
well educated in the military science—in fact, I have
already said that, because I have said he was a
West Pointer. He knew all that was worth knowing
in that specialty and was able to reason well upon
his knowledge, but his reasoning faculty did not
shine when he was discussing other things. Johnson
was a member of Trinity, and was easily the most
brilliant member of the club. But his fine light
shone not in public, but in the privacy of the club,
and his qualities were not known outside of Hartford.

I had long been suffering from these intolerable
and inexcusable exudations of misplaced piety, and
for years had wanted to enter a protest against them,
but had struggled against the impulse and had always been able to conquer it, until now. But this
time —— was too much for me. He was the
feather that broke the camel's back. The substance
of his wandering twaddle—if by chance it had substance—was that there is nothing in dreams.
Dreams merely proceed from indigestion—there is
no quality of intelligence in them—they are thoroughly fantastic and without beginning, logical se-
quence, or definite end. Nobody, in our day, but

the stupid or the ignorant attaches any significance to them. And then he went on blandly and pleasantly to say that dreams had *once* had a mighty importance, that they had had the illustrious honor of being used by the Almighty as a means of conveying desires, warnings, commands, to people whom He loved or hated—that these dreams are set down in Holy Writ; that no sane man challenges their authenticity, their significance, their verity.

I followed —— and I remember with satisfaction that I said not one harsh thing, vexed as I was, but merely remarked, without warmth, that these tiresome damned prayer-meetings might better be adjourned to the garret of some church, where they belonged. It is *centuries* ago that I did that thing. It was away back, back, back, so many, many years ago—and yet I have always regretted it, because from that time forth, to the last meeting which I attended (which would be at the beginning of the spring of 1891) the piety ending was never used again. No, perhaps I am going too far; maybe I am putting too much emphasis upon my regret. Possibly when I said that about regret, I was doing what people so often unconsciously do, trying to place myself in a favorable light after having made a confession that makes such a thing more or less difficult. No, I think it quite likely that I never regretted it at all.

Anybody could see that the "piety ending" had no importance, for the reason that it was manifestly perfunctory. The club was *founded* by a great clergyman; it always had more clergymen in it than good people. Clergymen are not able to sink the shop without falling under suspicion. It was quite natural that the original members should introduce that kind of ending to their speeches. It was also quite natural that the rest of the membership, being church members, should take up the custom, turn it into a habit, and continue it without ever happening to notice that it was merely a mouth function, had no heart in it, and therefore was utterly valueless to themselves and to everybody else.

I do not now remember what form my views concerning dreams took at that time. I don't remember now what my notion about dreams was then, but I do remember telling a dream by way of illustrating some detail of my speech, and I also remember that when I had finished it Reverend Doctor Burton made that remark which contained that word I have already spoken of sixteen or seventeen times as having been uttered by my mother, in some such connection, forty or fifty years before. I was probably engaged in trying to make those people believe that now and then, by some accident, or otherwise, a dream which was prophetic turned up in the dreamer's mind. The date of my memorable dream was about the beginning of May, 1858. It was a remarkable dream, and I had been telling it several times every year for more than fifteen years—and now I was telling it again, here in the club.

In 1858 I was a steersman on board the swift and popular New Orleans and St. Louis packet, *Pennsylvania,* Captain Kleinfelter. I had been lent to Mr. Brown, one of the pilots of the *Pennsylvania,* by my owner, Mr. Horace E. Bixby, and I had been steering for Brown about eighteen months, I think. Then in the early days of May, 1858, came a tragic trip—the last trip of that fleet and famous steamboat. I have told all about it in one of my books, called *Life on the Mississippi.* But it is not likely that I told the dream in that book. I will ask my secretary to see—but I will go on and dictate the dream now, and it can go into the waste basket if it shall turn out that I have already published it. It is impossible that I can have published it, I think, because I never wanted my mother to know about that dream, and she lived several years after I published that volume.

I had found a place on the *Pennsylvania* for my brother Henry, who was two years my junior. It was not a place of profit, it was only a place of promise. He was "mud" clerk. Mud clerks received no salary, but they were in the line of promotion. They could become, presently, third clerk and second clerk, then chief clerk—that is to say, purser. The dream begins when Henry had been mud clerk about three months. We were lying in port at St. Louis. Pilots and steersmen had nothing to do during the three days that the boat lay in port in St. Louis and New Orleans, but the mud clerk had to begin his labors at dawn and continue them into the night, by the light of pine-knot torches. Henry and I, moneyless and unsalaried, had billeted ourselves upon our brother-in-law, Mr. Moffett, as night lodgers while in port. We took

our meals on board the boat.   No, I mean *I* lodged
at the house, not Henry. He spent the *evenings*
at the house, from nine until eleven, then went to
the boat to be ready for his early duties.   On the
night of the dream he started away at eleven, shak-
ing hands with the family, and said good-by according to custom.   I may mention that handshaking
as a good-by was not merely the custom of that
family, but the custom of the region—the custom
of Missouri, I may say.   In all my life, up to that
time, I had never seen one member of the Clemens
family kiss another one—except once.   When my
father lay dying in our home in Hannibal, Missouri
—the 24th of March, 1847—he put his arm around
my sister's neck and drew her down and kissed her,
saying, "Let me die."   I remember that, and I
remember the death rattle which swiftly followed
those words, which were his last.   These good-bys
were always executed in the family sitting room on
the second floor, and Henry went from that room
and downstairs without further ceremony.   But this
time my mother went with him to the head of the
stairs and said good-by again.   As I remember it,
she was moved to this by something in Henry's
manner, and she remained at the head of the stairs
while he descended.   When he reached the door he
hesitated, and climbed the stairs and shook hands
good-by again.   In the morning, when I awoke, I
had been dreaming, and the dream was so vivid, so
like reality, that it deceived me, and I thought it
was real.   In the dream I had seen Henry a corpse.
He lay in a metallic burial case.   He was dressed

in a suit of my clothing, and on his breast lay a great bouquet of flowers, mainly white roses, with a red rose in the center. The casket stood upon a couple of chairs. I dressed, and moved toward that door, thinking I would go in there and look at it, but I changed my mind. I thought I could not yet bear to meet my mother. I thought I would wait awhile and make some preparation for that ordeal. The house was in Locust Street, a little above Thirteenth, and I walked to Fourteenth and to the middle of the block beyond before it suddenly flashed upon me that there was nothing real about this—it was only a dream. I can still feel something of the grateful upheaval of joy of that moment, and I can also still feel the remnant of doubt, the suspicion that maybe it was real, after all. I returned to the house almost on a run, flew up the stairs two or three steps at a jump, and rushed into that sitting room, and was made glad again, for there was no casket there.

We made the usual eventless trip to New Orleans —no, it was not eventless, for it was on the way down that I had the fight with Mr. Brown [1] which resulted in his requiring that I be left ashore at New Orleans. In New Orleans I always had a job. It was my privilege to watch the freight piles from seven in the evening until seven in the morning, and get three dollars for it. It was a three-night job and occurred every thirty-five days. Henry always joined my watch about nine in the evening, when his own duties were ended, and we often

---

[1] See *Life on the Mississippi.*

walked my rounds and chatted together until midnight. This time we were to part, and so the night
before the boat sailed I gave Henry some advice.
I said: "In case of disaster to the boat, don't lose
your head—leave that unwisdom to the passengers
—they are competent—they'll attend to it. But
you rush for the hurricane deck, and astern to the
solitary lifeboat lashed aft the wheelhouse on the
port side, and obey the mate's orders—thus you
will be useful. When the boat is launched, give
such help as you can in getting the women and
children into it, and be sure you don't try to get
into it yourself. It is summer weather, the river
is only a mile wide, as a rule, and you can swim
ashore without any trouble." Two or three days
afterward the boat's boilers exploded at Ship Island,
below Memphis, early one morning—and what happened afterward I have already told in *Life on the
Mississippi*. As related there, I followed the
Pennsylvania about a day later, on another boat, and
we began to get news of the disaster at every port
we touched at, and so by the time we reached
Memphis we knew all about it.

I found Henry stretched upon a mattress on the
floor of a great building, along with thirty or forty
other scalded and wounded persons, and was
promptly informed, by some indiscreet person, that
he had inhaled steam, that his body was badly
scalded, and that he would live but a little while;
also, I was told that the physicians and nurses were
giving their whole attention to persons who had a
chance of being saved. They were short-handed

in the matter of physicians and nurses, and Henry and such others as were considered to be fatally hurt were receiving only such attention as could be spared, from time to time, from the more urgent cases. But Doctor Peyton, a fine and large-hearted old physician of great reputation in the community, gave me his sympathy and took vigorous hold of the case, and in about a week he had brought Henry around. He never committed himself with prognostications which might not materialize, but at eleven o'clock one night he told me that Henry was out of danger and would get well. Then he said, "At midnight these poor fellows lying here and there and all over this place will begin to mourn and mutter and lament and make outcries, and if this commotion should disturb Henry it will be bad for him; therefore ask the physicians on watch to give him an eighth of a grain of morphine, but this is not to be done unless Henry shall show signs that he is being disturbed."

Oh, well, never mind the rest of it. The physicians on watch were young fellows hardly out of the medical college, and they made a mistake—they had no way of measuring the eighth of a grain of morphine, so they guessed at it and gave him a vast quantity heaped on the end of a knife blade, and the fatal effects were soon apparent. I think he died about dawn, I don't remember as to that. He was carried to the dead-room and I went away for a while to a citizen's house and slept off some of my accumulated fatigue—and meantime something was happening. The coffins provided for the dead were of unpainted white pine, but in this instance some of the ladies of Memphis had made up a fund of sixty dollars and bought a metallic case, and when I came back and entered the dead-room Henry lay in that open case, and he was dressed in a suit of my clothing. I recognized instantly that my dream of several weeks before was here exactly reproduced, so far as these details went —and I think I missed one detail, but that one was immediately supplied, for just then an elderly lady entered the place with a large bouquet consisting mainly of white roses, and in the center of it was a red rose, and she laid it on his breast.

I told the dream there in the club that night just as I have told it here, I suppose.

[*New York, January 15, 1906*

REVEREND DOCTOR BURTON swung his leonine head around, focused me with his eye, and said:

"When was it that this happened?"

"In June, '58."

"It is a good many years ago. Have you told it several times since?"

"Yes, I have, a good many times."

"How many?"

"Why, I don't know how many."

"Well, strike an average. How many times a year do you think you have told it?"

"Well, I have told it as many as six times a year, possibly oftener."

"Very well, then, you've told it, we'll say, seventy or eighty times since it happened?"

"Yes," I said, "that's a very conservative estimate."

"Now then, Mark, a very extraordinary thing happened to me a great many years ago, and I used to tell it a number of times—a good many times—every year, for it was so wonderful that it always astonished the hearer, and that astonishment gave me a distinct pleasure every time. I never suspected that that tale was acquiring any auxiliary advantages through repetition until one day after I had been telling it ten or fifteen years it struck me that either I was getting old and slow in delivery, or that the tale was longer than it was when it was born. Mark, I diligently and prayerfully examined that tale, with this result: that I found that its proportions were now, as nearly as I could make out, one part fact, straight fact, fact pure and undiluted, golden fact, and twenty-four parts embroidery. I never told that tale afterward—I was never able to tell it again, for I had lost confidence in it, and so the pleasure of telling it was gone, and gone permanently. How much of this tale of yours is embroidery?"

"Well," I said, "I don't know. I don't think any of it is embroidery. I think it is all just as I have stated it, detail by detail."

"Very well," he said, "then it is all right, but I wouldn't tell it any more; because if you keep on, it will begin to collect embroidery sure. The safest thing is to stop now."

That was a great many years ago. And to-day is the first time that I have told that dream since Doctor Burton scared me into fatal doubts about it. No, I don't believe I can say that. I don't believe that I ever had any doubts whatever concerning the salient points of the dream, for those points are of such a nature that they are *pictures,* and pictures can be remembered, when they are vivid, much better than one can remember remarks and unconcreted facts. Although it has been so many years since I have told that dream, I can see those pictures now just as clearly defined as if they were before me in this room. I have not told the entire dream. There was a good deal more of it. I mean I have not told all that happened in the dream's fulfillment. After the incident in the death-room I may mention one detail, and that is this. When I arrived in St. Louis with the casket it was about eight o'clock in the morning, and I ran to my brother-in-law's place of business, hoping to find him there, but I missed him, for while I was on the way to his office he was on his way from the house to the boat. When I got back to the boat the casket was gone. He had had it conveyed out to his house. I hastened thither, and when I arrived the men were just removing the casket from the vehicle to carry it upstairs. I stopped that procedure, for I did not want my mother to see the dead face, because one side of it was drawn and distorted by the effects of the opium. When I went upstairs there stood the two chairs which I had seen in my dream, and if I had arrived there two or three minutes later the casket would have been resting upon those two chairs, just as in my dream of several weeks before.

A very curious thing happened at the house of James Goodwin, father of Rev. Francis Goodwin and also father of the great Connecticut Mutual Insurance Company. Mr. James Goodwin was an old man at the time that I speak of, but in his young days, when he used to drive stage between Hartford and Springfield, he conceived the idea of starting a Mutual Insurance Company, and he collected a little capital in the way of subscriptions—enough to start the business in a modest way—and he gave away the rest of the stock where he could find people willing to accept it (though they were rather scarce)—and now he had lived to see that stock worth 250 and nobody willing to sell at that price, or any other. He had long ago forgotten how to drive stage—but it was no matter. He was worth seven millions, and didn't need to work for a living any longer. Rev. Frank Goodwin, his son, an Episcopal clergyman, was a man of many accomplishments; and, among others, he was an architect. He planned and built a huge granite mansion for his father, and I think it was in this mansion that that curious thing happened. No, it happened in Francis Goodwin's own house in the neighborhood. It happened in this way. Frank Goodwin had a burglar alarm in his house. The annunciator was right at his ear, on the port side of his bed. He would put the whole house on the alarm—every window and every door—at bedtime; then, at five o'clock in the morning, the cook would descend from her bedroom and open the kitchen door, and that would set the alarm to buzzing in Goodwin's ear. Now as that happened every morning straight along, week in and week out, Goodwin soon became so habituated to it that it didn't disturb him. It aroused him, partly, from his sleep sometimes—sometimes it probably did not affect his sleep at all, but from old habit he would automatically put out his left hand and shut off that alarm. By that act he shut off the alarm from the entire house, leaving not a window or a door on it from five o'clock in the morning thenceforth until he should set the alarm the next night at bedtime.

The night that I speak of was one of those dismal New England November nights, close upon the end of the month, when the pestiferous New England climate furnishes those regions a shake-down just in the way of experiment and to get its hand in for business when the proper time comes, which is December. Well, the wind howled and the snow blew along in clouds when we left that house about midnight. It was a wild night. It was like a storm at sea, for boom and crash and roar and furious snow-drive. It was no kind of a night for burglars to be out in, and yet they *were* out. Goodwin was in bed, with his house on the alarm by half past twelve. Not very long afterward the burglars arrived. Evidently they knew all about the burglar alarm, because, instead of breaking into the kitchen, they sawed their way in—that is to say, they sawed a great panel out of the kitchen door and stepped in without alarming the alarm. They went all over the house at their leisure; they collected all sorts of trinkets and trumpery, all of the silverware. They carried these things to the kitchen, put them in bags, and then they gathered together a sumptuous supper, with champagne and Burgundy and so on, and ate that supper at their leisure. Then when they were ready to leave—say at three o'clock in the morning—the champagne and the Burgundy had had an influence, and they became careless for a moment; but one moment was enough. In that careless moment a burglar unlocked and opened the kitchen door, and of course the alarm went off. Rev. Mr. Goodwin put out his left hand and shut off the alarm and went on sleeping peacefully, but the burglars bounded out of the place and left all their swag behind them. A burglar alarm is a valuable thing if you know how to utilize it.

When Reverend Frank was finishing his father's mansion, I was passing by one day. I thought I would go in and see how the house was coming along, and in the first room I entered I found Mr. Goodwin and a paperhanger. Then Mr. Goodwin told me this curious story. He said: "This room has been waiting a good while. This is Morris paper, and it didn't hold out. You will see there is one space there, from the ceiling halfway to the floor, which is blank. I sent to New York and ordered some more of the paper—it couldn't be furnished. I applied in Philadelphia and in Boston, with the same result. There was not a bolt of that paper left in America, so far as any of these people knew. I wrote to London. The answer came back in those same monotonous terms—that paper was out of print—not a yard of it to be found. Then I told the paperhanger to strip the paper off and we would replace it with some other pattern, and I was very sorry, because I preferred that pattern to any other. Just then a farmer-looking man halted in front of the house, started to walk that single-plank approach that you just walked, and came in; but he saw that sign up there—'No admittance'—a sign which did not obstruct your excursion into this place—but it halted him. I said: 'Come in! Come in!' He came in, and, this being the first room on the route, he naturally glanced in. He saw the paper on the wall and remarked, casually: 'I am acquainted with that pattern. I've got a bolt of it at home down on my farm in Glastonbury.' It didn't take long to strike up a trade with him for that bolt, which had been lying in his farmhouse for he didn't know how long, and he hadn't any use for it—and now we are finishing up that lacking patch there."

MRS MORRIS'S ILLNESS TAKES A SERIOUS TURN

Cabinet Officers Urge President to Disavow Violence to Her

A DISCUSSION IN THE CASE

Mr. Sheppard Criticizes the President and Republican Leaders Try to Stop Him.

(Special to The New York Times.)

WASHINGTON, Jan. 10.—Mrs. Minor Morris, who on Thursday was dragged from the White House, is to-night in a critical condition.

She seemed to be on the road to recovery on Saturday, and her physicians held out hopes that she would be able to be out by Monday. At the beginning of this week her condition took an unfavorable turn, and she has been growing steadily worse. She had a congestive chill to-day and has continued to grow worse. It is evident to-night that her nervous system has suffered something approaching a collapse.

The bruises inflicted upon her by the policemen have not disappeared, a striking evidence of their severity. Her arms, shoulders, and neck still bear testimony to the nature of her treatment. Mentally and physically she is suffering severely.

It was learned to-day that two Cabinet officers, one of whom is Secretary Taft, have been laboring with the President for two days to get him to issue a statement disavowing the action of Assistant Secretary Barnes, who ordered Mrs. Morris expelled, and expressing his regret for the way she was treated. They have also urged him to promise to take action which will make impossible the repetition of such an occurrence.

The President has held out stoutly against the advice of these two Cabinet officers. He authorized Mr. Barnes to make the statement that he gave out, in which the treatment of Mrs. Morris was justified, and it is not easy to take the other tack now. On high authority, however, it is learned that the two Cabinet officers have not ceased their labors. They both look on the matter not as "a mere incident," but as a serious affair.

The Morris incident was brought up in the House to-day

just before adjournment by Mr. Sheppard of Texas. He was recognized for fifteen minutes, in the ordinary course of the debate on the Philippine Tariff bill, and began at once to discuss the resolution he introduced Monday calling for an investigation of the expulsion. He excused himself for speaking on the resolution at this time, saying that as it was not privileged he could not obtain its consideration without the consent of the Committee on Rules.

He went on to describe the incident at the White House. He had proceeded only a minute or two when he was interrupted by General Grosvenor, who rose to the point of order that the remarks were not germane to the Philippine Tariff bill.

"I will show the gentleman that it is germane," cried Mr. Sheppard. "It is just as proper for this country to have a Chinese wall around the White House as it is to have such a wall around the United States."

"Well, if he thinks it is proper to thus arraign the President and his household," said Mr. Grosvenor, "let him go on."

"If the President had heard the howl of a wolf or the growl of a bear from the adjacent offices," retorted Mr. Sheppard, "the response would have been immediate, but the wail of an American woman fell upon unresponsive ears."

There had been several cries of protest when General Grosvenor interrupted Mr. Sheppard, many of whose Democratic friends gathered about him and urged him to proceed. They applauded his reply to Mr. Grosvenor, and the Ohioan did not press his point.

"These unwarrantable and unnecessary brutalities," continued Mr. Sheppard, "demand an investigation. Unless Congress takes some action we shall soon witness in a free republic a condition where citizens cannot approach the President they have created without fear of bodily harm from arbitrary subordinates."

Mr. Sheppard had nearly reached the close of his remarks when Mr. Payne, the titular floor leader of the Republicans, renewed the Grosvenor point of order. Mr. Olmstead of Pennsylvania, in the chair, however, ruled that with the House sitting in Committee of the Whole on the state of the Union, remarks need not be germane.

Mr. Payne interrupted again, to ask a question.

"If a gentleman has the facts upon which to found his attack," he said, "does he not think the police court is the better place to air them?"

"The suggestion is a reflection upon the gentleman himself, although he is a friend of mine," replied Sheppard.

When the speech was finished Grosvenor got the floor and said he had been aware of the rules when he did not press his point.

"But I made the point," he continued, "merely to call the attention of the young gentleman from Texas in a mild and fatherly manner to my protest against his remarks. I hoped he would refrain from further denunciation of the President. He has introduced a resolution which is now pending before the proper committee. That resolution asks for facts and I supposed that the gentleman would wait for the facts until that resolution is brought into the House.

"I know no difference in proper conduct between the President's office and household and the humblest home in this Nation, but I don't believe a condition has arisen such that the husband of this woman cannot take care of the situation."

A high government official to-night added to the accounts of the expulsion an incident, which he said was related to him by an eye-witness. While the policemen and their negro assistant were dragging Mrs. Morris through the grounds the scene was witnessed by the women servants, some of whom called out, "Shame!" One of the policemen pressed his hand down on Mrs. Morris's mouth to stifle her cries for help, and at that sight a man servant, a negro, rushed forward and shouted:

"Take your hand off that white woman's face! Don't treat a white woman that way!"

The policeman paid no attention to the man, and continued his efforts to stifle Mrs. Morris's cries.

The reason I want to insert that account of the Morris case, which is making such a lively stir all over the United States, and possibly the entire world, in these days, is this. Some day, no doubt, these autobiographical notes will be published. It will be after my death. It may be five years from now, it may be ten, it may be fifty—but whenever the time shall come, even if it should be a century hence—I claim that the reader of that day will find the same strong interest in that narrative that the world has in it to-day, for the reason that the account speaks of the thing in the language we naturally use when we are talking about something that has just happened. That form of narrative is able to carry along with it for ages and ages the very same interest which we find in it to-day. Whereas if this had happened fifty years ago, or a hundred, and the historian had dug it up and was putting it in *his* language, and furnishing you a long-distance view of it, the reader's interest in it would be pale. You see, it would not be *news* to him, it would be history; merely history; and history can carry on no successful competition with *news,* in the matter of sharp interest. When an eye-witness sets down in narrative form some extraordinary occurrence which he has witnessed, that is *news*— that is the news form, and its interest is absolutely indestructible; time can have no deteriorating effect upon that episode. I am placing that account there largely as an experiment. If any stray copy of this book shall, by any chance, escape the paper-mill for a century or so, and then be discovered and read, I am betting that that remote reader will find that it is still *news* and that it is just as interesting as any news he will find in the newspapers of his day and morning—if newspapers shall still be in existence then—though let us hope they won't.

These notions were born to me in the fall of 1867, in Washington. That is to say, thirty-nine years ago. I had come back from the *Quaker City* excursion. I had gone to Washington to write *The Innocents Abroad*, but before beginning that book it was necessary to earn some money to live on meantime, or borrow it—which would be difficult, or to take it where it reposed unwatched—which would be unlikely. So I started the first Newspaper Correspondence Syndicate that an unhappy world ever saw. I started it in conjunction with William Swinton, a brother of the admirable John Swinton. William Swinton was a brilliant creature, highly educated, accomplished. He was such a contrast to me that I did not know which of us most to admire, because both ends of a contrast are equally delightful to me. A thoroughly beautiful woman and a thoroughly homely woman are creations which I love to gaze upon, and which I cannot tire of gazing upon, for each is perfect in her own line, and it is *perfection,* I think, in many things, and perhaps most things, which is the quality that fascinates us. A splendid literature charms us; but it doesn't charm *me* any more than its opposite does—"hogwash" literature. At another time I will explain that word, "hog-wash" and offer an example of it which lies here on the bed—a book which was lately sent to me from England, or Ireland.

Swinton kept a jug. It was sometimes full, but seldom as full as himself—and it was when he was fullest that he was most competent with his pen. We wrote a letter apiece once a week and copied them and sent them to twelve newspapers, charging each of the newspapers a dollar apiece. And although we didn't get rich, it kept the jug going and partly fed the two of us. We earned the rest of our living with magazine articles. My trade in that line was better than his, because I had written six letters for the New York *Tribune* while I was out on the *Quaker City* excursion, fifty-three for the *Alta Californian,* and one pretty breezy one for the New York *Herald* after I got back, and so I had a good deal of a reputation to trade on. Every now and then I was able to get twenty-five dollars for a magazine article.

I had a chance to write a magazine article about an ancient and moss-grown claim which was disturbing Congress that session, a claim which had been disturbing Congress ever since the War of 1812, and was always getting paid, but never satisfied. The claim was for Indian corn and for provender consumed by the American troops in Maryland or somewhere around there, in the War of 1812. I wrote the article, and it is in one of my books, and is there called "Concerning the Great Beef Contract." It was necessary to find out the price of Indian corn in 1812, and I found that detail a little difficult. Finally I went to A. R. Spofford, who was the Librarian of Congress then—Spofford the man with the prodigious memory—and I put my case before him. He knew every volume in the Library, and what it contained, and where it was located. He said promptly, "I know of only two sources which promise to afford this information, 'Tooke on Prices' " (he brought me the book) "and the New York *Evening Post*. In those days newspapers did not publish market reports, but about 1809 the New York *Evening Post* began to print market reports on sheets of paper about note-paper size, and fold these in the journal." He brought me a file of the *Evening Post* for 1812. I examined "Tooke" and then began to examine the *Post*—and I was in a great hurry. I had less than an hour at my disposal. But in the *Post* I found a personal narrative which chained my attention at once. It was a letter from a gentleman who had witnessed the arrival of the British and the burning of the Capitol. The matter was bristling with interest for him and he delivered his words hot from the bat. That letter must have been read with fiery and absorbing interest three days later in New

York, but not with any more absorbing interest than the interest which was making my blood leap fifty-nine years later. When I finished that account I found I had used up all the time that was at my disposal, and more.

[*New York, January 15th, continued*

[*Dictated on January 16th*

THAT incident made a strong impression upon me. I believed I had made a discovery—the discovery already indicated—the discovery of the wide difference in interest between "news" and "history"; that news is history in its first and best form, its vivid and fascinating form, and that history is the pale and tranquil reflection of it.

This reminds me that in this daily dictation of autobiographical notes I am mixing these two forms together all the time. I am hoping by this method of procedure to secure the values of both. I am sure I have found the right way to spin an auto-biography at last, after my many experiments. Years ago I used to make skeleton notes to use as texts in writing autobiographical chapters, but really those notes were worth next to nothing. If I expanded them upon the page at once, while their interest was fresh in my mind, they were useful, but if I left them unused for several weeks, or several months, their power to suggest and excite had usually passed away. They were faded flowers, their fragrance was gone. But I believe in this present plan. When you arrive with your stenographic plant at eleven, every morning, you find me placid and comfortable in bed, smoking, untroubled by the fact that I must presently get to work and begin to dictate this history of mine. And if I were depending upon faded notes for inspiration, I should have trouble and my work would soon become distasteful. But by my present system I do not need any notes. *The thing uppermost in a person's mind* is the thing to talk about or write about. The thing of new and immediate interest is the pleasantest text he can have—and you can't come here at eleven o'clock, or any other hour, and catch me without a new interest—a perfectly fresh interest—because I have either been reading the infernal newspapers and got it there, or I have been talking with somebody; and in either case the new interest is present—the interest which I most wish to dictate about. So you see the result is that this narrative of mine is sure to begin every morning in diary form, because it is sure to begin with something which I have just read, or something which I have just been talking about. That text, when I am done with it—if I ever get done with it, and I don't seem to get done with any text—but it doesn't matter, I am not interested in getting done with anything. I am only interested in talking along and wandering around as much as I want to, regardless of results to the future reader. By consequence, here we have diary and history combined; because as soon as I wander from the present text—the thought of to-day—that digression takes me far and wide over an uncharted sea of recollection, and the result of that is *history*.

Consequently my autobiography is diary and history combined. The privilege of beginning every day in the diary form is a valuable one. I may even use a larger word, and say it is a precious one, for it brings together widely separated things that are in a manner related to each other, and consequently pleasant surprises and contrasts are pretty sure to result every now and then.

Did I dictate something about John Malone three or four days ago? Very well, then, if I didn't I must have been talking with somebody about John Malone. I remember now, it was with Mr. Volney Streamer. He is a librarian of the Players' Club. He called here to bring me a book which he has published, and, in a general way, to make my acquaintance. I was a foundation member of the Players' Club, but ceased to be a member three years ago, through an absurdity committed by the management of that club, a management which has always been idiotic; a management which from the beginning has been selected from, not the nearest asylum in the city, but the most competent one (and some time I wish to talk about that). Several times, during this lapse of three years, old friends of mine and comrades in the club—David Munro, that charming Scot, editor of the *North American Review;* Robert Reid, the artist; Saint-Gaudens, the sculptor; John Malone, the ex-actor; and others— have been resenting the conduct of that management—the conduct, I mean, which resulted in my segregation from the club—and they have always been trying to find a way of restoring me to the fold without damaging my pride. At last they found a way. They made me an honorary member. This handsome honor afforded me unlimited gratification and I was glad to get back under such flattering conditions. (I don't like that word, but let it go, I can't think of the right one at the moment.) Then David Munro and the others put up the fatted calf for the lost sheep in the way of a dinner to me. Midway of the dinner I got a glimpse, through a half-open pantry door, of that pathetic figure, John Malone. There he was, left out, of course. Sixty-five years old; and his history may be summarized—his history for fifty years—in those two words, those eloquent words—"left out." He has been left out, and left out, and left out, as the years drifted by for nearly two generations. He was always expecting to be counted in. He was always pathetically hoping to be counted in; and that hope never deserted him through all those years, and yet was never in any instance realized. During all those years that I used to drop in at the Players' for a game of billiards and a chat with the boys, John Malone was always there until midnight and after. He had a cheap lodging in the Square—somewhere on Gramercy Park, but the club was his real home. He told me his history once. His version of it was this:

He was an apprentice in a weekly little newspaper office in Willamette, Oregon, and by and by Edwin Booth made a one-night stand there with his troupe, and John got stage-struck and joined the troupe, and traveled with it around about the Pa-

cific coast in various useful histrionic capacities—
capacities suited to a beginner, sometimes assisting
by appearing on the stage to say, "My lord, the
carriage waits," later appearing armored in shining tin, as a Roman soldier, and so on, gradually
rising to higher and higher eminences, and by and
by he stood shoulder to shoulder with John McCullough, and the two stood next in rank after Edwin
Booth himself on the tragic stage. It was a question which of the two would succeed Booth when
Booth should retire or die. According to Malone,
his celebrity quite equaled McCullough's in those
days, and the chances were evenly balanced. A
time came when there was a great opportunity—
a great part to be played in Philadelphia. Malone
was chosen for the part. He missed his train. John
McCullough was put into that great place and
achieved a success which *made* him for life. Malone
was sure that if he had not missed the train he would
have achieved that success himself; he would have
secured the enduring fame which fell to John
McCullough's lot; he would have moved on through
life serene, comfortable, fortunate, courted, admired, applauded, as was John McCullough's case
from that day until the day of his death. Malone
believed with all his heart that fame and fortune
were right there within his reach at that time, and
that he lost them merely through missing his train.
He dated his decline from that day. He declined,
and declined, and declined, little by little, and little
by little, and year after year, until there came a
time when he was no longer wanted on the stage;

when even minor part after minor part slipped from his grasp; and at last engagements ceased altogether—engagements of any kind. Yet he was always believing, and always expecting, that a turn of fortune would come; that he would get a chance on the stage in some great part; and that *one* chance, he said, was all he wanted. He was convinced that the world would not question that he was the rightful successor of Edwin Booth, and from that day forth he would be a famous and happy and fortunate man. He never gave up that hope. Three or four years ago, I remember his jubilation over the fact that he had been chosen by some private theatrical people to play Othello in one of the big theaters of New York. And I remember his grief and deep depression when those private theatrical people gave up the enterprise, at the last moment, and canceled Malone's engagement, snatching from him the greatness which had once more been just within his reach.

As I was saying, at mid-dinner that night I saw him through the half-open door. There he remained through the rest of the dinner, "left out," always left out. But at the end of the speeches, when a number of us were standing up in groups and chatting, he crept meekly in and found his way to the vacant chair at my side, and sat down. I sat down at once and began to talk with him. I was always fond of him—I think everybody was. And presently the president of the New York City College came and bent over John and asked me something about my last summer, and how I had liked it up in the New Hampshire hills, at Dublin. Then, in order to include John in the conversation, he asked him if he was acquainted with that region and if he had ever been in Dublin. Malone said dreamily, and with the air of a man who was trying to think up long-gone things, "How does it lie as regards Manchester?" President Finley told him, and then John said, "I have never been to Dublin, but I have a sort of recollection of Manchester. I am pretty sure I was there once—but it was only a one-night stand, you know."

It filled my soul with a gentle delight, a gracious satisfaction, the way he said that—"Only a one-night stand." It seemed to reveal that in his half century of daydreaming he had been an Edwin Booth and unconscious that he was only John Malone—that he was an Edwin Booth, with a long and great and successful career behind him, in which "one-night stands" sank into insignificance and the memory unused to treasuring such little things could not keep tally of them. He said it with the splendid indifference and serenity of a Napoleon who was making an indolent effort to remember a skirmish in which a couple of soldiers had been killed, but was not finding it really worth while to dig deep after such a fact.

Yesterday I spoke to Volney Streamer about John Malone. I had a purpose in this, though I did not tell Streamer what it was. David Munro was not able to be at that dinner, and so, to get satisfaction, he is providing another, for the 6th of February. David told me the guests he was inviting, and

said that if there was anybody that I would like to
invite, think it over and send him the name. I did
think it over, and I have written down here on
this pad the name of the man I selected—John
Malone—hoping that he would not have to be left
out this time, and knowing he wouldn't be left out
unless David should desire it, and I didn't think
David would desire it. However, I took the opportunity to throw out a feeler or two in talking
with Volney Streamer, merely asking him how John
Malone stood with the membership of the Players'
now—and that question was quickly and easily answered—that everybody liked John Malone and
everybody pitied him.

Then he told me John Malone's history. It differed in some points from the history which Malone had given me, but not in essentials, I should
say. One fact came out which I had not known
about—that John was not a bachelor, but had a
married daughter living here somewhere in New
York. Then, as Streamer went on, came this surprise: that *he* was a member of Edwin Booth's company when John Malone joined it a thousand years
ago, and that he had been a comrade of John's in
the company all over the Pacific coast and the rest
of the states for years and years. There, you see,
an entire stranger drops in here in the most casual
way, and the first thing I know he is an ancient and
moss-grown and mildewed comrade of the man who
is for the moment uppermost in my mind. That is
the way things happen when you are doing a diary
and a history combined, and you can't catch these

things in any other way but just that. If you try
to remember them, with the intention of writing
them down in the form of history a month or a
year hence, why, when you get to them the juice is
all out of them—you can't bring to mind the details.
And moreover, they have lost their quality of surprise and joy, anyway. That has all wasted and
passed away.

Very well. Yesterday Rev. Joe Twichell arrived from Hartford to take dinner and stay all
night and swap some lies, and he sat here by the
bed the rest of the afternoon, and we talked, and
I told him all about John Malone. Twichell came
in after breakfast this morning (the 16th) to chat
again, and he brought me this, which he had cut
out of the morning paper:

VETERAN ACTOR DEAD

John Malone Was Historian of The Players' Club

John Malone, the historian of the Players' Club and one
of the oldest actors in the country, was stricken with
apoplexy yesterday afternoon in front of Bishop Greer's
residence, 7 Gramercy Park, a few doors from the club.
Bishop Greer saw him fall, and, with the assistance of his
servants, carried Mr. Malone into his house. He was unconscious, and the Bishop telephoned to Police Headquarters.

An ambulance was sent from Bellevue Hospital, and Mr.
Malone was taken to the institution by Dr. Hawkes. Later
the Players' had him removed to the Post-Graduate Hospital, where he died last night.

Mr. Malone was sixty-five years old, and supported all the notable actors of a past generation. For a long time he was associated with Booth and Barrett. He had appeared on the stage but infrequently of late years, devoting the greater part of his time to magazine work. He lived with a married daughter in West 147th Street, but visited the Players' Club nearly every day. He was on his way to the club when stricken.

So there is another surprise, you see. While Twichell and I were talking about John Malone he was passing from this life. His disappointments are ended. At last he is not "left out." It was a long wait, but the best of all fortunes is his at last.

I started to say, a while ago, that when I had seemingly made that discovery of the difference between "news" and "history" thirty-nine years ago, I conceived the idea of a magazine, to be called *The Back Number* and to contain nothing but ancient news; narratives culled from moldy old newspapers and moldy old books; narratives set down by eye-witnesses at the time that the episodes treated of happened.

ABOUT GENERAL SICKLES

[*New York, January 16th, continued*

[*Dictated Wednesday, January 17th*

WITH considerable frequency, since then, I have tried to get publishers to make the experiment of such a magazine, but I was never successful. I was never able to convince a publisher that *The Back Number* would interest the public. Not one of them was able to conceive of the idea of a sane human being finding interest in stale things. I made my latest effort three years ago. Again I failed to convince. But I, myself, am not convinced. I am quite sure that *The Back Number* would succeed and become a favorite. I am also sure of another thing—that *The Back Number* would have this advantage over any other magazine that was ever issued, to wit: that the man who read the first paragraph in it would go on and read the magazine entirely through, skipping nothing—whereas there is no magazine in existence which ever contains three articles which can be depended upon to interest the reader. It is necessary to put a *dozen* articles into a magazine of the day in order to hit six or eight tastes. One man buys the magazine for one of its articles, another is attracted by another, another by a third; but no man buys the magazine because of the whole of its contents. I contend that *The Back Number* would be bought for the whole of its contents and that each reader would read the whole.

Mr. Paine, you and I will start that magazine, and try the experiment, if you are willing to select the ancient news from old books and newspapers and do the rest of the editorial work. Are you willing?

Mr. Paine. "I should be very willing, when we get time to undertake it."

"Very well, then we will, by and by, make that experiment."

Twichell and I stepped across the street, that night, in the rain, and spent an hour with General Sickles. Sickles is eighty-one years old, now. I had met him only once or twice before, although there has been only the width of Ninth Street between us for a year. He is too old to make visits, and I am too lazy. I remember when he killed Philip Barton Key, son of the author of "The Star-spangled Banner," and I remember the prodigious excitement it made in the country. I think it cannot be far from fifty years ago. My vague recollection of it is that it happened in Washington and that I was there at the time.[1]

I have felt well acquainted with General Sickles for thirty-eight or thirty-nine years, because I have known Twichell that long. Twichell was a chaplain in Sickles's brigade in the Civil War, and he was always fond of talking about the general. Twichell was under Sickles all through the war. Whenever he comes down from Hartford he makes it his duty to go and pay his respects to the general. Sickles is a genial old fellow; a handsome and stately military figure; talks smoothly, in well-constructed English—I may say perfectly constructed English. His talk is full of interest and bristling with points, but as there are no emphases scattered through it anywhere, and as there is no animation in it, it soon

---

[1] Key was shot by Sickles as a result of a complication which concerned Sickles's wife.

becomes oppressive by its monotony and it makes the listener drowsy. Twichell had to step on my foot once or twice. The late Bill Nye once said, "I have been told that Wagner's music is better than it sounds." That felicitous description of a something which so many people have tried to describe, and couldn't, does seem to fit the general's manner of speech exactly. His talk is much better than it is. No, that is not the idea—there seems to be a lack there somewhere. Maybe it is another case of the sort just quoted. Maybe Nye would say that "it is better than it sounds." I think that is it. His talk does *not* sound entertaining, but it *is* distinctly entertaining.

Sickles lost a leg at Gettysburg, and I remember Twichell's account of that circumstance. He talked about it on one of our long walks, a great many years ago, and, although the details have passed out of my memory, I still carry the picture in my mind as presented by Twichell. The leg was taken off by a cannon ball. Twichell and others carried the general out of the battle, and they placed him on a bed made of boughs, under a tree. There was no surgeon present, and Twichell and Rev. Father O'Hagan, a Catholic priest, made a makeshift tourniquet and stopped the gush of blood—*checked* it, perhaps is the right term. A newspaper correspondent appeared first. Gen. Sickles considered himself a dying man, and (if Twichell is as truthful a person as the character of his cloth requires him to be) General Sickles put aside everything connected with a future world in order to go out of

this one in becoming style. And so he dictated his
"last words" to that newspaper correspondent.
That was Twichell's idea—I remember it well—
that the general, no doubt influenced by the fact
that several people's last words have been so badly
chosen—whether by accident or intention—that they
have outlived all the rest of the man's fame, was
moved to do his last words in a form calculated
to petrify and preserve them for the future generations. Twichell quoted that speech. I have forgotten what it was, now, but it was well chosen for
its purpose.

Now when we sat there in the general's presence,
listening to his monotonous talk—it was about himself, and is always about himself, and always seems
modest and unexasperating, inoffensive—it seemed
to me that he was just the kind of man who would
risk his salvation in order to do some "last words"
in an attractive way. He murmured and warbled,
and warbled, and it was all just as simple and pretty
as it could be. And also I will say this: that he
never made an ungenerous remark about anybody.
He spoke severely of this and that and the other
person—officers in the war—but he spoke with dignity and with courtesy. There was no malignity in
what he said. He merely pronounced what he evidently regarded as just criticisms upon them.

I noticed then, what I had noticed once before,
four or five months ago, that the general valued
his lost leg away above the one that is left. I am
perfectly sure that if he had to part with either of
them he would part with the one that he has got.

I have noticed this same thing in several other generals who had lost a portion of themselves in the Civil War. There was General Fairchild of Wisconsin. He lost an arm in one of the great battles. When he was consul-general in Paris and we Clemenses were sojourning there some time or other, and grew to be well acquainted with him and with his family, I know that whenever a proper occasion —an occasion which gave General Fairchild an opportunity to elevate the stump of the lost arm and wag it with effect, occurred—that is what he did. It was easy to forgive him for it, and I did it.

General Noyes was our minister to France at the time. He had lost a leg in the war. He was a pretty vain man, I will say that for him, and anybody could see—certainly I saw—that whenever there was a proper gathering around, Noyes presently seemed to disappear. There wasn't anything left of him but the leg which he didn't have.

Well, General Sickles sat there on the sofa, and talked. It was a curious place. Two rooms of considerable size—parlors opening together with folding-doors—and the floors, the walls, the ceilings cluttered up and overlaid with lion skins, tiger skins, leopard skins, elephant skins; photographs of the general at various times of life—photographs *en civil;* photographs in uniform; gushing sprays of swords fastened in trophy form against the wall; flags of various kinds stuck here and there and yonder; more animals; more skins; here and there and everywhere more and more skins; skins of wild creatures, always, I believe; beautiful skins. You couldn't walk across that floor anywhere without stumbling over the hard heads of lions and things. You couldn't put out a hand anywhere without laying it upon a velvety, exquisite tiger-skin or leopard skin, and so on—oh, well, all the kinds of skins were there; it was as if a menagerie had undressed in the place. Then there was a most decided and rather unpleasant odor, which proceeded from disinfectants and preservatives and things such as you have to sprinkle on skins in order to discourage the moths—so it was not altogether a pleasant place, on that account. It was a kind of museum, and yet it was not the sort of museum which seemed dignified enough to be the museum of a great soldier —and so famous a soldier. It was the sort of museum which should delight and entertain little boys and girls. I suppose that that museum reveals a part of the general's character and make. He is sweetly and winningly childlike.

Once, in Hartford, twenty or twenty-five years ago, just as Twichell was coming out of his gate one Sunday morning to walk to his church and preach, a telegram was put into his hand. He read it immediately, and then, in a manner, collapsed. It said, "General Sickles died last night at midnight."

Well, you can see, now, that it wasn't so. But no matter—it was so to Joe at the time. He walked along—walked to the church—but his mind was far away. All his affection and homage and worship of his general had come to the fore. His heart was full of these emotions. He hardly knew where he was. In his pulpit, he stood up and began the service, but with a voice over which he had almost no command. The congregation had never seen him thus moved, before, in his pulpit. They sat there and gazed at him and wondered what was the matter; because he was now reading, in this broken voice and with occasional tears trickling down his face, what to them seemed a quite unemotional chapter—that one about Moses begat Aaron, and Aaron begat Deuteronomy, and Deuteronomy begat St. Peter, and St. Peter begat Cain, and Cain begat Abel—and he was going along with this, and half crying—his voice continually breaking. The congregation left that church that morning without being able to account for this most extraordinary thing—as it seemed to them. That a man who had been a soldier for more than four years, and who had preached in that pulpit so many, many times on really moving subjects, without even the quiver of a lip, should break all down over the begattings, was a thing which they couldn't understand. But there it is—any one can see how such a mystery as that would arouse the curiosity of those people to the boiling-point.

Twichell has had many adventures. He has more adventures in a year than anybody else has in five. One Saturday night he noticed a bottle on his wife's dressing bureau. He thought the label said "Hair Restorer," and he took it in his room and gave his head a good drenching and sousing with it and carried it back and thought no more about it. Next morning when he got up his head was a bright green!

He sent around everywhere and couldn't get a substitute preacher, so he had to go to his church himself and preach—and he did it. He hadn't a sermon in his barrel—as it happened—of any lightsome character, so he had to preach a very grave one— a very serious one—and it made the matter worse. The gravity of the sermon did not harmonize with the gayety of his head, and the people sat all through it with handkerchiefs stuffed in their mouths—any way to try to keep down their joy. And Twichell told me that he was sure he never had seen his congregation—he had never seen the whole body of his congregation—the *entire* body of his congregation—absorbed in interest in his sermon, from beginning to end, before. Always there had been an aspect of indifference, here and there, or wandering, somewhere; but this time there was nothing of the kind. Those people sat there as if they thought, "Good for this day and train only; we must have all there is of this show, not waste any of it." And he said that when he came down out of the pulpit more people waited to shake him by the hand and tell him what a good sermon it was, than ever before. And it seemed a pity that these people should do these fictions in such a place—right in the church —when it was quite plain they were not interested in the sermon at all; they only wanted to get a near view of his head.

Well, Twichell said—no, Twichell didn't say, *I* say, that as the days went on and Sunday followed Sunday, the interest in Twichell's hair grew and grew; because it didn't stay green. It took on deeper and deeper shades of green; and then it would change and become reddish, and would go from that to some other color; but it was never a solid color. It was always mottled. And each Sunday it was a little more interesting than it was the Sunday before —and Twichell's head became famous while his hair was undergoing these various and fascinating mottlings. And it was a good thing in several ways, because the business had been languishing a little, and now a lot of people joined the church so that they could have the show, and it was the beginning of a prosperity for that church which has never diminished in all these years. Nothing so fortunate ever happened to Joe as that.

But I have wandered from that tree where General Sickles lay bleeding and arranging his last words. It was three-quarters of an hour before a surgeon could be found, for that was a tremendous battle and surgeons were needed everywhere. When the surgeon arrived it was after nightfall. It was a still and windless July night, and there was a candle burning—I think somebody sat near the general's head and held this candle in his hand. It threw just light enough to make the general's face distinct, and there were several dim figures waiting around about. Into this group, out of the darkness, bursts an aide; springs lightly from his horse; approaches this white-faced expiring general; straightens himself up soldier fashion; salutes; and reports in the most soldierly and matter-of-fact way that he has carried out an order given him by the general, and that the movement of the regiments to the supporting point designated has been accomplished.

The general thanked him courteously. I am sure Sickles must have been always polite. It takes *training* to enable a person to be properly courteous when he is dying. Many have tried it. I suppose very few have succeeded.

[*New York, Thursday, January 18, 1906*

SENATOR TILLMAN of South Carolina has been making a speech—day before yesterday—of frank and intimate criticism of the President—the President of the United States, as he calls him; whereas, so far as my knowledge goes, there has been no such functionary as President of the United States for forty years, perhaps, if we except Cleveland. I do not call to mind any other President of the United States—there may have been one or two— *perhaps* one or two, who were not always and persistently presidents of the Republican party, but were now and then for a brief interval really Presidents of the United States. Tillman introduces into this speech the matter of the expulsion of Mrs. Morris from the White House, and I think his arraignment of the President was a good and capable piece of work. At any rate, his handling of it suited me very well and tasted very good in my mouth. I was glad that there was somebody to take this matter up, whether from a generous motive or from an ungenerous one, and give it an airing. It was needed. The whole nation, and the

entire press, have been sitting by in meek and slav-
ish silence, everybody privately wishing—just as was
my own case—that some person with some sense of
the proprieties would rise up and denounce this outrage as it ought to be denounced.   Tillman makes
a point which charms me.   I wanted to use it myself, days ago, but I was already arranging a scheme
in another matter of public concern which may invite a brick or two in my direction, and one entertainment of this sort at a time is plenty for me.
That point was this: that the President is always
prodigal of letters and telegrams to Tom, Dick,
and Harry, about everything and nothing.   He
seems never to lack time from his *real* duties to
attend to duties that do not exist.   So, at the very
time when he should have been throwing off one or
two little lines to say to Mrs. Morris and her friends
that, being a gentleman, he was hastening to say he
was sorry that his assistant secretary had been turning the nation's official mansion into a sailor boarding-house, and that he would admonish Mr. Barnes,
and the rest of the reception-room garrison, to deal
more gently with the erring in future, and to ab-
stain from any conduct in the White House which
would rank as disgraceful in any other respectable
dwelling in the land. . . .

I don't like Tillman.   His second cousin killed
an editor, three years ago, without giving that editor a chance to defend himself.   I recognize that it
is almost always wise, and is often in a manner
necessary, to kill an editor, but I think that when
a man is a United States Senator he ought to re-

quire his second cousin to refrain as long as he can, and then do it in a handsome way, running some personal risk himself. I have not known Tillman to do many things that were greatly to his credit during his political life, but I am glad of the position which he has taken this time. The President has persistently refused to listen to such friends of his as are not insane—men who have tried to persuade him to disavow Mr. Barnes's conduct and express regret for that occurrence. And now Mr. Tillman uses that point which I spoke of a minute ago, and uses it with telling effect. He reminds the Senate that at the very time that the President's dignity would not allow him to send to Mrs. Morris or her friends a kindly and regretful line, he had time enough to send a note of compliment and admiration to a prize-fighter in the far West. If the President had been an unpopular person, that point would have been seized upon early, and much and disastrous notice taken of it. But, as I have suggested before, the nation and the newspapers have maintained a loyal and humiliated silence about it, and have waited prayerfully and hopefully for some reckless person to say the things which were in their hearts, and which they could not bear to utter. Mrs. Morris embarrasses the situation, and extends and keeps alive the discomfort of eighty millions of people, by lingering along near to death, yet neither rallying nor dying; to do either would relieve the tension. For the present, the discomfort must continue. Mr. Tillman certainly has not chloroformed it.

We buried John Malone this morning. His old friends of the Players' Club attended in a body. It was the second time in my life that I had been present at a Catholic funeral. And as I sat in the church my mind went back, by natural process, to that other one, and the contrast strongly interested me. That first one was the funeral of the Empress of Austria, who was assassinated six or eight years ago. There was a great concourse of the ancient nobility of the Austrian Empire; and as that patchwork of old kingdoms and principalities consists of nineteen states and eleven nationalities, and as these nobles came clothed in the costumes which their ancestors were accustomed to wear on state occasions three, four, or five centuries ago, the variety and magnificence of the costumes made a picture which cast far into the shade all the notions of splendor and magnificence which in the course of my life I had accumulated from the opera, the theater, the picture galleries, and from books. Gold, silver, jewels, silks, satins, velvets—they were all there in brilliant and beautiful confusion, and in that sort of perfect harmony which Nature herself observes and is master of, when she paints and groups her flowers and her forests and floods them with sunshine. The military and civic milliners of the Middle Ages knew their trade. Infinite as was the variety of the costumes displayed, there was not an ugly one, not one that was a discordant note in the harmony, or an offense to the eye. When those massed costumes were still, they were transcendently beautiful; when the mass stirred, the slightest movement set the jewels and metals and bright colors afire and swept it with flashing lights which sent a sort of ecstasy of delight through me.

But it was different this morning. This morning the clothes were all alike. They were simple and devoid of color. The Players were clothed as they are always clothed, except that they wore the high silk hat of ceremony. Yet, in its way, John Malone's funeral was as impressive as had been that of the Empress. There was no inequality between John Malone and the Empress except the artificial inequalities which have been invented and established by man's childish vanity. The Empress and John were just equals in the essentials of goodness of heart and a blameless life. Both passed by the onlooker, in their coffins, respected, esteemed, honored; both traveled the same road from the church, bound for the same resting-place—according to Catholic doctrine, Purgatory—to be removed thence to a better land or to remain in Purgatory accordingly as the contributions of their friends, in cash or prayer, shall determine. The priest told us, in an admirably framed speech, about John's destination, and the terms upon which he might continue his journey or must remain in Purgatory. John was poor; his friends are poor. The Empress was rich; her friends are rich. John Malone's prospects are not good, and I lament it.

Perhaps I am in error in saying I have been present at only two Catholic funerals. I think I was present at one in Virginia City, Nevada, in the neighborhood of forty years ago—or perhaps it was down in Esmeralda, on the borders of California— but if it happened, the memory of it can hardly be said to exist, it is so indistinct. I *did* attend one or two funerals—maybe a dozen—out there; funerals of desperadoes who had tried to purify society by exterminating other desperadoes—and *did* accomplish the purification, though not according to the program which they had laid out for this office.

Also, I attended some funerals of persons who had fallen in duels—and maybe it was a duelist whom I helped to ship. But would a duelist be buried by the church? In inviting his own death, wouldn't he be committing suicide, substantially? Wouldn't that rule him out? Well, I don't remember how it was, now, but I think it was a duelist.

[*New York, Friday, January 19, 1906*

About Dueling

In those early days dueling suddenly became a fashion in the new territory of Nevada, and by 1864 everybody was anxious to have a chance in the new sport, mainly for the reason that he was not able to thoroughly respect himself so long as he had not killed or crippled somebody in a duel or been killed or crippled in one himself.

At that time I had been serving as city editor on Mr. Goodman's Virginia City *Enterprise* for a matter of two years. I was twenty-nine years old. I was ambitious in several ways, but I had entirely escaped that particular fashion. I had had no desire

to fight a duel. I had no intention of provoking
one. I did not feel respectable, but I got a certain
amount of satisfaction out of feeling safe. I was
ashamed of myself, the rest of the staff were
ashamed of me—but I got along well enough. I
had always been accustomed to feeling ashamed of
myself, for one thing or another, so there was no
novelty for me in the situation. I bore it very well.
Plunkett was on the staff. R. M. Daggett was on
the staff. These had tried to get into duels, but,
for the present, had failed and were waiting. Goodman was the only one of us who had done anything to
shed credit upon the paper. The rival paper was
the Virginia *Union*. Its editor for a little while
was Fitch, called the "silver-tongued orator of Wisconsin"—that was where he came from. He tuned
up his oratory in the editorial columns of the *Union,*
and Mr. Goodman invited him out and modified him
with a bullet. I remember the joy of the staff when
Goodman's challenge was accepted by Fitch. We
ran late that night, and made much of Joe Goodman. He was only twenty-four years old; he lacked
the wisdom which a person has at twenty-nine, and
he was as glad of being *it* as I was that I wasn't.
He chose Major Graves for his second (that name
is not right, but it's close enough, I don't remember
the major's name). Graves came over to instruct
Joe in the dueling art. He had been a major under
Walker, the "gray-eyed man of destiny," and had
fought all through that remarkable man's filibuster-
ing campaign in Central America. That fact gauges
the major. To say that a man was a major under

Walker, and came out of that struggle ennobled by Walker's praise, is to say that the major was not merely a brave man, but that he was brave to the very utmost limit of that word. All of Walker's men were like that. I knew the Gillis family intimately. The father made the campaign under Walker, and with him one son. They were in the memorable Plaza fight, and stood it out to the last against overwhelming odds, as did also all of the Walker men. The son was killed at the father's side. The father received a bullet through the eye. The old man—for he was an old man at the time—wore spectacles, and the bullet and one of the glasses went into his skull, and the bullet remained there. There were some other sons—Steve, George, and Jim, very young chaps—the merest lads—who wanted to be in the Walker expedition, for they had their father's dauntless spirit. But Walker wouldn't have them; he said it was a serious expedition, and no place for children.

The major was a majestic creature, with a most stately and dignified and impressive military bearing, and he was by nature and training courteous, polite, graceful, winning; and he had that quality which I think I have encountered in only one other man—Bob Howland—that quality which resides in the eye; and when that eye is turned upon an individual or a squad, in warning, that is enough. The man that has that eye doesn't need to go armed; he can move upon an armed desperado and quell him and take him prisoner without saying a single word. I saw Bob Howland do that once—a slender, good-natured, amiable, gentle, kindly little skeleton of a man, with a sweet blue eye that would win your heart when it smiled upon you, or turn cold and freeze it, according to the nature of the occasion.

The major stood Joe up straight; stood Steve Gillis up fifteen paces away; made Joe turn his right side toward Steve, cock his navy six-shooter— that prodigious weapon—and hold it straight down against his leg; told him that *that* was the correct position for the gun—that the position ordinarily in use at Virginia City (that is to say, the gun straight up in the air, bring it slowly down to your man) was all wrong. At the word "One," you must raise the gun slowly and steadily to the place on the other man's body that you desire to convince. "One, two, three—fire—Stop!" At the word "stop," you may fire—but not earlier. You may give yourself as much time as you please *after* that word. Then, when you fire, you may advance and go on firing at your leisure and pleasure, if you can get any pleasure out of it. And, in the meantime, the other man, if he has been properly instructed and is alive to his privileges, is advancing on *you,* and firing—and it is always likely that more or less trouble will result.

Naturally, when Joe's revolver had risen to a level it was pointing at Steve's breast, but the major said: "No, that is not wise. Take all the risks of getting murdered yourself, but don't run any risk of murdering the other man. If you survive a duel you want to survive it in such a way that the memory of it will not linger along with you through the rest of your life, and interfere with your sleep. Aim at your man's leg; not at the knee, not above the knee, for those are dangerous spots. Aim below the knee; cripple him, but leave the rest of him to his mother."

By grace of these truly wise and excellent instructions, Joe tumbled his man down with a bullet through his lower leg, which furnished him a permanent limp. And Joe lost nothing but a lock of hair, which he could spare better then than he could now. For when I saw him here a year ago his crop was gone; he had nothing much left but a fringe, with a dome rising above.

About a year later I got *my* chance. But I was not hunting for it. Goodman went off to San Francisco for a week's holiday, and left me to be chief editor. I had supposed that that was an easy berth, there being nothing to do but write one editorial per day; but I was disappointed in that superstition. I couldn't find anything to write an article about, the first day. Then it occurred to me that inasmuch as it was the 22d of April, 1864, the next morning would be the three-hundredth anniversary of Shakespeare's birthday—and what better theme could I want than that? I got the Cyclopædia and examined it, and found out who Shakespeare was and what he had done, and I borrowed all that and laid it before a community that couldn't have been better prepared for instruction about Shakespeare than if they had been prepared by art. There wasn't *enough* of what Shakespeare had done to make an editorial

of the necessary length, but I filled it out with what
he hadn't done—which in many respects was more
important and striking and readable than the hand-
somest things he had really accomplished. But next
day I was in trouble again. There were no more
Shakespeares to work up. There was nothing in
past history, or in the world's future possibilities,
to make an editorial out of suitable to that community; so there was but one theme left. That theme
was Mr. Laird, proprietor of the Virginia *Union*.
His editor had gone off to San Francisco, too, and
Laird was trying his hand at editing. I woke up
Mr. Laird with some courtesies of the kind that
were fashionable among newspaper editors in that
region, and he came back at me the next day in a
most vitriolic way. So we expected a challenge from
Mr. Laird, because according to the rules—according to the etiquette of dueling as reconstructed and
reorganized and improved by the duelists of that
region—whenever you said a thing about another
person that he didn't like, it wasn't sufficient for
him to talk back in the same, or a more offensive
spirit; etiquette required him to send a challenge.
So we waited for a challenge—waited all day. It
didn't come. And as the day wore along, hour
after hour, and no challenge came, the boys grew
depressed. They lost heart. But I was cheerful;
I felt better and better all the time. They couldn't
understand it, but *I* could understand it. It was
my *make* that enabled me to be cheerful when other
people were despondent. So then it became necessary for us to waive etiquette and challenge Mr.

Laird. When we reached that decision, they began
to cheer up, but *I* began to lose some of my animation. However, in enterprises of this kind you
are in the hands of your friends; there is nothing
for you to do but to abide by what they consider
to be the best course. Daggett wrote a challenge
for me, for Daggett had the language—the right
language—the convincing language—and I lacked
it. Daggett poured out a stream of unsavory epi-
thets upon Mr. Laird, charged with a vigor and
venom of a strength calculated to persuade him;
and Steve Gillis, my second, carried the challenge
and came back to wait for the return. It didn't
come. The boys were exasperated, but I kept my
temper. Steve carried another challenge, hotter
than the other, and we waited again. Nothing came
of it. I began to feel quite comfortable. I began
to take an interest in the challenges myself. I had
not felt any before; but it seemed to me that I was
accumulating a great and valuable reputation at no
expense, and my delight in this grew and grew as
challenge after challenge was declined, until by midnight I was beginning to think that there was nothing
in the world so much to be desired as a chance to
fight a duel. So I hurried Daggett up; made him
keep on sending challenge after challenge. Oh, well,
I overdid it. I might have suspected that that would
happen—Laird was a man you couldn't depend on.

The boys were jubilant beyond expression. They
helped me make my will, which was another discomfort—and I already had enough. Then they
took me home. I didn't sleep any—didn't want to

sleep. I had plenty of things to think about, and less than four hours to do it in—because five o'clock was the hour appointed for the tragedy, and I should have to use up one hour—beginning at four—in practicing with the revolver and finding out which end of it to level at the adversary. At four we went down into a little gorge, about a mile from town, and borrowed a barn door for a mark—borrowed it of a man who was over in California on a visit— and we set the barn door up and stood a fence rail up against the middle of it. The rail was no proper representative of Mr. Laird, for he was longer than a rail and thinner. Nothing would ever fetch him but a line shot, and then, as like as not, he would split the bullet—the worst material for duel- ing purposes that could be imagined. I began on the rail. I couldn't hit the rail; I couldn't hit the barn door. There was nobody in danger except stragglers around on the flanks of that mark. I was thoroughly discouraged, and I didn't cheer up any when we presently heard pistol shots over in the next little ravine. I knew what that was—that was Laird's gang out practicing him. They would hear my shots, and of course they would come up over the ridge to see what kind of a record I was making —see what their chances were against me. Well, I hadn't any record; and I knew that if Laird came over that ridge and looked at my barn door without a scratch on it, he would be as anxious to fight as I was—or as I had been at midnight, before that disastrous acceptance came.

Now just at this moment a little bird, no bigger

than a sparrow, flew along by and lit on a sage-bush about thirty yards away. Steve whipped out his revolver and shot its head off. Oh, he was a marksman—much better than I was. We ran down there to pick up the bird, and just then, sure enough, Mr. Laird and his people came over the ridge, and they joined us. And when Laird's second saw that bird with its head shot off, he lost color, and you could see that he was interested.

He said:

"Who did that?"

Before I could answer, Steve spoke up and said quite calmly, and in a matter-of-fact way, "Clemens did it."

The second said, "Why, that is wonderful! How far off was that bird?"

Steve said, "Oh, not far—about thirty yards."

The second said, "Well, that is astonishing shooting. How often can he do that?"

Steve said, languidly, "Oh, about four times out of five!"

I knew the little rascal was lying, but I didn't say anything. The second said:

"Why, that is *wonderful* shooting! Why, I supposed he couldn't hit a church!"

He was supposing very sagaciously, but I didn't say anything. Well, they said good morning. The second took Mr. Laird home, a little tottery on his legs, and Laird sent back a note in his own hand declining to fight a duel with me on any terms whatever.

Well, my life was saved—saved by that accident.

I don't know what the bird thought about that interposition of Providence, but I felt very, very comfortable over it—satisfied and content. Now we found out, later, that Laird had hit *his* mark four times out of six, right along. If the duel had come off, he would have so filled my skin with bullet holes that it wouldn't have held my principles.

By breakfast time the news was all over town that I had sent a challenge and Steve Gillis had carried it. Now that would entitle us to two years apiece in the penitentiary, according to the brand-new law. Governor North sent us no message as coming from himself, but a message *came* from a close friend of his. He said it would be a good idea for us to leave the territory by the first stage-coach. This would sail next morning at four o'clock—and in the meantime we would be searched for, but not with avidity; and if we were in the territory after that stage-coach left, we would be the first victims of the new law. Judge North was anxious to have some victims for that law, and he would absolutely keep us in the prison the full two years. He wouldn't pardon us out to please anybody.

Well, it seemed to me that our society was no longer desirable in Nevada; so we stayed in our quarters and observed proper caution all day—except that once Steve went over to the hotel to attend to another customer of mine. That was a Mr. Cutler. You see, Laird was not the only person whom I had tried to reform during my occupancy of the editorial chair. I had looked around and selected several other people, and delivered a

new zest of life into them through warm criticism
and disapproval—so that when I laid down my editorial pen I had four horse-whippings and two duels
owing to me. We didn't care for the horse-whippings; there was no glory in them; they were not
worth the trouble of collecting. But honor required
that some notice should be taken of that other duel.
Mr. Cutler had come up from Carson City, and
sent a man over with a challenge from the hotel.
Steve went over to pacify him. Steve weighed only
ninety-five pounds, but it was well known throughout the territory that with his fists he could whip
anybody that walked on two legs, let his weight and
science be what they might. Steve was a Gillis,
and when a Gillis confronted a man and had a proposition to make the proposition always contained
business. When Cutler found that Steve was my
second he cooled down; he became calm and rational,
and was ready to listen. Steve gave him fifteen
minutes to get out of the hotel, and half an hour to
get out of town, or there would be results. So *that*
duel went off successfully, because Mr. Cutler went
off toward Carson, a convinced and reformed man.

I have never had anything to do with duels since.
I thoroughly disapprove of duels. I consider them
unwise, and I know they are dangerous. Still, I
have always taken a great interest in other people's
duels. One always feel an abiding interest in any
heroic thing which has entered into his own experience.

In 1878, fourteen years after my unmaterialized
duel, Messieurs Fortu and Gambetta fought a duel

which made heroes of both of them in France, and
made them ridiculous throughout the rest of the
world. I was living in Munich that fall and winter,
and I was so interested in that duel that I wrote
a long account of it, and it is in one of my books,
somewhere [1]—an account which had some inaccuracies in it, but as an exhibition of the *spirit* of that
duel, I think it was correct and trustworthy.

---

[1] *A Tramp Abroad.*

INDEX

363

END VOL. I